Introduction

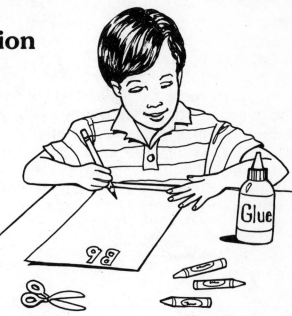

The purpose of this book is to introduce children to the letters of the alphabet by providing activities that combine all areas of the curriculum while utilizing a thematic, multi-sensory approach. By participating in exciting "hands-on" activities built around different letters, your students will experience success and therefore gain confidence while developing listening, speaking, reading, and writing skills.

Each chapter is organized into categories which encompass writing, reading, poetry, dramatization, science (including ecology), math, social studies, cooking, art, music and games. Appropriate activities are described in each area which can be used as a springboard for unit study. Holiday activities are also included when applicable. There are literature suggestions relevant to specific activities as well as a comprehensive list at the end of each chapter.

Through our combined 100+ years of early childhood teaching and administrative experience, we, as authors of this book, have found that the more modalities provided for students, the greater the percentage of skill mastery. Based on this conviction, we have developed the materials in this book as a demonstration of this philosophy.

This book is not intended to replace current curriculum, but rather to enhance, expand and supplement it. It is compatible with any early childhood curriculum.

Suggestions for Using This Book

As you introduce each letter, read through the appropriate chapter and select the activities that would best suit the interest and abilities of your class. Be sure to stress the sound of the highlighted letter with each activity. Each chapter includes a group of pictures pertinent to the letter being studied. These pictures can be enlarged, colored and cut out to make flash cards or incorporated into bulletin boards depicting the current letter. As each new letter is completed, incorporate the new flash cards into a set to use as a means of reviewing and distinguishing between the letters. Copies of the pictures could be distributed to the students for them to make their own sets of flash cards or to be used in various art projects.

Also included in this book are ideas for in-school "book publishing." These ideas involve classroom books as well as individual children's books. Suggestions for laminating and binding are included as well. We are confident the hands-on, multi-sensory activities in this book will help make learning exciting for you and your students.

Cooperative Learning

Frequent opportunities are provided for cooperative learning experiences in order to enhance young children's confidence. When forming the groups, make certain that children with different skill levels are included in each one. Put extremely shy children with those who are outgoing and have more nurturing personalities.

Parent Connection

As you begin each letter unit, make copies of the note to parents on page 3. (Make one copy first, fill in the blanks and then copy enough for each child to take a letter home.) Parent involvement in, and awareness of, what is taking place in the classroom has been proven to be a very positive influence on the educational growth of students. Many of the chapters include suggestions for field trips which will help expand young children's background knowledge. These field trips offer excellent opportunities for parent involvement.

_____
date

Dear Parents:

We are beginning a unit of study on the letter _____ . We are very excited about the learning that will take place across the curriculum as we study our letter. You can help at home by:

a. reading books to your child to reinforce the letter sound. (See book list attached.)

b. helping your child create the letter from clay, with paint or by tracing it in sand.

c. helping your child find magazine pictures to cut out that begin with the featured letter. Have your child paste the pictures on paper to form a collage.

d. asking your child to tell you about the special letter activity he/she worked on in school today.

We need your help in school! If you can contribute in any of the ways listed below, please check and return the form.

Thank you for your continued support.

_____
teacher

- -

I can do one or more of the following:

☐ read a book to the class

☐ help with a letter project

☐ read a book to individual students

_____   _____
date   parent

3

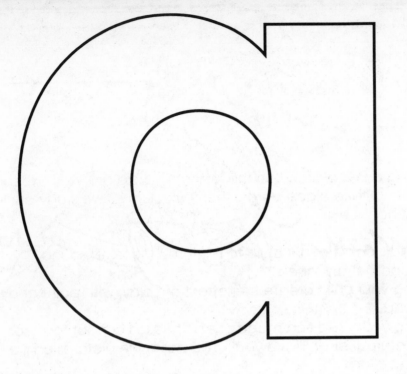

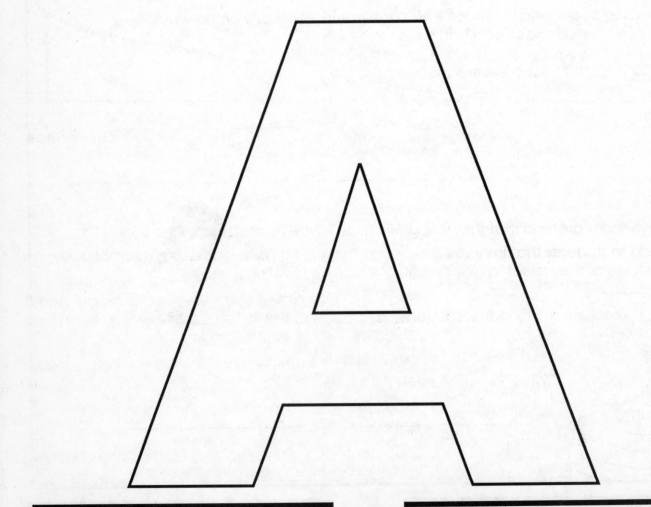

Ape Faces

Dramatics

Directions:

1. Have the children sit on the floor in pairs facing each other.
2. Have them pretend that they are apes. (One is Ape A, and one is Ape B.)
3. Stress to students that they use their faces, making no noise and doing minimal body gestures as they react to different situations. (See situations below.)

Situation 1—Both apes are eating bananas, but Ape B drops its banana on the ground below the tree in which the two apes are sitting.

Situation 2—A butterfly lands on Ape A's finger, and it lets Ape B hold it, too.

Situation 3—Ape B sees a dangerous lion approaching and tries to warn Ape A.

Situation 4—The apes are sitting on the ground below a tree when they suddenly feel raindrops.

Amusing Poetry

An Anaconda's Answer

"Baby Anaconda, get outta my way!"
  said the boa constrictor one day in May.
"Little Anaconda, you're ugly and small!"
  teased the boa constrictor one day in fall.
"Why Anaconda, you're skinny as a string!"
  mocked the boa constrictor one day in spring.
"Hey Anaconda, what happened to you?"
  "Time went on, and I grew and grew and grew!
Next time you come to me and want to tease,
  I'll wrap myself 'round you, and you'll feel my squeeze!"

For the Record: An anaconda is one of the world's largest snakes. It can grow to be about 29 ½ feet long. A boa constrictor usually only grows to a maximum of 18 ¼ feet long.

Apples

Apples, apples, way up in the tree
  Looking down so shiny at me!
Apples, apples, I would like to know
  Why you chose a place so high to grow?

For the Record: There are more than 1,000 varieties of cultivated apples.

April Fool's Day

A Broken Nose

Help me, help me! I just broke my nose!
How do you know?
Listen!

(Put both hands opened flat on both sides of the nose. Insert a thumbnail behind your front teeth and quickly scrape your nail against them. Bend your nose at the same time. It will sound as if it is cracked!)

click... click... click!

A Is for Apple

Art

Objective: To make prints using apples

Materials: apples cut vertically into halves, tempera paint, shallow dishes, large sheets of paper, crayons

Directions:

1. Show students how to dip ½ of an apple into a shallow dish of paint. Be sure they wipe off excess paint.

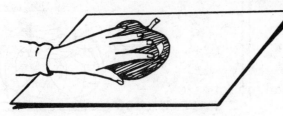

2. Have students slowly press the apple onto the paper. They can make pictures using the apple forms.

3. Students can use crayons to decorate around the apple imprints. Encourage them to turn the imprints into things like cars, trees, flowers, etc., by using crayons to add details.

a

Amazing Ants

Bulletin Board Suggestions:

The Ants Go Marching

Anteaters grow over six feet long and have a tongue over a foot long. Make your own giant anteater. (Enlarge the pattern on page 9.) Staple it to your bulletin board or tape it to a wall. Draw and cut out an anthill and place it next to the anteater. Have students make ants out of construction paper and attach them to the anteater's tongue and to the anthill. Title the board **The Ants Go Marching . . .**

Active Ants

Make a large ant farm with lots of tunnels. Place ants made from the pattern in the tunnels. Title the board **Active Ants**

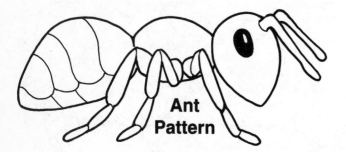

Ant Pattern

Astronaut Accessory

Objective: To make an astronaut helmet

Materials: brown grocery bag (one per student), crayons, scissors

Directions:
1. Cut off the top part of the bag so that when it is put over a student's head, it sits on his/her shoulders.
2. Help each student cut a large hole out of his/her grocery bag for his/her face.
3. Have students decorate the bag to look like an astronaut's helmet.

Patterns for Bulletin Boards

**Add red ribbon
for tongue.**

IF8661 The Alphabet

Admiring Absorption

Science

Objective: To demonstrate how plants absorb fluids

Materials: white carnations, water, food coloring, glass or jar, measuring cup, scissors

Directions:
1. Cut the stem of the flowers so that about 6 inches of them remain.
2. Mix a colored water solution in a glass or jar. Add 10 drops of food coloring to $\frac{1}{2}$ cup of water.
3. Place a flower in the water. Wait several hours.
4. Observe how the petals gradually change color.
5. Repeat with other flowers in different colored solutions.

Abracadabra: Attraction Action

Objective: To show how a magnet's magnetic field can be strong enough to attract and magnetize objects without touching them

Materials: strong horseshoe magnet, steel nail, tacks

Directions:

1. Hold one end of a horseshoe magnet very close to a nail without touching it.

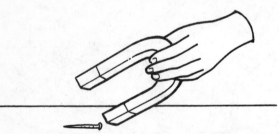

2. Slowly raise the magnet and note how it controls the nail.

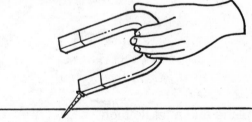

3. Put tacks at the base of the nail and note their attraction to the nail.

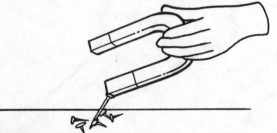

4. Discuss how a magnet has a magnetic field that radiates from its poles.

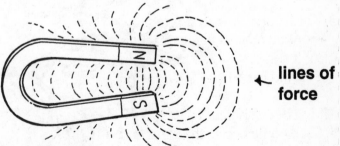

← **lines of force**

Suggested Reading: *Experiments with Magnets* by Helen J. Challand

Alien Aviation

Objective: To make alien flying saucers

Materials: several large, durable, dull white paper plates per student; one small, dull paper bowl per student; glue; construction paper; glitter; scissors; watercolors; crayons; markers. (Optional: pompons, tiny wiggle eyes, pipe cleaners)

Directions:

1. Depending on the thickness of the paper plates used, it might be necessary to have students glue several together to make a sturdy base. This helps the flying saucers fly better.

2. Students should turn the glued plates upside-down. Have them securely glue an upside-down paper bowl on top.

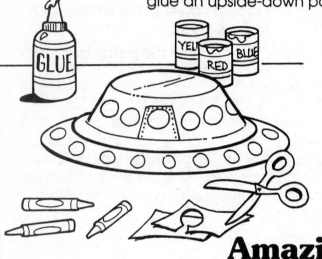

3. Have students make markings using crayons and then paint the flying saucer. They can use markers for further detail, if desired.

4. Let students decorate their flying saucers with construction paper portholes and doors. Glitter may be added for flashing lights.

5. If this is an art project only, students can turn their saucers into alien creatures with pompons, eyes and pipe cleaners. Do not do this if the children will fly saucers.

Amazing Poetry

Read the poems below to your students. See if they can pick out "a" sounds.

Aviation

Superman knows how to fly
　　Unless Kryptonite's around;
Then he can flap and flap his arms,
　　But he won't get off the ground!

An airplane and a jet fly high
　　And glide gently through the air;
But with engines, wheels, and a need for gas,
　　They can require so much care!

A helicopter flies straight up.
　　Watch as its blades start to spin—
But it can only go so high
　　And can't fly in lots of wind!

If I had my choice, I'd be a bird
　　And fly better than the rest.
Just like the well-known saying goes,
　　"Mother Nature does it best!"

A Field Trips and Follow-Up Activities

Objective: To use a field trip to motivate students in art, writing and reading activities

Suggested Field Trips: apple orchard, ambulance service, acrobat (gymnastic) training school, advertising agency, apiary, aviary

Class Thank-You Banner

Materials: large sheet of paper (cut approximately 10' x 3'), assorted colors of 9" x 12" sheets of construction paper, scissors, glue, thin black markers

Directions: Have each child use the smaller sheets of construction paper to create a picture of something he/she saw on the field trip. Encourage students to make fairly large pictures of different objects. Students can use the thin markers to add small details to the pictures. On the banner, write the name of the place you visited in large letters across the middle. Then, glue the children's pictures around the letters. Finally, have each child dictate a sentence near his/her picture that describes it such as, "The tractor was very big," or "The apples were red, yellow and green," or "The apple cider was delicious." Have students sign their names. Send the completed banner to the place of the field trip.

Individual Thank-You Letters

Materials: construction paper, crayons/markers

Directions: Discuss the field trip. Have each child draw a picture about the trip and dictate one or two related sentences below it. Have students sign their names.

Class Trip Book

Materials: 18" x 24" sheets of white construction paper, crayons, markers

Directions: Have the children brainstorm everything they can remember about the field trip. Together, write a story about the trip that has the same number of sentences as there are students in the class. Write each sentence at the bottom of a piece of white construction paper. Then have students illustrate the pages. Number and laminate each page. Share the story with another class by having each child hold up his/her page and describe what's happening in the illustration. Display the pages chronologically around the room or compile them into a class big book.

The apples were red, yellow, and green.

IF8661 The Alphabet

A Pictures for Miscellaneous Activities

Book List

Adler, D. (1989). *A Picture Book of Abraham Lincoln.* New York: Holiday House.

Christian, M. (1981). *April Fool.* New York: Macmillan.

Collington, P. (1987). *The Angel and the Soldier Boy.* New York: Knopf.

Eichenberg, F. (1952). *Ape in a Cape.* New York: Harcourt, Brace and World.

Hoban, J. (1989). *Amy Loves the Rain.* New York: Harper and Row.

Kunhardt, E. (1993). *Honest Abe.* New York: Greenwillow Books.

Rice, E. (1981). *Benny Bakes a Cake.* New York: Greenwillow Books.

Seuss, Dr. (1947). *McElligot's Pool.* New York: Random House.

Stadler, J. (1985). *Snail Saves the Day.* New York: Crowell.

Steig, W. (1971). *Amos and Boris.* New York: Farrar, Strauss and Giroux.

Stevenson, J. (1988). *We Hate Rain!* New York: Greenwillow Books.

Bb

Beach Scene

Art

Materials: sand or rice, glue, crayons or paint, paintbrushes, shells (pasta), Bristol board

Directions: Develop an awareness of a beach ecosystem and create a beach scene. After discussing what you might find at a beach, (or after taking a trip to the beach if possible), give each child a sheet of Bristol board. Have students draw a line toward the bottom of their boards to mark where the sand will be placed. (Model this first.) Next, have the students color or paint the water, sky, sea gulls, etc. Then, have them use a paintbrush to spread glue on the bottom of their papers. Sand or rice should be put on top of the glue next. Have students let their pictures rest for a count of ten. Then, they shake off the excess sand or rice. Tell the students to glue on the shells.

This can also be done with a shoe box to create a diorama.

Build a Bus

Objective: yellow and black construction paper, scissors, pencils, paste, white crayons

Directions: Give each child a pre-cut yellow rectangle, and a pre-cut yellow square. Have them paste the two together to create the body of a bus.

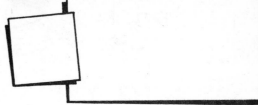

Next have them fold a black piece of paper in half, and draw one circle. When the children have cut the circles out, they can paste them on. Or, if you'd like, you may fasten them on with paper fasteners so they move. The children can add windows, doors, a driver, children, etc. Have the children write "bus" on the bus.

Extension Activities: song – "The Wheels on the Bus" (see page 25)

Writing/ Reading

"B" Is for Book

Objective: To enhance students' vocabulary of nouns beginning with B

Materials: a copy for each student of an 8 1/2" x 11" sheet of paper with "B is for ___."

Directions: Help children select a noun beginning with the sound for "B" and illustrate it. Label it. Papers can be assembled to make a class book.

Beautiful Babies Book

Materials: photo album

Directions: Mount children's baby photos in an album. Write the child's name under each photo.

Title the album **Beautiful Babies**.

Bunny Basket

Art

Materials: one half-pint milk carton for each child, construction paper (white and a variety of colors), scissors, stapler, crayons or markers, grass (commercial or thin strips cut from green crêpe, cellophane or tissue paper), small balls of cotton

Method:

1. Cut the tops off of the milk cartons.

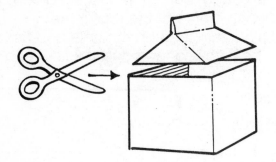

2. Cover the outside of the carton with construction paper.

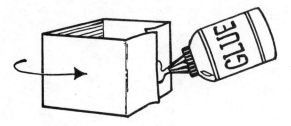

3. Cut 1/2" wide strips of construction paper for the handles. The children should decorate their handles. Attach the handles to the inside of the milk carton with a stapler.

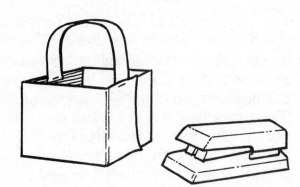

4. Provide children with a bunny face copied on a piece of 6" x 8 1/2" white paper. Cut it out.

5. Glue the face to the front of the carton.

6. Children should paste or glue a cotton ball on the back of the carton for the tail.

7. Put grass in each basket.

Writing/ Reading

"B" Letter Recognition

Directions: A student wears a "B" necklace for a day. This could be a child whose name begins with B, the birthday boy, etc. Another possibility includes creating several necklaces so that a group of children can wear the necklaces on Monday, a second group on Tuesday, and so on. This way, each child gets a turn. To make the necklace, put "B" on a round piece of cardboard. Punch a hole at the top of the cardboard. String yarn through the hole and tie a knot. Be sure the yarn is long enough to fit over a child's head.

Materials: letter B cutout, hole punch, yarn, cardboard

Extension Activities: Allow students to decorate the letters. This activity could be done for each letter of the alphabet.

Big Books

Objective: To introduce big books if you haven't already If you have utilized big books, you can simply stress the initial consonant sounds in the words "big" and "book."

Suggested Reading:

Hairy Bear by Gardiner and Elizabeth Fuller
The Three Billy Goats Gruff by Paul Galdone
How Big Is Big? by Avelyn Davis
Who Sank the Boat? by Pamela Allen
Billy Balloon by Blackburn and Handy
Mrs. Wishy Washy by Joy Cowley

Theme Backpack, Bag or Box

Objective: To stress that backpack, bag, box and book all begin with the letter "B ."

Materials: a bag, box or backpack, thematic books

Directions: In a bag, box or backpack, place several books on one subject relating to an area of study you are currently working on. (For example, if you are working on community helpers, place books about community helpers in the box/bag.) You can include fiction, nonfiction and periodicals.

Suggested Reading:
The books in your bag, box or backpack!

A "B" Field Trip and Follow-Up

Objective: To use the field trip as motivation for writing

Suggested Trips:
bakery
bagel bakery
beach
barn
bank

Class Thank-You Letter

Materials: large chart paper, markers/crayons

Directions: Discuss the trip. Encourage the use of complete sentences. Encourage the expansion of vocabulary. Ask students questions like, "What did you see? What did you like? What did you find out? Who showed you around? How can you say thank you? How do you write a letter?" Discuss the form of the letter. Have the children contribute (dictate) sentences for the letter. Write them on a chart. Have the children sign their names.

Blowing Bubbles   Science

Objective: To allow children to experiment with air and water

Materials: straw, bucket of water

Directions: Blow through a straw in the air. What do you see? feel?

Blow through a straw in water. What do you think is in the bubbles?

Beans and Bulbs

Science

Objective: To teach students about planting, comparing and classifying beans and bulbs

Materials: bulbs (onion, tulip, radish), beans (lima, black, navy, pinto, garbanzo, lentil, kidney), soil, potting containers, water, paper towels, chart paper, crayons

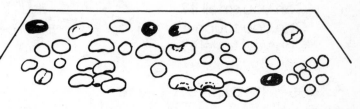

Directions:

1. Display all beans on a table. The students can then compare and classify the beans by shape, color and size. Repeat the activity using the bulbs. (Depending on the class size and/or time restraint, you may want to work this activity with small groups.)

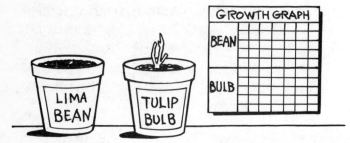

2. Next, plant a bean and a bulb. Through this activity, you can teach children what plants need to grow. To bring in math, graph the growth of the two plants over a month's period of time.

3. With a remaining bean, you can demonstrate a seedling. Place a bean in a wet paper towel. Over a number of days, the bean will sprout and grow.

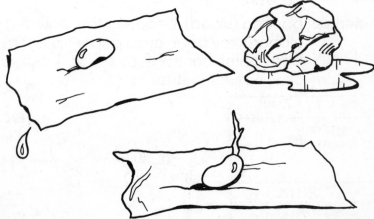

Suggested Reading:

 The Carrot Seed by Ruth Krauss
 Jack and the Beanstalk
 The Plant Sitter by Graham Green
 Seeds and More Seeds by Millicent E. Selsam

Balloon Experiments

Science

Objective: To predict outcomes and make observations

Materials: balloons, pin, bucket of water

Directions:

1. Have a student blow up a balloon.
2. Ask the following questions:
   What happened to the balloon? (It got bigger.)
   What do you think is inside?
   Can you see it?
   Can you feel it?
   Can you smell it?
   Can you touch it?
   Can you taste it?
   Can you hear it?
3. Have students let the balloon go. Ask students what happened and why.

4. Have a student blow up another balloon. Have him/her stick a pin in it. Ask what happened and what came out of the balloon.
5. Have a student blow up yet another balloon. He/she should let the air out in a pail of water. Ask the students: What happened? What do you see? What do you think is in the bubbles? Why do you think that?

Buoyancy

Objective: To discover that some materials are buoyant

Materials: banana (sliced), bead, button, bow (ribbon), toy boat, brass paper fastener, bag, water, container (preferably a clear one), large sheet of paper, marker

IT FLOATS
1. toy boat
2 banana slice

IT SINKS
1. paper fastener
2. button

Directions: Fill the container with water. One by one, drop the listed items into the water to test for buoyancy. Make a list of items that are buoyant and those that are not.

Suggested Reading:
Who Sank the Boat? (Big Book) by Pamela Allen

Bird Feeder

Science

Objective: To observe the construction of a simple bird feeder, to learn how to care for a bird feeder and to observe birds feeding

Materials: a large plastic bleach bottle, an aluminum pie tin, scissors, glue, string, birdseed

Directions:

1. With scissors, cut an arch-shaped opening into the side of the bottle.

2. Glue the pie tin onto the bottom of the bottle.

3. Tie a sturdy piece of string around the neck of the bottle.

4. Ask students the following questions:
   Where will the food go?
   Where will the birds perch?
   What kind of foods do birds like?
   Where shall we hang our bird feeder? (Encourage children to suggest a place near a classroom window.)

Extension Activities:

Observations of feeding can lead to further discussions of bird identification and habitat.

Feeders can also be made from pine cones rolled in peanut butter, plastic baskets, milk cartons and tin cans.

Suggested Reading:

Bird Talk by Roma Gans
Birds in Wintertime by Allen Eitzen
The Good Bird by Peter Wezel

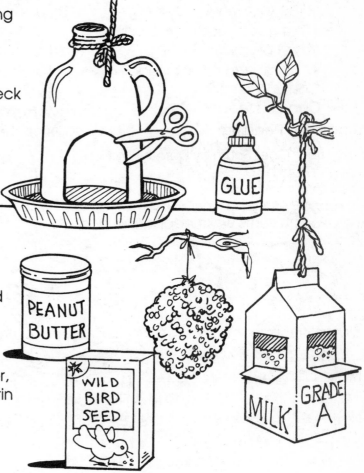

Button Classification

Objective: To sort or classify various buttons by shape, color or size attributes

Materials: buttons of assorted sizes, shapes and colors

Directions: Have students sort or classify buttons according to color, size, shape, pattern, etc.

Bear Week

Science

Objective: To become familiar with several kinds of bears and to have the opportunity to share favorite bears with the others

Materials: Discuss various types of bears:

> brown bears
> grizzly bears
> polar bears

Have a Teddy Bear Day at school. Encourage children to bring their teddy bears to school to share.

Suggested Reading:

Buzzy Bear Goes South by Dorothy Marion
Bears in Pairs by Niki Yektai
Baby Bears and How They Grow—Books for
   Young Explorers by National Geographic Society
Brown Bear, Brown Bear by Bill Martin, Jr.
Blueberries for Sal by Robert McCloskey
Ira Sleeps Over by Bernard Waber

Big and Little

Objective: To become familiar with the concept of "opposite" in terms of size

Materials: concrete objects such as large and small crayons, blocks, chairs, scissors, etc.

Directions:
1. Present children with one big and one little block.
2. Ask students how these blocks are different and how they are the same.
2. Guide students into telling the difference in size, using the terms big and little.
4. Use other materials in the same manner.

Extension Activity:

Give each child a piece of drawing paper. Ask each to draw two similar things—one big and one little. Encourage the children to keep their drawings simple; a big circle and a little circle, a house and a skyscraper, etc. Label the pictures using the terms "big" and "little."

Suggested Reading:

Goldilocks and the Three Bears by Janet Stevens
Big Ones, Little Ones by Tana Hoban

Bread Sculpture

Objective: To create sculptures from a bread mixture

Materials: 3 cups flour
1 1/2 cups salt
3 teaspoons oil
5 tablespoons warm water
paint and paintbrushes
cookie sheets
acrylic spray
oven

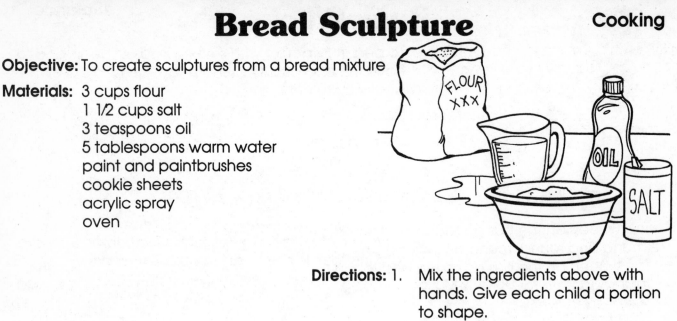

Directions:

1. Mix the ingredients above with hands. Give each child a portion to shape.

2. When sculptures are complete, place them on a cookie sheet.

3. Bake at 275 degrees for 25 minutes on the lowest oven rack.*

4. Let them stand overnight before painting.

5. For a final finish, you may want to use an acrylic spray.

*Thick pieces may need to bake longer.

"B" Poems and Finger Plays

Little Boy Blue by Mother Goose

Little Boy Blue
    come blow your horn!
The sheep's in the meadow,
    the cow's in the corn.
Where's the little boy that
    looks after the sheep?
He's under the haystack,
    fast asleep!

Bo Peep by Mother Goose

Little Bo Peep, she lost her sheep
And didn't know where to find them.
Let them alone and they'll come home
Wagging their tails behind them.

Band

Music

Activities: Create a rhythm band in your own classroom! Discuss which senses the children will utilize most. Ask the children to name as many instruments as they can.

The Wheels on the Bus

1. The wheels on the bus go round and round,
   Round and round, round and round,
   The wheels on the bus go round and round,
   All through the town.
   (Roll hands over each other.)

2. The doors on the bus go open and shut,
   Open and shut, open and shut,
   The doors on the bus go open and shut,
   All through the town.
   (Hold palms forward and turn hands out and in.)

3. The money on the bus goes clink, clink, clink,
   ("Twinkle" or flutter fingers on both hands like coins falling.)

4. The driver on the bus says, "Please move back."
   (Make "move to the rear" gesture.)

5. The windows on the bus go open and shut,
   (Move hands up, then down - or however the windows on the buses in your community move.)

6. The horn on the bus goes beep, beep, beep,
   (Pretend to beep the horn on each word "beep.")

7. The children on the bus go bump, bump, bump,
   (Bounce up and down as if on a bumpy ride.)

8. The daddy on the bus tips his hat,
   (Tip hat.)

9. The baby on the bus goes, "Wah, wah wah!"
   (Pretend to cry like a baby, wiping tears with fists.)

10. The mother on the bus goes, "Shh, shh, shh."
    (Put index finger to lips.)

Bone Soup

Objective: To make a pot of bone soup based upon the book, *Stone Soup*

Materials: book - *Stone Soup* by Marcia Brown
vegetables such as carrots, celery, parsley, potatoes
1 onion
soup greens
1 beef soup bone
large pot with cover
hot plate or stove
peeler, knife, spoon
small dishes and spoons (for each child)
bread
butter

Directions: 1. Read *Stone Soup* to the class.

2. Discuss with the class the reasons for using a bone rather than stones.

3. Have children bring the necessary ingredients to school.

4. Put a beef soup bone in the soup pot.

5. Peel and wash the vegetables with the children.

6. Children place all the ingredients in a large pot.

7. Cover the contents of the pot with water.

8. Place the pot on the hot plate or stove, boil, cover and simmer until done.

9. Serve to the children in small dishes with bread and butter.

Book List

Ancona, G. (1979). *It's a Baby!* New York: Dutton.

Barton, B. (1986). *Boats.* New York: Harper and Row.

Barton, B. (1973). *Buzz, Buzz, Buzz,* New York: Macmillan.

Berenstain, S. and Berenstain, J. (1971). *The B Book.* New York: Random House.

Berenstain, S. and Berenstain, J. (1987). *The Berenstain Bears on the Job.* New York: Random House.

Berenstain, S. (1964). *The Bike Lesson.* New York: Beginner Books.

Brown, M. (1962). *Benjy's Blanket.* New York: Franklin Watts.

Brown, M. (1989). *Big Red Barn.* New York: Harper and Row.

de Paola, T. (1979). *Big Anthony and the Magic Ring.* New York: Harcourt Brace Jovanovich.

Flack, M. (1958). *Ask Mr. Bear.* New York: Macmillan.

Freeman, D. (1977). *Beady Bear.* New York: Penguin Books.

Galdone, P. (1985). *Three Bears.* Ticknor & Fields.

Gans, R. (1971). *Bird Talk.* New York: Crowell.

Gibbons, G. (1983). *Boat Book.* New York: Holiday House.

Hoban, R. (1960). *Bedtime for Frances.* New York: Harper and Row.

Ipcar, D.Z. (1972). *The Biggest Fish in the Sea.* New York: Viking Press.

Kellogg, S. (1991). *Jack and the Beanstalk.* New York: Morrow Junior Books.

Lamorisse, A. (1957). *The Red Balloon.* Garden City, New York: Doubleday.

Lionni, L. (1959). *Little Blue and Little Yellow.* McDowell, Obolensky.

Marino, D. (1961). *Buzzy Bear Goes South.* New York: Franklin Watts.

Martin, Jr., B. (1983). *Brown Bear, Brown Bear.* New York: Henry Holt & Co.

Mayer, M. (1980). *Bubble Bubble.* New York: Macmillan.

McCloskey, R. (1977). *Blueberries for Sal.* New York: Viking Press.

Parish, P. (1963). *Amelia Bedelia.* New York: Harper and Row.

Rice, E. (1981). *Benny Bakes a Cake.* New York: Greenwillow Books.

Ueno, N. (1973). *Elephant Buttons.* New York: Harper and Row.

Vincent, G. (1985). *Breakfast Time, Ernest and Celestine.* New York: Greenwillow Books.

Wezel, P. (1964). *The Good Bird.* New York: Harper and Row.

Wildsmith, B. (1981). *Bear's Adventure.* New York: Pantheon Books.

Wildsmith, B. (1974). *The Lazy Bear.* New York: Franklin Watts.

Yektai, N. (1987). *Bears in Pairs.* New York: Bradbury Press.

Zolotow, C. (1960). *Big Brother.* New York: Harper and Row.

B Pictures for Miscellaneous Activities

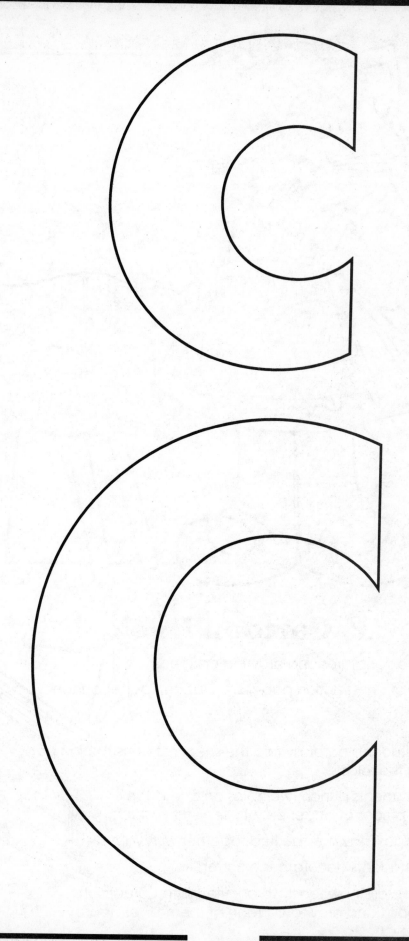

Cc

Cartoon Book

Objective: To practice signatures and drawing cartoons

Materials: 4-6 sheets of construction paper per student, paper punch, yarn, scissors, thin markers

Directions:
1. Have students carefully fold the sheets of construction paper into fourths and cut on the folds.

2. Next, students punch two holes on one edge of all the pieces of paper exactly the same place.

3. The pages may now be tied together with yarn.

4. Have students decorate the cover.

5. Students are now ready to ask friends to autograph their book and draw a cartoon of themselves nearby.

Creative Collage

Art

Objective: To encourage individual creativity

Materials: paste, construction paper, scissors, assorted materials such as scraps of colored construction paper, tissue paper, ribbons, corrugated paper, packaging materials, fabrics, etc.

Directions: Explain to the children that a collage is an art form. Model how to create various designs by cutting the scrap materials into the size and shape desired and pasting them on a piece of construction paper. (This is a good time to introduce the children to abstract art.) Explain that the finished product does not have to represent objects such as a house, tree, flower, person, etc. You might want to show the children works by Paul Klee, Georges Braque or Pablo Picasso.

Some children may be more comfortable with more conventional types of work. Model how to use the scrap materials to create houses, people, trees, flowers, cars, etc.

After the children have created several collages, encourage them to move away from a completely flat presentation. A house can have a door that opens. A bird can have wings that can be moved, etc. In the more abstract representation, folding, twisting and curling of the scraps can be used to create three-dimensional creative collages.

Suggested Reading:
Pezzetino by Leo Lionni

A Coin Shower

Science

Objective: To clean dirty coins

Materials: dull penny, glass jar with a lid. lemon juice, salt, tablespoon

Directions:

1. Carefully lower a penny into the jar

2. Add 2 tablespoons of salt and 4 tablespoons of lemon juice.

3. Shake the jar very hard until the coin is clean. (The lemon's acid chemically removes the dull copper oxide coating on the penny. The salt acts as an abrasive to speed up the process.)

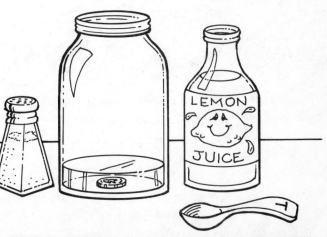

Class Cookbook

Materials: paper, pencils, book rings, construction paper

Directions: Discuss with the students what a recipe is. Using rebus pictures, write a simple recipe (such as cream cheese and crackers) on the board. Demonstrate how the recipe is followed. To create your classroom cookbook, you can:

1. Ask students to bring in a favorite simple recipe from home. (Send a note to parents.) The students can then illustrate the dish or some of the ingredients.

2. Ask students to write or dictate to you the directions of something they know how to make. Ask them what their favorite food is. Ask how they think it is made. Next, have students illustrate their pages.

Make a copy of each recipe for each student. Have him/her design a cover on construction paper. Bind recipes together with book rings.

"C" Word Caterpillar

Objective: To create a caterpillar using circles having the letter "C"

Materials: pre-cut circles of various colors having the letter "C", pencils and markers

Directions: Give each child a pre-cut circle. Each child will trace the **C** on his/her circle in pencil. Place the circles in a chain fashion to form a caterpillar's body. Create a face on a larger circle, add antennae and place it on the left side of the caterpillar's body to promote left to right progression.

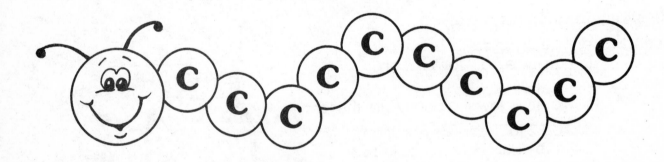

Clouds

Science

Objective: To become familiar with clouds

Materials: 18" x 12" sheets of paper divided into three sections with thick lines, cotton balls, dryer lint or grey flannel, glue, crayons

Directions: Have students place the papers horizontally and tell them that they will be making three kinds of clouds, one in each section.

Students will create fat, fluffy (cumulus) clouds in one section of their paper by gluing on cotton balls.

In another section, create thin, airy (stratus) clouds, by having the students stretch out the cotton balls before gluing them on.

In the last section, create dark, stormy (cirrus) clouds, by gluing on dark dryer lint that you have collected or grey flannel. Have students illustrate under them. Students may decorate the rest of the page with crayon, coloring the sky around the clouds.

Cookie Counting Book

Materials: drawing paper, crayons, stapler, staples

Directions: On each sheet of paper, write a number from one to five. Children draw and decorate the correct number of cookies corresponding to the number on their page. Give them all the help they need. Help the children put the pages in numerical order. Add a cover and staple pages into a book.

To make the activity more fun, have some cookies on hand to pass around while the class is working on their cookie counting books!

Carrot Top Experiment

Science

Objective: To find out what will happen if a carrot top is put in water

Materials: two or more carrots, water, 2 dishes

Directions: Cut off the tops of two carrots. One should have some green sprouts, and one should not.

Place each top in a separate dish with enough water to just reach the top of the carrot.

What happens to a carrot top when placed in water?					
What happened to water level?					
DAY 1	2	3	4	5	6
7	8	9	10	11	12
What happened to each carrot?					
DAY 1	2	3	4	5	6
7	8	9	10	11	12

Record the changes on the chart daily:

What happened to the water level?

What happened to each carrot?

Variables can be added by placing one carrot in the sun and one in the closet.

Suggested Reading:

The Carrot Seed by Ruth Krauss

Conservation

Objective: To discuss the meaning of conservation and why it is important

To demonstrate the meaning of conservation

Materials: cup, pitcher, water, large sheet of paper, marker

Directions: Explain to the students that conservation means saving by eliminating waste. Next, hold up the cup and a pitcher of water. Ask the students, "What would you do if you were thirsty?" After the students have responded, pour some water into the cup, allowing some to spill on the floor. Ask the students, "Can I drink the water off the floor?" (NO) The water on the floor is waste. Water has not been conserved. Next, make a class list that tells ways to conserve water and/or electricity. Be sure to discuss the importance of conserving our natural resources. **Caution! Clean up the spilled water right away so no one slips on the wet floor.**

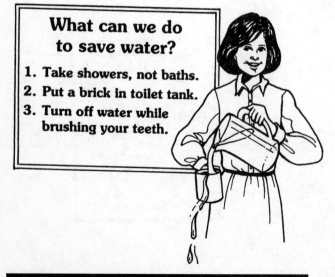

What can we do to save water?

1. Take showers, not baths.
2. Put a brick in toilet tank.
3. Turn off water while brushing your teeth.

Color Graph

Math

Materials: poster-size graph paper, pre-cut cars in several colors, glue or tape

Directions: Discuss the purpose of a graph with the class. Show the children a prepared graph with each row designated by a different-colored car. One at a time, have children select a car in their favorite color and attach it with glue or tape to the graph in the corresponding row. After each child has had a turn, count the cars in each row to determine the most favorite and least favorite color. Note any ties.

Explain that color graphs may be used to survey many different color preferences. For example: favorite color of shoes, favorite color of house, favorite color of crayon

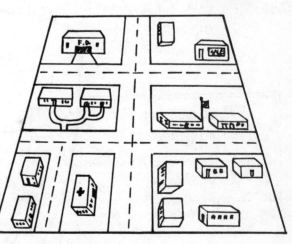

Community

Social Studies

Objective: To become familiar with the buildings/ services that make up a community

Materials: shoe boxes, paint, scissors, mural paper

Directions: Lay the mural paper flat on a table or on the floor. Draw the main street(s) in your town (or make up your own), leaving enough room for "shoe box buildings." After a discussion or community walk, have students choose buildings in the community to create. (Some buildings to include may be the firehouse, police station, grocery store, school, park, city hall, etc.) Students can paint the shoe boxes and add windows, doors, etc. Next, place each building on the mural paper.

Suggested Reading:
Dan, Dan the Flying Man by Gardiner and Elizabeth Fuller
Katy and the Big Snow by Virginia Lee Burton

Christopher Columbus

"Oh, No!"

Objective: To introduce the children to Christopher Columbus and the discovery of America
To introduce students to the concept that the world is round

Directions: Use a toy or a paper boat on a flat surface to illustrate that years ago, people thought that the world was flat. They thought that if they kept on sailing, they would fall off the end of the Earth.

Use a globe to illustrate to the children what Christopher Columbus wanted to do and how he "bumped" into America before he could get to the Indies.

Suggested Reading:
A Book About Christopher Columbus by Ruth Belov Gross

Crazy Cups

Objective: Make a bulletin board using the pattern below. Have each child color his/her own "Crazy Cup."

"C" Finger Play

Poetry

Cats-A-Counting

One little cat looking for some milk
Her fur is smooth, smooth as silk. (Stroke hand.)

Two little cats on the run. (Run two fingers.)
They are looking for some fun.

Three little cats walking into town.
    (Walk three fingers.)
Two are striped and one is brown.

Four little cats and a fifth one too,
They are out looking for you and you and you.
    (Point to children.)

                    by Ada Frischer

Suggested Reading:
    Poems - "The Owl and the
    Pussy Cat" by Edward Lear
    "Pussy Cat Pussy Cat
    Where Have You Been"

Caps For Sale

Dramatization

Materials: book - *Caps for Sale* by Slobodkina, several Frisbees™

Frisbees stack very well and can make excellent caps and promote balance as well! See who can walk across the classroom with a Frisbee™ or two balanced on his/her head.

Community Walk

Suggested Trips

Objective: To walk around the community
and make a class book about
the experience

Individual Books

Materials: construction paper, markers/crayons/pencils, binding materials

Directions: Take a walk in your community. After class discussion about the walk, each child
can dictate his/her own story about the walk and then illustrate it. An individual
book is then assembled for each child. This will produce a number of books that
can be circulated "library fashion" among the children in the class. It is a good
idea to make a cover, title page and author page. On the author page, write
some information about the author.

e.g., Allison is in kindergarten. She is five years old. She lives in _____
with her mother, father and sister. She likes to ride her bicycle. Allison wants
to be a doctor when she grows up. This is her first book.

A photograph of the author next to the biography makes this a very special
"publication."

"No Cook" Candy

Cooking

1. Wash [hands].

2. Mix 2 [spoons] of [jar] peanut butter
   and 1 [spoon] of [honey jar] honey.

3. Add 2 [spoons] of [box] powdered milk.

4. Mix in 10 [raisins] raisins.

5. Roll into [balls] balls.

6. Roll in [crackers] graham cracker crumbs.

7. Look [eyes] , smell [nose] , taste [mouth] .

Note: You can make your own graham cracker crumbs. Just put crackers in a plastic bag and have children use a rolling pin to make the crumbs.

This is an individual recipe for each child.

Carrot Salad

Grate carrots. Add crushed, canned pineapple to taste. Add raisins and some vanilla yogurt to moisten.

Cocoa

Add cocoa to hot tap water and mix with sugar.

C Pictures for Miscellaneous Activities

Book List

Bridwell, N. *Clifford.* (series) New York: Scholastic.

Carle, E. (1973). *Have You Seen My Cat?* New York: Franklin Watts.

Carle, E. (1988). *The Mixed-Up Chameleon.* New York: Harper and Row.

Carle, E. (1976). *The Very Hungry Caterpillar.* Cleveland, OH: Collins + World.

de Paola, T. (1975). *The Cloud Book.* New York: Holiday House.

Freeman, D. (1982). *Corduroy.* Somers, New York: Live Oak Media.

Gag, W. (1928). *Millions of Cats.* New York: Coward McCann.

Gray, W. (1976). *Camping Adventure.* Washington, D.C.: National Geographic Society - series.

Green, C. (1983). *Hi, Clouds.* Chicago, IL: Childrens Press.

Krauss, R. (1945). *The Carrot Seed.* New York: Harper and Brothers.

Numeroff, L.J. (1985). *If You Give a Mouse a Cookie.* New York: Harper and Row.

Rey, H.A. (1973). *Curious George.* Boston, Massachusetts: Houghton Mifflin.

Seuss, Dr. (1985). *The Cat in the Hat.* New York: Random House.

Slobodkina, E. (1947). *Caps for Sale.* New York: Scholastic.

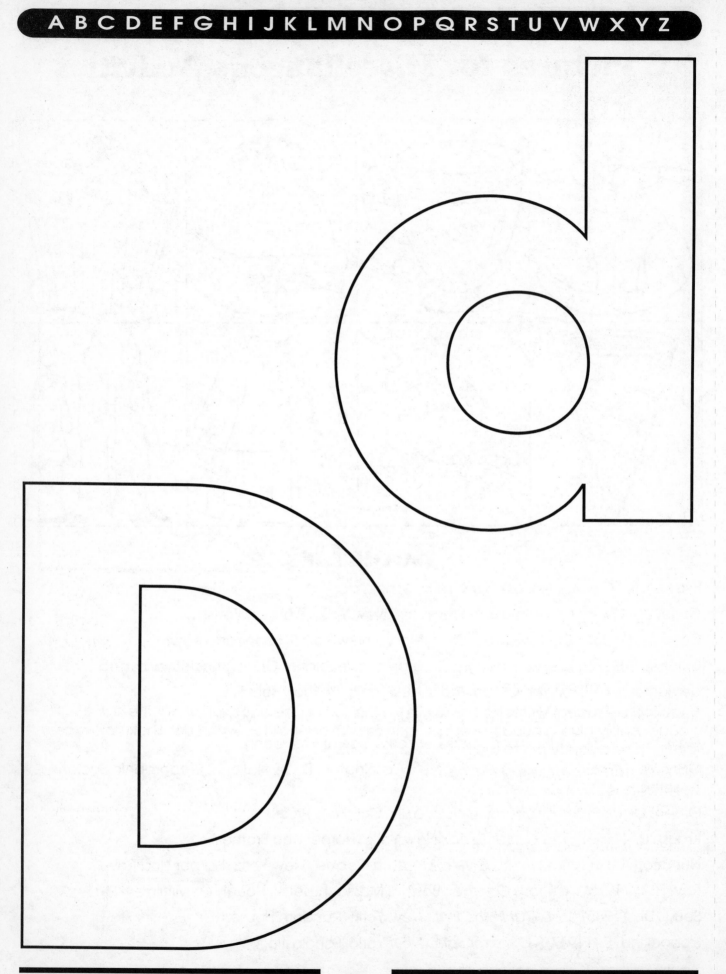

Dd

Deputizes

Art/ Social Studies

Preparation: Enlarge the deputy star badge pattern. Make a copy of the enlarged pattern on gray construction paper for each student.

Directions: Student writes his/her name on the line on the badge. Cut out the star badge. Apply glue around the edge. Sprinkle with silver glitter. When dry, shake off excess glitter. Tape a safety pin to the back of each badge.

Place all completed badges in a shoe box that has been decorated to resemble a strong box. Each day select one or more badges from the box. These students will be your helpers (deputies) for the day.

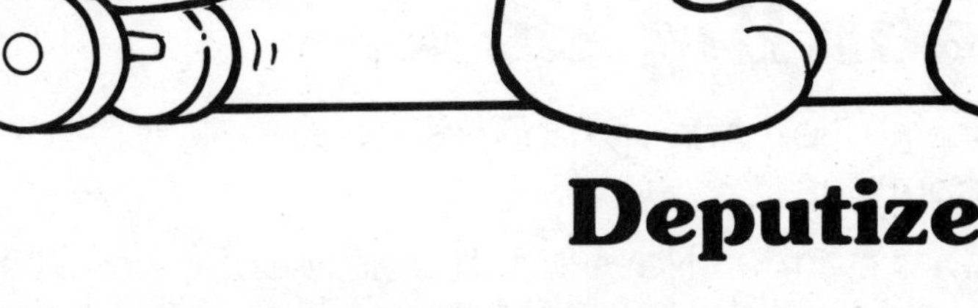

Deputy Tom

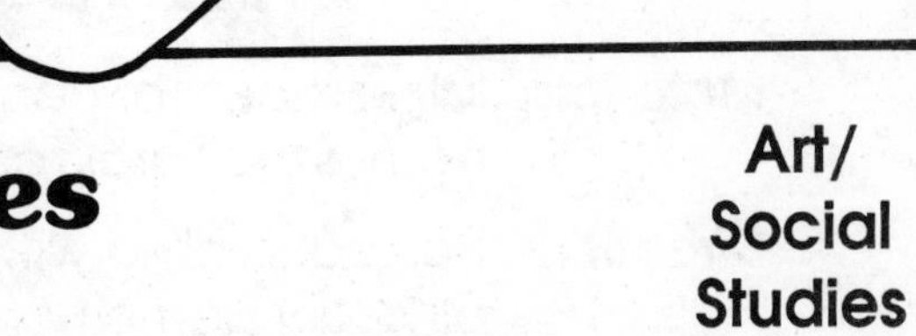

Orange Delight

Cooking

(Makes about 24 servings)

Ingredients: 12 oranges (optional) or plastic cups

12 cups orange juice

4 pints vanilla ice cream

4 cups crushed ice

small bottle seltzer water

Directions:
1. (Optional) Cut oranges into halves. Remove the fruit from the skin with a sharp knife. Use the skin to make beverage cups and cut the pieces of fruit to add later for garnish.

2. Freeze orange juice for about 10-15 minutes.

3. Pour 3 cups of orange juice, 1 pint of ice cream, 1 cup of ice and a dash of seltzer into the blender. Blend until slushy.

4. Repeat step #3 three more times.

5. Pour mixture into orange skin halves or cups and garnish with small orange pieces.

Dinosaur Big Book

Materials: large sheets of construction paper, markers, notebook rings, dinosaur names on cards, container

Directions: Pair each child with a partner. Have each pair select a card with a dinosaur name from a container. This will be their very own dinosaur to describe and illustrate. Working together, the pairs will blend their talents and skills to design at least one page of the book. When completed, bind the big book with notebook rings.

You could also use this method to create a class book about dogs.

Suggested Reading:
Refer to **Dinosaurs** page 43.

Dinosaurs

Art

Materials: clay (assorted colors), clay tools or toothpicks, plastic dinosaur models or pictures

Directions:
1. After reading and discussing dinosaur books, explain to students that they will create their own dinosaur from clay. Display the plastic models or pictures.

2. Ask students to choose which dinosaur they would like to create. (Distinctive dinosaurs that turn out well are the Stegosaurus, Tyrannosaurus Rex, Anklyosaurus and the Apatasaurus.)

3. Next, give each student some clay to soften and form into a ball.

4. Instruct students to pinch out a neck, head and tail from the ball.

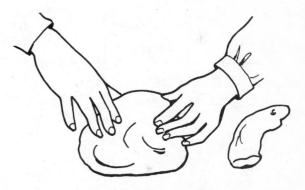

5. Give the children additional clay for the legs, horns, spikes and bony plates.

6. Using the clay tools, add eyes and an open mouth. Children may want to add teeth, claws, etc.

Extension Activity:
Cover the bottom of a large box with sand. Add a lake, trees, mountains and a volcano. Place dinosaurs in sand for display.

Suggested Reading:
My Visit to the Dinosaurs by Aliki
Dinosaur Mania by Edward Radlauer
If a Dinosaur Came to Dinner by Jane Belk Moncure
Danny and the Dinosaur by Syd Hoff
There Used To Be a Dinosaur in My Backyard by B.G. Hennessy
Dinosaurs by Books for Young Explorers National Geographic Society

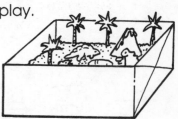

Daisy Power

Materials: To create daisy pencils that rest in a decorated pencil holder

Materials: small coffee cans with lids (one per student), construction paper, double-sided tape, glue, pencils (without erasers), pompons, felt, sequins and glitter (optional), green pipe cleaners (optional), scissors

Directions:

1. Instruct students to remove the coffee can lid. Have them cover the sides of the can using construction paper and secure it with tape.

2. Students should decorate the can with construction paper patterns they make.

3. Using a small pointed object, have students punch several small holes in the can's lid. Students should make the same number of holes as the number of pencils they will decorate as daisies. Set the can aside.

4. Daisy pencils can be made by gluing a pompon to the top of the pencil and adding felt petals and leaves. To make leaves that can be posed, have students wrap small pieces of green pipe cleaners around the pencil "stem" first. The leaves may be glued on top of the pipe cleaner.

5. Tell students to decorate their flowers with sequins, glitter, faces, etc.

6. Have students place the pencil flowers in the holes in the coffee can lid. Students now have a flowerpot pencil holder that "kind of grows on you!"

Design

Art

Objective: To color an abstract design

Materials: construction paper, crayons or markers, white paper

Directions: Tell students that they are going to color a curved-line design. Each design will be very different and distinct - an original creation.

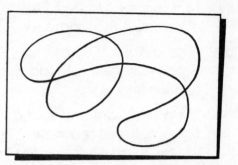

To have children physically "feel" a curved line, have the class line up single file and follow you around the tables and around the desks and chairs. Be sure to curve the line of children as you lead - no sharp corners or angles!

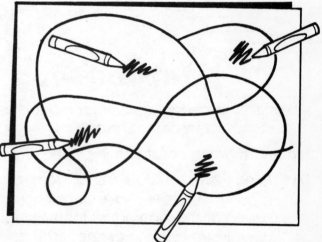

Encourage the children to use many different colors. Mounted on black construction paper and displayed in the classroom, these designs help the children feel a great sense of pride and accomplishment.

Science

Decompose

Objective: To expose children to some materials that decompose, and to create an awareness that some materials do not decompose

Materials: plastic objects (straw, utensil), vegetable or fruit (Lettuce leaf works well), rock, a paper item (plate, napkin), soil, paper, pen or pencil, potting containers (optional)

Directions: In potting containers, or outdoors, bury all four types of items separately. Allow two (or more) weeks to pass*, then dig up all four items. Discuss what you have found. Make a chart listing the biodegradable materials.

*To incorporate math, mark the "dig-up" day on your calendar. Keep a daily tally of the number of days before "dig-up" day.

Suggested Reading:
   It Was Just a Dream by Chris Van Allsburg

Does It Decompose?	
YES	NO
lettuce	rock
apple	wash cloth
banana peel	plastic straw
bread	ribbon
pickle	button
leaf	shoe string
tissue	plastic bag
	eraser

Dot-to-Dot

Math

Objective: To design a cover for a book using the dot-to-dot technique

Materials: white construction paper, crayons

Directions: Place ten dots in a random fashion on a paper. Make copies on construction paper for the students. Have children connect the dots in any order by drawing lines. A design will appear. Have the children color the individual sections of the design with different crayons.

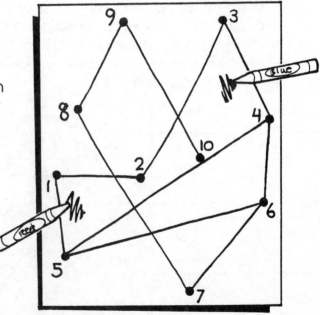

Dentist

Social Studies

Objective: To become familiar with the role of the dentist

Materials: copies of the chart below

Directions: Discuss the role of dentists - what they do, why people go to them and how they help people. This is also a good opportunity to stress good health habits and the care of teeth. Involve parents by sending home a "tooth brushing chart" at the beginning of each month (with an accompanying explanatory letter). At the end of the month, if all the children have brought their charts back to school properly checked, you might want to have a special class celebration for "D" Day - (Dental Health Day). Invite a dentist or a dental hygienist to visit the class. Have him or her demonstrate proper brushing techniques.

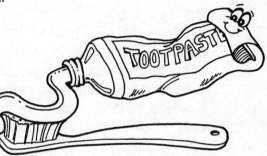

Suggested Reading:

Dr. DeSoto by William Steig
I Can Be a Doctor by Rebecca Hankin
I Can Be a Dentist by Ray Broekel
Curious George Goes to the Hospital by H.A. Rey

I brushed my teeth today!

S	M	T	W	Th	F	S

Dominoes

Show children how to build dominoes so they will knock each other down when the first one is toppled.

Duck, Duck, Goose

Variations of this game can be played by asking children to think of other animals that begin with the sound for "D."

dog, dog, CAT!

i.e. dog, dog, cat
donkey, donkey, horse
deer, deer, goat
dromedary, dromedary, camel
dinosaur, dinosaur, elephant
dormouse, dormouse, chipmunk
Dalmatian, Dalmatian, poodle

The child who is tapped with the animal name that does not begin with "D" is the one who must get up and chase the "tapper" around the circle.

A Delicious, Delightful Dessert

Cooking

Objective: Melt semi-sweet chocolate chips. Dip slices of banana and whole strawberries into the melted chocolate. Put them on waxed paper to cool and solidify. Enjoy!

Doughnuts

Materials: tube of biscuits, oil, sugar, cinnamon, electric fry pan, paper towels

Directions: Separate the biscuits. Roll and reshape each one into a circle. Fry in oil in an electric fry pan until brown. Drain on paper towels. Sprinkle with either confectioners sugar or a sugar and cinnamon mixture.

Five Little Ducks

Poetry

There were five little ducks, not any more.
One swam away, and then there were four.

There were four little ducks nesting near the tree.
One swam away, and then there were three.

The three little ducks looked at the sky so blue.
One swam away, and then there were two.

Those two little ducks were looking for some fun.
One swam away, and then there was one.

That one little duck who was swimming all alone,
He looked up and said, "Where have all the others gone?"

by Ada Frischer

Drum

Music

Play a march such as "Yankee Doodle" on a piano or play a tape or record. Have one or two children beat the rhythm on a drum. The rest of the class can clap or march to the rhythm.

Suggested Trips

- Have a doctor and/or dentist visit the classroom or arrange for your class to visit them.
- Dinosaur exhibit (if available)
- Dairy farm

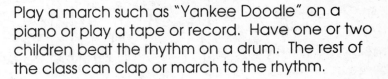

Museum of
Natural History

D Pictures for Miscellaneous Activities

Enlarge the cards to make flash cards for use throughout the study of the "D" sound.

Book List

Aliki. (1981). *Digging Up Dinosaurs.* New York: Harper and Row.

Berenstain, S. and Berenstain, J. (1987). *The Berenstain Bears Go to the Doctor.* New York: Random House.

Berenstain, S. and Berenstain, J. (1981). *The Berenstain Bears Visit the Dentist.* New York: Random House.

Freeman, D. (1977). *Dandelions.* Penguin Books.

Hankin, R. (1985). *I Can Be a Doctor.* Chicago, Illinois: Childrens Press.

Hoban, T. (1977). *Dig, Drill, Dump, Fill.* New York: Greenwillow Books.

Hoff, S. (1978). *Danny and the Dinosaur.* New York: Harper and Row.

Mayer, M. (1977). *Just Me and My Dad.* Western Publishing.

McCloskey, R. (1976). *Make Way for Ducklings.* New York: Penguin Books.

Most, B. (1984). *What Ever Happened to the Dinosaurs?* New York: Harcourt Brace Jovanovich.

Wildsmith, B. (1984). *Daisy.* New York: Pantheon Books.

Zion, G. (1956). *Harry the Dirty Dog.* New York: Harper and Row.

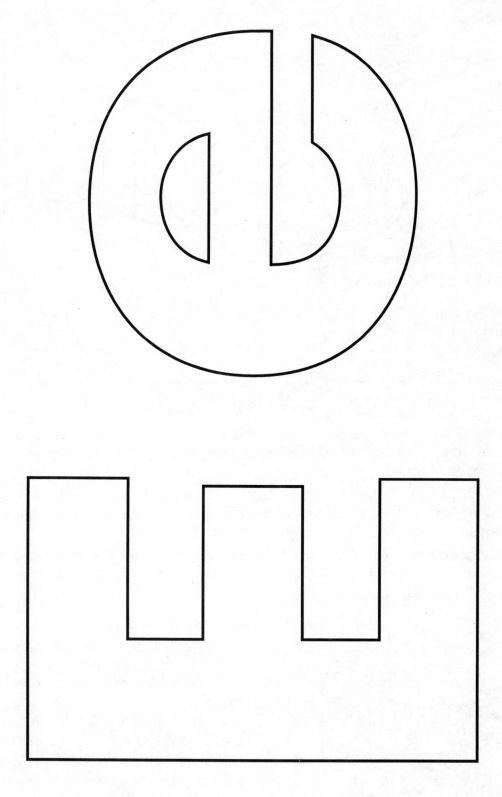

Ee

"Egg"citing Eggs

Art/Science

Objective: To demonstrate nature's beautiful colors and how they can be used to color eggs (This may also be tied in to show how people of some cultures, such as Native Americans, used natural dyes to paint their faces and bodies.)

Materials: stove, pot, water, boiled eggs, vinegar, natural plants or juices (i.e.,spinach leaves, beet juice, deeply colored onion skins, dandelion flowers, strawberries, grape juice, blueberries), vegetable oil on a cloth

Directions:
1. Make each individual dye by boiling the plant matter in water until the water absorbs the color. Strain and cool. More plant matter will create a stronger dye.

2. Drop several boiled eggs and a few drops of vinegar into the pot containing the natural dye. Gently simmer for approximately $1/2$ hour. Remove the eggs and dry completely. Rub a little oil on the eggs to enhance the color and make them shine.

3. Peel the eggs, if desired, to see if the dye was strong enough to penetrate the shell.

"Eventually, My Dear!"

"Mama, Mama," I cried,
"I never will see
Way, way up high
Over any tall tree!"
"Have patience, my dear!"
She comforted me.

I stretched, and I stretched
Until my neck hurt,
But my clearest view
Was still lots of dirt.
"Your time will come soon,"
Said Mom, the expert.

I made a monkey
Pull hard on my neck.
My muscles were sore,
And my back felt a wreck.
"Don't worry!" said Mom,
And she gave me a peck.

I had friends on the ground,
But it didn't seem fair
That my family could see
Way up in the air.
"We love you, my son,"
Said Mom, "Anywhere!"

Little by little
My legs grew stronger,
And each day it seemed
My neck became longer.
"You'd have noticed it
But you're headstrong, dear!"

One day after sleeping,
I opened my eyes—
Saw treetops below me . . .
I had reached my full size!
I bent down to kiss Mom—
She had tears in her eyes!

So now I stand proudly—
Almost 20 feet high.
My friends on the ground
Say that I touch the sky!
Mama is so smart,
And now I know why!

E's Are Not I's, or Are They?

Letter Recognition

Objective: To write and recognize the letter "e"

Directions:

1. On a sheet of paper, write pairs of the letter "e" numerous times. Be sure to leave enough space so that students can turn the "e's" into eyes for people or imaginative pictures. (See illustration.)

2. Make a copy of the page for each student.

3. Have students trace the "e's" and create wonderful works of "e" art.

EAST

IF8661 The Alphabet

Enchanted Elves

Art

Objective: To create and decorate elf ornaments

Materials: one small pine cone per student, green tempera paint, paintbrushes, hair spray, white glue, tape, glitter (optional), one small Styrofoam ball or large bead per student, green construction paper, one thin piece of wire per student, yarn, scissors, two tiny wiggly eyes per student, one tiny pompon per student, thin markers, one green pipe cleaner per student, hard candy wrapped in cellophane

Directions:

1. Have students paint the pine cones with green paint. When dry, they spray them with hair spray.

2. Students then glue a Styrofoam ball or large bead to the pine cone for a head.

3. Next, have students glue triangular shoes made from green construction paper to the bottom of the pine cone. Show students how to use scissors to curl the tops.

4. Yarn may be glued to the head for hair.

5. Then, have students glue a construction paper hat to the head.

6. An elf's face may be created by gluing on wiggly eyes and a tiny pompon nose. A thin marker may be used to draw in the mouth and cheeks.

7. Wrap a pipe cleaner securely around the neck for arms. Have students bend it at the elbows.

8. Tape a piece of candy to the ends of the pipe cleaner for hands.

9. Have students attach a thin piece of wire around the neck and form a loop so it can be hung from a tree either in the classroom or at home.

10. Glitter may be glued to the tops of the pine cone for a sparkled effect.

Follow-Up Fun: Elves are famous for making and giving gifts anonymously, so have your students become elves. Have each child draw and color a picture of an elf. Instruct them not to sign their name on the pictures. Collect the drawings. Secretly, tape a piece of hard candy to each picture (so you become an elf, too). Put each drawing in an envelope and seal it. Let each child take an envelope with instructions not to open it until he/she gets home.

"If I Were Elastic . . ." Game

"If I were elastic," said the snake,
"I'd never get a stomachache.
I'd stretch my stomach and make plenty of room
To allow me lots more food to consume.
I'd gulp a mouse, a cat, a horse.
There'd still be lots of room, of course!

Objective: To guess objects hidden in a sock

Materials: long, thin socks, wiggle eyes, glue, objects to hide in the socks, rubber bands

Directions: 1. Make five snakes by gluing wiggle eyes onto the toe area of each sock.

2. Fill each snake with five objects. Secure each end with a rubber band.

A jack?

3. Divide the class into five groups.

4. Give each group a snake.

5. Give them several minutes to guess what objects their snake "swallowed."

6. The group who guesses the most correct objects wins.

7. After the game, it might be fun to "turn the tables on the snakes" and eat gummy snakes (or worms).

For the Record: Large pythons usually eat animals the size of a house cat, but they sometimes kill animals as large as a wild pig (about 100 pounds) and swallow them whole!

George Eastman—"Say Cheese"

Science

Objective: To learn about the history of the camera, to take photographs, and to write captions for photographs

Materials: a camera, film

Background Information: Before cameras, people could project images onto a screen or piece of paper, but they weren't permanent. In 1826, a French inventor named Joseph Niépce took the first actual photograph. Other inventors continued to improve photography, but George Eastman, an American, invented a machine for coating the glass plates in cameras, and he even perfected flexible roll film so that people didn't have to process their own. In 1888, Eastman produced a light camera, the Kodak, that sold for $25. By 1900, he sold a camera that cost $1. This way, millions of people could become amateur photographers.

click

Directions:

1. Read about and discuss George Eastman's amazing discovery.

2. Discuss how to correctly use a camera.

3. Pair up students.

4. Let each child photograph his/her partner doing a favorite activity at school.

5. Let students mount the photographs on a bulletin board with the title: "We Oughta Be in Pictures!"

Long Live the King!

Suggested Reading: *My Camera* by George Ancona
I Can Be a Photographer by Christine Osinski

Eggplants, Eggplants, Everywhere!

Objective: To count the number of eggplants hidden in the picture

Math

Materials: an eggplant picture (below), crayons

Directions: Observe and discuss what an eggplant is. (The eggplant probably came from India. Its egg-shaped fruit grows on a bush. It can be purple, yellow, brown, white or striped. The fruit of the eggplant is sometimes called a garden egg.)

Give each child the picture below containing the hidden eggplants to color. Together count the number of hidden eggplants.

Extinct and Extraordinary

Science

Objective: To create dioramas depicting dinosaurs in their habitats

Materials: one shoe box (or larger box) per student, clay (brown, green or gray), construction paper, scissors, glue, stones, twigs, soil, cotton, miscellaneous items (See directions), pictures of dinosaurs

Suggestion: Read several books to students about dinosaurs and their habitats

Suggested Reading: *Dinosaur Bones* by Aliki
My Visit to the Dinosaurs by Aliki

Directions:

1. Have students cover the outside of their shoe box with construction paper. Show them how to trace each side, cut it out, and glue it onto the box.

2. Now, have students create the dinosaurs' habitats inside the box. Stress creativity! Suggestions include:

   Sky—Cover the inside of the box with blue construction paper by once again tracing the sides, cutting and gluing the paper to the sides of the box.

   Trees—Glue twigs onto green construction paper.

   Clouds—Glue cotton to sky.

   Water—Glue either blue construction paper or blue cellophane to base.

   Grass—Glue real grass or Easter basket grass to bottom of box.

   Eggs—Use white jellybeans with twigs (for nests).

   Rocks—Use different sizes of stones.

3. Let students make clay dinosaurs. (Have pictures available for reference.)

4. Display students' dioramas on a table with the title "A Look Into the Past."

"A Look Into the Past"

E Pictures for Miscellaneous Activities

Enlarge the pictures below to make flash cards, bulletin board characters or characters to be used in a story.

Book List

Aliki. (1988). *Dinosaur Bones*. New York: Crowell.

Aliki. (1985). *My Visit to the Dinosaurs*. New York: Crowell.

Balian, L. (1980). *Leprechauns Never Lie*. Nashville, TN: Abingdon.

Boynton, S. (1979). *Hester in the Wild*. New York: Harper and Row.

Brewster, P. (1981). *Ellsworth and the Cats from Mars*. New York: Houghton Mifflin.

Calhoun, M. (1962). *Hungry Leprechaun*. New York: Morrow.

Carlstrom, N. (1988). *Better Not Get Wet*. New York: Macmillan.

Dos Santos, J. (1982). *Henri and the Loup-Garou*. New York: Pantheon.

Fort, P. (1988). *Redbird*. New York: Orchard Books.

Jonas, A. (1985). *The Trek*. New York: Greenwillow Books.

Kennedy, R. (1979). *The Leprechaun's Story*. New York: Dutton.

Low, A. (1982). *Genie and the Witch's Spells*. New York: Knopf.

Polacco, P. (1988). *Rechenka's Eggs*. New York: Philomel Books.

Seuss. (1940). *Horton Hatches the Egg*. New York: Random House.

Small, D. (1985). *Imogene's Antlers*. New York: Crown Publishers.

Stevenson, J. (1990). *Emma at the Beach*. New York: Greenwillow Books.

Stevenson, J. (1983). *What's Under My Bed?* New York: Greenwillow Books.

Vaës, A. (1982). *The Porcelain Pepper Pot*. Boston, MA: Little, Brown.

Westcott, N. (1981). *The Giant Vegetable Garden*. Boston, MA: Little, Brown.

More E Pictures for Miscellaneous Activities

Enlarge the pictures below to make flash cards, bulletin board characters or characters that can be used in a story.

Book List

Ancona, G. (1992). *My Camera.* New York: Crown Publishers.

Brown, R. (1985). *The Big Sneeze.* New York: Lothrop, Lee and Shepard Books.

Dodds, D. (1989). *Wheel Away!* New York: Harper and Row.

Hayes, S. (1988). *Eat Up, Gemma.* New York: Lothrop, Lee and Shepard Books.

Khalsa, D. (1988). *Sleepers.* New York: Crown Publishers.

Osinski, C. (1986). *I Can Be a Photographer.* Chicago, IL: Children's Press.

Peet, B. (1978). *Eli.* Boston, MA: Houghton Mifflin.

Rockwell, A. and Rockwell, H. (1985). *The Emergency Room.* New York: Macmillan.

Unstead, R.J. (1978). *See Inside an Egyptian Town.* New York: Warwick Press.

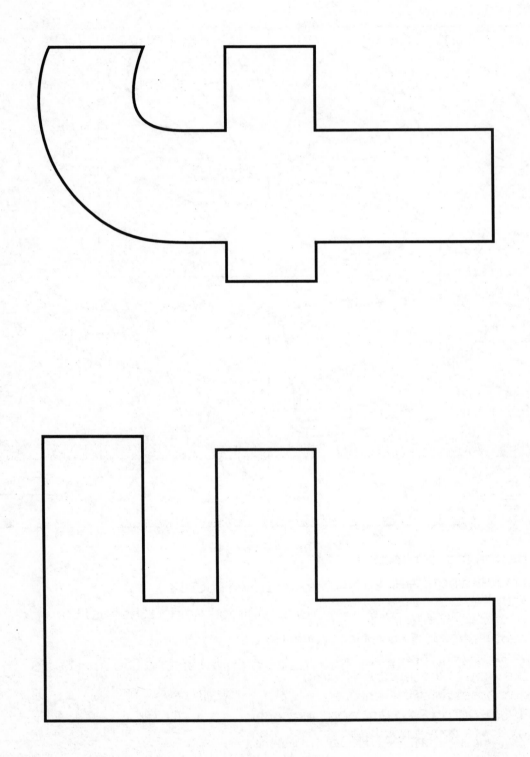

ABCDEFGHIJKLMNOPQRSTUVWXYZ

Ff

I Like My Friend Because . . .

Social Studies

Objective: paper, crayons/marker

Directions: Discuss what "friend" means with the class. Why do you like your friend? What does your best friend do that you like? Why do you think your friend likes you? Get several different responses from the children. Give each child a paper on which to draw a picture of a friend.

Fall Trees

Art

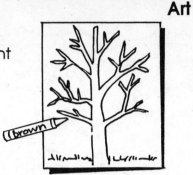

Objective: To create fall trees and colors using fingers and paint

Directions: smocks, cray-pas or crayons, light-colored construction paper, five shallow cups of paint (red, orange, yellow, brown and green)

1. Using brown cray-pas or brown crayons, have children draw and color a tree trunk.

2. Set up a table with the five cups of paint. Working with five children at a time, have each child stand in front of one color of paint and with one finger, have each child paint leaves on and around his/her tree.

Paper Plate Fish

Objective: To create a fish from a paper plate and to become familiar with characteristics of a fish (gills, fins, scales, etc.)

Materials: a paper plate for each student, scissors, pencils, three 2" x 1" strips of paper for each student, glue, crayons

Directions:
1. Give each child a paper plate and instruct him/her to create the mouth of the fish with two lines to create a "piece of pie." The students or you will cut the "pie piece" out and glue it to the opposite side of the plate to create a tail.

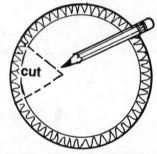

2. With their crayons, the students can add scales.

3. Give each student three strips of paper. They will glue them on the body of the fish to create gills. Also give them precut fins and an eye to glue in place.

Suggested Reading:

The Biggest Fish in the Sea by Dahlov Ipcar
A Fish Out of Water by P.D. Eastman

Swimmy by Leo Lionni
Fish Is Fish by Leo Lionni

Farm Animals

Science

Objective: To help children recognize common farm animals and make farm animal sounds

Materials: opaque projector, oaktag, markers, scissors, cards below

Directions: To make farm animal flashcards, cut out the animal pictures below on the dotted lines. Use an overhead projector to enlarge them on oaktag. Color them with markers.

Hold each card up and ask the children to name the animal. Then have the children make the appropriate animal sounds. Sing "Old MacDonald Had a Farm" and read *On the Farm* by Richard Scarry.

My Feelings Book

Objective: To write and illustrate a book about feelings

Materials: 2 sheets of white paper for each child, crayons or markers, a copy of the sentence strips below for each student

Directions: After reading and discussing books that relate to feelings, have students complete the sentence strips at the bottom of the page with your help. Cut out the strips and glue each one on a separate piece of paper.

Next, have each student illustrate his/her feelings.

Suggested Reading:

Books that deal with happy emotions:
The Happy Day by Ruth Krauss
Happiness is Smiling by Katharine Gehm

Books that deal with sad emotions:
The Cow Who Said Oink by Bernard Most
Little Blue and Little Yellow by Leo Lionni
Sylvester and the Magic Pebble
    by William Steig

I am happy when _____ .

I am sad when _____ .

My Family

Objective : To draw families

Materials: a 9" x 12" sheet of white paper for each student, crayons

Directions: Discuss families and the various make-up of families. Ask volunteers to discuss the members and make-up of their families. Next, tell students they will draw a picture of their family. Create a bulletin board with the finished pictures, entitled "The Ones We Love."

There are 4 people in my house.   This is our house.

Baby Farm Animals

Science

Objective: To help children recognize baby farm animals and their names
To help children recognize farm products

Materials: colored index cards, crayons, pictures of adult farm animals, pictures of baby farm animals, pictures of farm animal products, paste

Directions: Make a concentration game for the children by pasting pictures of baby farm animals and their matching words on the back of index cards. Several different games may be designed. (Use different-colored index cards for each game.)

1. identical baby farm animal matched to identical baby farm animal
2. adult farm animal matched to offspring (Use the pictures from page 65.)
3. baby farm animal picture matched to baby farm animal word
4. adult farm animal matched to product

Other suggestions: duck - duckling - eggs; hen - chick - eggs; cow - calf - milk; sheep - lamb - wool; goat - kid - milk, cheese; goose - gosling - down; pig - piglet - pork

Fall Season

Science

Objective: To help children become aware of the change of the summer season to fall

Materials: crayons, 9" x 12" sheets of oaktag, green construction paper, stapler

Directions: Discuss the change of the season to fall as it relates to the leaves. Explain that leaves change color in the fall.

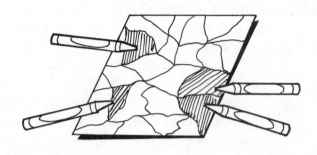

1. To make a model of a fall leaf, give the children a piece of oaktag. Have them color it with the beautiful colors of fall: orange, red, yellow and brown. They should blend in these colors and cover the entire sheet.

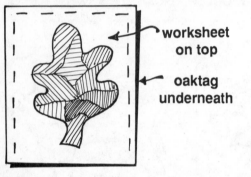

worksheet on top

oaktag underneath

2. Next, give the children a precut leaf outline.

3. Staple or glue the sheet with the leaf outline to the colored oaktag. The leaf will appear to have beautiful fall colors.

Forests

Science

Objective: To become aware of how animals need forests and the effects on these animals when forests are cut down

Materials: mural paper, assorted paints, brushes, smocks, black marker

Directions: • Discuss what animals live in a forest. Divide the mural paper in half by drawing a thick black vertical line down the center. On the first half of the paper, have students draw a forest. (Be sure students include animals.)

• On the second half of the mural paper, instruct students to draw tree stumps. Discuss what would happen to all the living creatures included in the first half.

Favorite Fruit Graph

Math

Objective: To create a bar graph

Materials: fruits, crayons, graph paper (Make your own using 1/2 inch squares.)

Directions: Have each child bring one favorite fruit to school. List all the fruits that have been brought to school on the graph paper and have each child record his/her own choice by coloring in a square next to his/her fruit choice. Tally the children's choice to find out which fruit is most popular

🍎 apple	▨								1
🍌 banana	▨	▨	▨						3
🍐 pear	▨	▨							2
🍊 orange	▨								1

After the graph is completed, use the fruit to make a fruit salad.

Fold into Fourths

Objective: To learn the concept of fourths

Materials: 8 1/2" x 11" drawing paper, crayons

Directions: Show the children the proper way to fold. Remind them to match the corners and then use their hands to crease the folds.

First they fold into halves, then into fourths. Direct them to draw an object in each fourth.

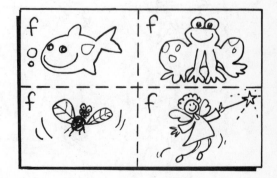

Fish in the Net

Materials: gym or large area

Directions: Line the class up at one end of the gym. Tell the students that they are now fish. You stand in the middle of the gym. You are the fisherman. To play the game, the fisherman calls out, "Fish in the net!" The students must then run across the gym to the other side without being tagged by you (fisherman). Any students tagged join hands with you and become part of the fisherman's net. The people standing in the center all shout out, "Fish in the net!" Without dropping hands, tney try to capture the fish as they run to the opposite sides of the gym. The game ends when all students but one have been caught. The winner then becomes the fisherman for the next game.

Follow My Feet

Materials: gym or large area

Directions: Talk about the importance of feet. Talk about the different ways people can move their feet. Let children take turns showing different ways to move their feet. Then, play "Follow My Feet" (a variation on "Follow The Leader.") Have children take turns being the leader.

As a rest time afterward to quiet the children, read *The Foot Book* by Dr. Seuss.

Families

Objective: To create a family mobile

Materials: a paper plate for each student, yarn, hole punch, 9" x 4" sheets of white paper, construction paper (assorted colors), crayons, paste or glue, scissors

Directions: Discuss what a family is. Ask several volunteer students to name the individuals who make up their families. Next, explain to students that they will create a family mobile.

colored paper

1. On the sheets of white paper, instruct students to daw and color each member of their family (one person per sheet).

2. Have students cut out each picture and paste it on construction paper. They should cut the construction paper to frame the individual portraits.

Punch holes.

3. Hole punch the frame and hole punch a spot on the rim of the paper plate.

4. Attach the frame to the plate with yarn. Repeat the same for each family member.

5. Next, punch two holes near the center of the plate. String one piece of yarn through the two holes so that the mobile can be hung.

Five Funny Fish

Poetry and Finger Plays/ Dramatization

Five funny fish swimming in the sea.
The first one said, "Look at me!"
The second one said, "The water is deep."
The third one said, "Don't fall asleep."
The fourth one said, "Let's swim away."
The fifth one said, "But not today."
Along came a man with a line and bait.
Five fish swam away. They didn't wait.
by Ada Frischer

Extension: Have the children dramatize the poem. Five children stand in front of the group representing fish 1, 2, 3, 4, 5. The "fish" act while the class recites the poem.

The Farmer in the Dell   Music

Using this tune, have the children suggest other verses about the farmer such as the farmer plows his field, the farmer plants his seeds, the farmer builds a fence, etc.

I see piglets
I see piglets.

I see piglets
on the farm,
on the farm.

Fudge

Cooking

Melt one large bag of chocolate bits in a double boiler.

Add - 1 can condensed milk - sweetened
1 teaspoon vanilla

Pour into a pan over waxed paper and let cool. Cut into squares.

Fun Fish Food

If possible, take your class to visit the seafood counter in your local grocery store. Arrange with the person in charge to have him/her talk to the children about the various kinds of fish and show them examples of freshwater fish, saltwater fish, shellfish, etc. Perhaps there will even be a live lobster tank.

Back at the classroom, let students sample some fish (tuna) using plastic forks, always bringing their attention to the "F" words.

is for fork.

Suggested Trips

Firehouse
Florist
Fish hatchery - aquarium
Farm
Factory

Book List

Anglund, J. (1958). *A Friend Is Someone Who Likes You.* New York: Harcourt Brace
   Jovanovich.

Carle, E. (1971). *Do You Want To Be My Friend?* New York: Crowell.

Coxe, M. (1990). *Whose Footprints?* New York: Crowell.

De Regniers, B.S. (1964). *May I Bring a Friend?* New York: Atheneum.

Eastman, P. D. (1986). *Sam and the Firefly.* New York: Beginner Books.

Elkin, B. (1957). *Six Foolish Fishermen.* New York: Macmillan.

Heine, H. (1986). *Friends.* New York: Macmillan.

Ipcar, D. (1972). *The Biggest Fish in the Sea.* New York: Viking Press.

Lionni, L. (1970). *Fish Is Fish.* New York: Pantheon Books.

Lionni, L. (1967). *Frederick.* New York: Pantheon Books.

Lobel, A. (1976). *Frog and Toad, All Year.* New York: Harper and Row.

Lobel, A. (1972). *Frog and Toad Together.* New York: Harper and Row.

McPhail, D. (1985). *Farm Morning.* San Diego, CA: Harcourt Brace Jovanovich.

Miller, J. (1992). *Farm Counting Book.* New York: Simon and Schuster Trade.

Palmer, H. (1967). *Fish Out of Water.* New York: Beginner Books.

Povensen, A. and Provensen, M. (1992). *Our Animal Friends at Maple Hill Farm.* New York:
   Random.

Rey, M. (1985). *Curious George at the Fire Station.* New York: Houghton Mifflin.

Rojankowsky, F. (1967). *Animals on the Farm.* New York: Knopf.

Ryder, J. (1977). *Fireflies.* New York: Harper and Row.

Seuss, Dr. (1960). *One Fish, Two Fish.* New York: Beginner Books.

F Pictures for Miscellaneous Activites

IF8661 The Alphabet

Gg

Gold Medals

Social Studies/
Self

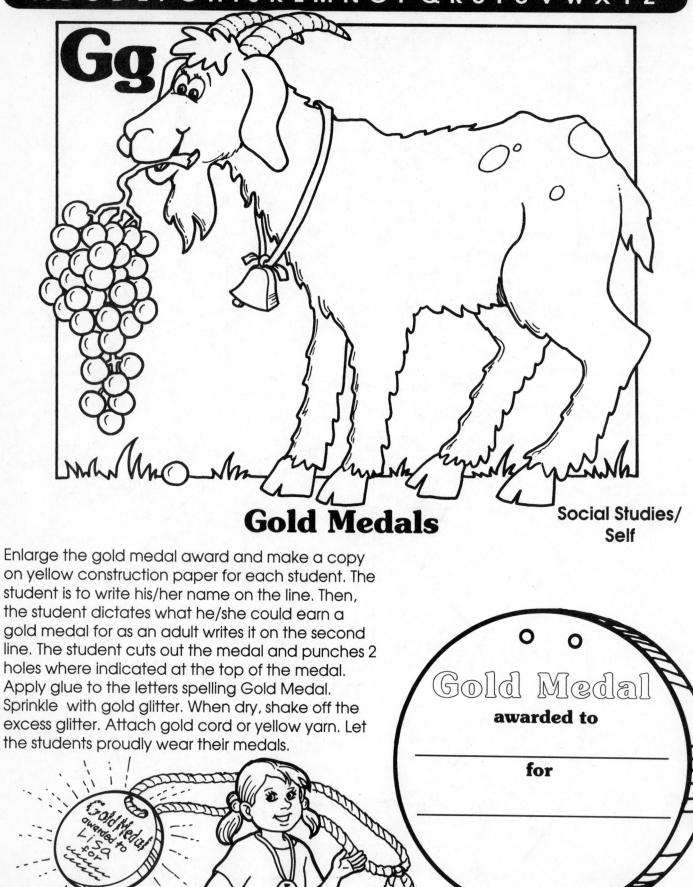

Enlarge the gold medal award and make a copy on yellow construction paper for each student. The student is to write his/her name on the line. Then, the student dictates what he/she could earn a gold medal for as an adult writes it on the second line. The student cuts out the medal and punches 2 holes where indicated at the top of the medal. Apply glue to the letters spelling Gold Medal. Sprinkle with gold glitter. When dry, shake off the excess glitter. Attach gold cord or yellow yarn. Let the students proudly wear their medals.

Gold Medal
awarded to
_____
for
_____

IF8661 The Alphabet

Giggle Book

Writing/ Reading

Objective: To create a page of a book full of nonsense situations to make students giggle

Materials: a sheet of white paper for each student, crayons, pencils, book rings or bindery

Directions: Ask the students, "Can you imagine a dog that said meow?" "Can you imagine a chair with ears?" "Can you imagine me with purple hair?" "All of these things would make me giggle!" Next, ask the students to imagine some things that would make them giggle. Discuss the students' responses. Give each student a sheet of white paper. Explain to students that they are to write and illustrate something that they think would make them giggle. Have students complete the sentence, "When I imagine _____ , I giggle." (For young students, run the partial statement off on a copy machine so that you or a volunteer may fill in the sentence as it is dictated by the child.) Have students illustrate their sentences. Create a cover, collect work and bind with book rings or bindery.

Suggested Reading: *Emma Giggled* by Lou Alpert

"Go Get the Green" Book

Objective: To provide alliteration with the hard sound for "G" and to emphasize the color green

Materials: white construction paper, crayons

Directions: Have each child complete the sentence, "Go get the green _____ ." Children may copy the sentence, or you may want to run off the sentence starter for them.

Children illustrate their sentences using lots of green in their pictures. Collect and assemble them into a book. The cover can be a design using blue and yellow paint mixed together - perhaps finger paint.

Suggested Reading: *Little Blue and Little Yellow* by Leo Lionni

Grandparents Day or Special Guest Day

Objective: To celebrate Grandparents Day or Special Guest Day

Social Studies

Directions: Send grandparents (or special guest) a note from the children. (See below.)

Plan a program for the special guests. Have the children show their guests around the room. Entertainment might consist of songs and a reading.

Prepare refreshments with the children for the guests.

Children will present their grandparents with the gift (**Grandparents Book**) that they have published. (See page 81.)

Suggested Reading:

Grandmother and I by Helen E. Buckley
Grandfather and I by Helen E. Buckley

Dear _____ ,

Please visit me in class on _____

from _____ to _____ o'clock.

This is a special day just for you.

Love,

_____

Glue and Glitter

Art

Objective: Create ghosts using glue and glitter

Materials: construction paper having pictures of ghosts, white glue, glitter

Directions: Using white glue, have children trace pictures of ghosts (you provide) on construction paper. Then have students sprinkle glitter over the glue. Allow the glue and glitter to dry for a few minutes before shaking off the excess. The extra glitter may be saved by pouring it back into the original container. Remind the children to apply the glitter before the glue dries, or else the glitter will not stick!

Science

Watching Grass Grow

Objective: To show children how to grow grass in small containers

Materials: grass seed, soil, egg cartons, markers, trays

Directions: Carefully poke two small holes in the bottom of each section of the egg carton. Separate each cup from the carton and have the children decorate them by drawing a face on two sides. For "growth insurance," you may want to provide two or three cups per child. Fill each cup with soil and sprinkle some grass seed on top. Press lightly into the soil, water gently, place in a sunny spot and wait for hair to grow!

Keep a record of how many days pass before the first "hair" is noticed.

Grumpy Gorilla

Creative Dramatics

Objective: To encourage children to be uninhibited in front of people

Materials: box or bag, oaktag, glue, scissors, cards below

Directions: Copy the cards below and glue them onto oaktag. Let the children take turns drawing a card out of a bag or box to act out. Children love to act! You can do them over and over. To build their vocabulary, talk about what they think the different adjectives mean. Add to the cards as needed.

glorious grasshopper	glowing grocer	gentle giant	ghastly grizzly bear
grumpy gorilla	gloating giraffe	gigantic gardener	glamorous goat
giggly gerbil	gloomy girl	grieving Guinea pig	gleeful ghost

Grocery Store

Dramatization

Objective: To act out a trip to the grocery store and to act as a grocer

Materials: toy cash register, play money, wallets or purses, empty cereal boxes, milk cartons, cans, egg cartons, plastic foods, toy grocery cart or shopping basket

Directions: Ask parents to help you collect the materials needed. Set up the grocery store in a corner of your room by placing items on shelves or tables. Set the cash register on a table near an imaginary door. Supply the register and purses/wallets with play money. Place basket or cart near the "Door." Your store is now ready for use!

Grandparents Book

Objective: To create a book about grandparents

Materials: 4 sheets of newsprint per child, crayons, pencils, stapler

Directions: Use the books below as an introduction to a discussion about grandparents. Have the children talk about things they do with grandparents, why they like to visit them, etc.

Fold and staple.

> *Grandmother and I* by Helen E. Buckley
> *Grandfather and I* by Helen E. Buckley
> *Grandparents Around the World* by Dorka Raynor

Each child will "publish" his/her own book. Give each child 4 pieces of newsprint. Have children fold them in half to make an 8-page book. Prepare 8 pages for each book as follows:

1. **Cover** - Discuss appropriate titles with the children. Write the title as selected by each child. Have the children design the cover.

2. **Dedication Page** - This book is dedicated to . . . - Take dictation from each child. Add a publication date to the page.

3. **These are my grandparents.** (Children will draw their grandparents.)

4. **My grandparents like . . .**

5. **I love my grandparents because . . .**

6. **My grandparents love me because . . .**

7. **This is what I like to do with my grandparents:**

For pages 4, 5, 6 and 7, take dictation from each child and have the children illustrate the text.

8. **Author's Page** - Each child can draw a picture of himself/herself or paste in a photograph on the page and write his/her name. Help students write a brief biography (age, grade, favorite food, school attending, what author would like to be, etc.).

Variation: Instead of pages 4, 5, 6 and 7, have each child dictate a story about his/her grandparents. Put two or three sentences on a page and have the child illustrate them.

In the event that a child does not have a grandparent, this book could be about "My Favorite Person" (friend, aunt, uncle, parent, etc.).

Coordinate this activity with Grandparents Day. (See Social Studies page 78.)

Granola

Using a granola cereal as a base, discuss with the children what healthy foods can be added to granola to make a good snack (i.e., raisins, sunflower seeds, cut-up dried fruits or fresh fruits).

Make selections using a voting system and then prepare the mix.

Poetry

The Ground Hog's Prediction

I saw a ground hog on Ground-Hog Day.
He looked for his shadow but he wanted to play.
He saw his shadow.
It scared him so.
He ran back in his hole and he said, "Oh no!"
    "It's not spring yet!
    Six more weeks of winter, I bet."

    by Ada Frischer

Let's Guess!

Math

Objective: To practice guessing (estimation)

Materials: containers, "G" items (gumballs, Goobers, giraffes, groceries, etc.)

Directions: Put a bunch of like items in a container (perhaps feature one each day). Have students write down how many of the item they believe are in the container.

Count the items together. Emphasize to students that no answer is wrong when estimating. Point out that it is good, however, to get as close to the actual number as possible.

Compare various containers of items. Ask questions like, "Why are there less items in this container than the other? How many of this item do you think will fit in this container?" Put items in and count together.

Suggested Trips

Greenhouse
Grocery store

Book List

Buckley, H.E. (1961). *Grandmother and I.* New York: Lothrop, Lee and Shepard.

Buckley, H.E. (1959). *Grandfather and I.* New York: Lothrop, Lee and Shepard.

Carle, E. (1977). *The Grouchy Ladybug.* New York: T.Y. Crowell.

Krauss, R. (1947). *Growing Story.* New York: Harper and Row.

Seuss, Dr. (1957). *How the Grinch Stole Christmas.* New York: Random House.

Showers, P. (1974). *Where Does the Garbage Go?* New York: Harper and Row.

G Pictures for Miscellaneous Activities

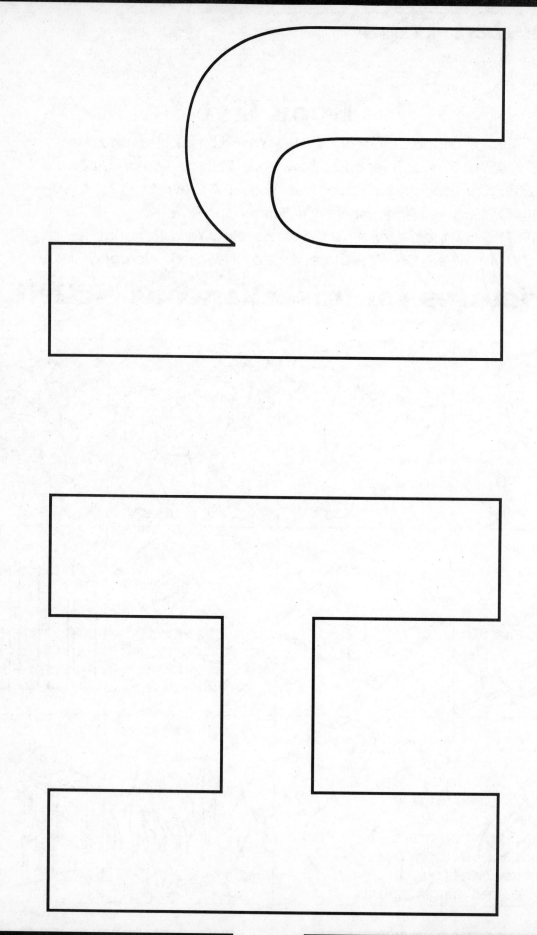

Hh

Hearts

Art

Objective: To create hearts from construction paper without using a pattern

Materials: 4" x 5" sheets of newsprint, 4" x 5" sheets of construction paper of various colors, scissors, hole punch, posterboard, optional - paste

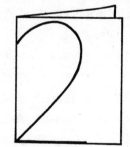

Directions: Fold the sheet of newsprint in half. (Newsprint is an inexpensive material to practice with, and it is easy to cut.) With the folded side on the left, make a two. (See illustration.)

Next, cut on the curve of the "2." Open and you have a heart!

When students have had the opportunity to practice with the newsprint, supply them with different sizes of construction paper. Make a heart collage by pasting hearts to posterboard, or create heart necklaces by punching holes and stringing them on yarn.

Hats

Art

Objective: To design a hat

Materials: paper plates, white glue, assorted materials such as crêpe paper, streamers, ribbons, buttons, beads, construction paper, tissue paper, shells, pasta shapes, glitter, gummed stars, feathers, artificial flowers, etc.

Directions: Tell the children that they are going to be hat designers and model for them some outlandish things they can do with the above materials. Make sure the materials are glued to the bottom side of the plate. Attach ribbon, yarn or cord to the sides so the hat can be tied under the chin. Have a "fashion" parade in school.

Suggested Reading:

Jennie's Hat by Ezra Jack Keats

Extension Activity:

Read the original poem on page 93, **All the Hats**. Make copies of it for the whole class. Mount them on light colored construction paper and let the children draw all kinds of hats all the way around the poem.

What Do You See in a Hole?

Objective: To encourage creative thinking

Directions: Lead a discussion about different kinds of holes and what you might see in them.

1. hole in a tree - squirrel
2. hole in grass - rabbit
3. hole in a house - mouse
4. hole in a hive - bees
5. hole in a doghouse - dog
6. hole in a sock - toe
7. hole in a glove - finger
8. hole in a leaf - ladybug, aphid, caterpillar
9. hole in an apple - worm

Give children each a large round circle ("a hole") on which to draw one of the above.

I Can Help With My Helping Hands

Objective: To write and illustrate how students can help and to trace their own helping hands

Materials: 12" x 18" sheets of white paper, crayons or markers, pencils, glue, scissors, paint (optional)

Directions: Discuss with students how they can help family and friends. Then pass out paper on which the words "I can help" are written at the top. On the paper have students work with a partner to trace both their right and left hands. Above the hands, students illustrate how they help.

Habitat

Objective: To become familiar with the word "habitat" and which animals live above, on and below the ground, and those that live in water

Materials: mural paper, magazines, scissors, crayons, glue

Directions: On mural paper, make four equal sections by drawing three vertical lines. Label each section "Trees - Above the Ground," "Land - On the Ground," "In the Dirt - Underground" and "Water." Have students cut out pictures of mammals, fish, insects, reptiles, etc., and glue them on the mural in the appropriate box. If the animal has a habitat of two categories, glue the picture on the line dividing the categories (For example, a frog lives on the ground as well as in the water.)

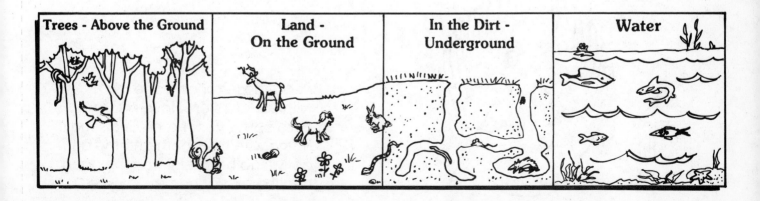

Health Habits

Social Studies

Objective: To reinforce good health habits such as "Cover your sneeze, please."

Preparation: Discuss good health habits with the children. Talk about why it is important to cover your sneeze. Keep a tissue box handy in the classroom and indicate its location to the children. Tissues should be thrown away after each use. If you have a sink in your classroom, hands should be washed. Read the poem on page 89.

Directions: Now that children have become aware of this health habit, they are ready to illustrate the poem.

On the paper plate, have students draw their face. Have them add eyes, nose, mouth and hair.

Each child will trace and cut out one hand. (They may need help cutting. Or, you could provide a hand previously prepared.) Paste or staple tissue over the nose and mouth and paste or staple the hand over the tissue. (See illustration.)

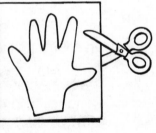

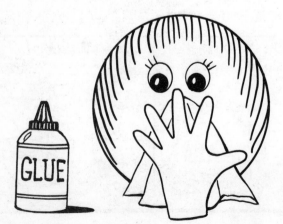

Read the letter on page 89 with the children. Have each child sign his/her name and send it home with the poem and the art activity to help reinforce this good health habit at home.

Dear Parents,

We are learning about good health habits in school. We read this poem, and I made a picture of myself covering my sneeze. Please help me remember this at home.

Love,

_____

Ahhhhh...

Cover Your Sneeze, Please

Please, please cover your sneeze.
Not your toes,
Not even your knees.
When you have a cold,
And maybe you wheeze,
Please, please cover your sneeze.

Please, please cover your sneeze.
We don't want your germs.
We want none of these.
Not us, not the bees,
Not the birds in the trees.
So, please, please cover your sneeze.

by Ada Frischer

TISSUE

Hearing - Match the Sounds

Science

Objective: To introduce the children to the sense of hearing

Materials: 10 toilet paper rolls, 20 squares of paper to cover the open ends of the rolls, 20 rubber bands, 10 paper clips, 10 staples, 2 erasers, 4 jingle bells, 12 identical wooden beads

Directions: Explain to the children that hearing is one of the five senses and that we hear through our ears. This is a good time to introduce some good ear safety habits.

- Don't scream in someone's ears.
- Don't play music or TV too loud.
- Don't stick things in your ears.

After some discussion about hearing, explain to the children that you are going to play a game, and that the sense of hearing is very important to the game.

Place one square of construction paper over the end of a paper roll and secure it with a rubber band. Put 5 paper clips in the roll and seal the other end with another square of construction paper. Shake it, so the children can hear the sound. Prepare another one, exactly the same. Now, shake this one alternately with the first one. Ask the children if they can tell you about the two sounds. (They are the same.)

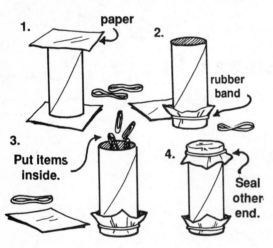

1. paper
2. rubber band
3. Put items inside.
4. Seal other end.

Now, prepare the remaining sets as follows:

5 staples in each of two rolls
1 eraser in each of two rolls
2 jingle bells in each of two rolls
6 identical wooden beads in each of two rolls

As you prepare each set with the children, demonstrate several times how each one sounds. Be sure the children are aware that two have the same sound.

Now, we are ready for the game. Mix up all the shakers and set them up as for a game of concentration.

Invite one child to come up and try two shakers. If they match, take them out of the game. See if the child can guess what is in them. If they do not match, the child puts them back in their original places. Continue the game until all five pairs are matched.

Hearing

Science

Objective: To utilize the sense of hearing by trying to discriminate between sounds

Materials: shoe box, small objects (marbles, rocks, M & M's, rulers), tape recording of household sounds (a door closing, water dripping, individual climbing stairs, etc.)

Directions: Discuss the sense of hearing with students. How do we hear? What do we hear with? Why do we have two ears? Next, have students close their eyes. Place one of the small objects you have collected in the shoe box. Have one student shake the box and allow him/her to guess the content. Repeat until all materials have been utilized. A second approach to this activity is to pre-record household sounds and then play each sound, allowing students to guess the source of the sound.

Is it a marble?

Hibernation

The sheep's wool grows thick in the winter.
The hair on the dog does too.
You can see many animals all year-round
When you visit them in the zoo.

But the bear sleeps all winter.
Into his cave he goes too.
A snake curls up in a hole in the ground
And sleeps all winter through.

The frog swims down into mud
And sleeps the winter away.
The ground hog tunnels into the ground
And comes out on Ground-Hog Day.

The frog and the ground hog
    The snake and the bear
Hibernation is their thing.
They sleep all winter
    when it is cold
And then they wake up in the spring.

        by Ada Frischer

Discuss with the children what various animals do in the winter and how nature prepares for cold winters. Stress hibernation.

Suggested Reading:
    The Happy Day by Ruth Krauss
    Buzzy Bear Goes South by Dorothy Marino

Half

Math

Objective: To identify half and visualize a half as two equal pieces of a whole

Materials: white squares or rectangles, crayons

Directions: Present a situation to your students in which they are asked to share something evenly with a brother or sister (a candy bar perhaps). Hold up a set of unifix cubes, or draw a rectangle on the board to represent the candy bar. Ask them how much they would get. How much would their brother/sister get? After showing the students half of several objects, distribute paper squares or rectangles. Show the students how to fold their shape in half. Next, have students color half.

Cooking

Honey Fruit Bits

Peel and cut apples and bananas into chunks. Dip in honey and then in graham cracker crumbs. Serve with toothpicks.

Horizontal

Math

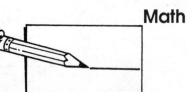

Objective: To help students understand the meaning of horizontal

Materials: 8 1/2 x 11" sheet of newsprint for each student, pencils

Directions: Give each student a piece of newsprint. Tell students to turn their paper horizontally. Demonstrate what that means. Have them draw a horizontal line to divide the paper in half.

Use this opportunity to explain vertical to students. Have them turn the back of their paper so it is vertical. Have students draw a vertical line to divide their paper in half.

Hexagon

Math

Objective: To recognize the hexagon shape

Directions: Explain that some shapes have a certain number of sides and that the number of sides determines the shape's name. Tell them that a hexagon has six sides. If you want, you could explain that "hex" is Latin for *six*.

Draw this hexagon shape on the chalkboard.

Poetry

All the Hats

There are big hats and little hats,
    Blues ones and red.
But the best hats are hats
    That fit on your head.
There are top hats and police hats
    And fire hats too.
And animal hats to wear
    At the zoo.
There are green hats and black hats,
    Pink ones and red.
But the best hats are hats
    That fit on your head.
                            by Ada Frischer

My Hat

I wear a hat upon my head
It keeps me warm and it's all red.
My sister's hat has ribbons and bows.
It keeps her ears warm
And not her nose.
        by Ada Frischer

The Hokey Pokey   Music

Directions: Gather students in a circle. Introduce the concept of right and left by asking students to hold up their left hand, their right foot, etc. Next, demonstrate how to place body parts "in" the circle and "out." Next, demonstrate the "Hokey Pokey" following the song below. Now, you are ready to play!

The Hokey Pokey

You put your right arm in
You take your right arm out
You put your right arm in and you shake it all
    about.
You do the Hokey Pokey (Shake arms in air.)
And you turn yourself around.
That's what it's all about. (Clap 2 times.)
Repeat the above using:
        your left arm
        your right leg
        your left leg
        your right hip
        Your left hip
        Your backside
        your whole self

Hundred

Math

Objective: To count orally to 100
To practice recognizing numerals 1 to 100

Materials: flashcards depicting the numbers 1 to 100

Directions: Young children enjoy showing their counting ability. Count to 100 beginning with one child and changing "counters" every five numbers.

Suggested Trips

Habitat (Nature Center)   Hardware Store
Horse farm   Hat factory

Book List

Aliki. (1962). *My Hands.* New York: Harper and Row.

Anno, M. (1985). *Anno's Hat Tricks.* New York: Philomel Books.

Asch, F. (1982). *Happy Birthday, Moon.* Englewood Cliffs, N.J.: Prentice Hall.

Burton, V. (1942). *The Little House.* New York: Houghton Mifflin.

Carle, E. (1987). *A House for a Hermit Crab.* Saxonville, MA: Picture Book Studio.

Castle, C. (1985). *The Hare and the Tortoise.* New York: Dial Books for Young Readers.

Cutts, D. (1979). *The House that Jack Built.* Mahwah, NJ: Troll Associates.

Galdone, P. (1968). *Henny Penny.* New York: Ticknor and Fields.

Galdone, P. (1985). *The Little Red Hen.* New York: Houghton Mifflin.

Geringer, L. (1985). *A Three Hat Day.* New York: Harper and Row.

Grimm, J. (1975). *Hansel & Gretel.* New York: Scribner.

Hurd, E. (1960). *Hurry, Hurry.* New York: Harper and Row.

Johnson, C. (1955). *Harold and the Purple Crayon.* New York: Harper and Row.

Keats, E.J. (1966). *Jenny's Hat.* New York: Harper and Row.

Krauss, R. (1949). *The Happy Day.* New York: Harper and Row.

Morris, A. (1989). *Hats, Hats, Hats.* New York: Lothrop, Lee and Shepard Books.

Seuss, Dr. (1963). *Hop on Pop.* New York: Beginner Books.

Seuss, Dr. (1940). *Horton Hatches the Egg.* New York: Random House.

Seuss, Dr. (1954). *Horton Hears a Who!* New York: Random House.

Zion, G. (1956). *Harry the Dirty Dog.* New York: Harper.

Zolotow, C. (1987). *The Hating Book.* New York: Harper and Row.

H Pictures for Miscellaneous Activities

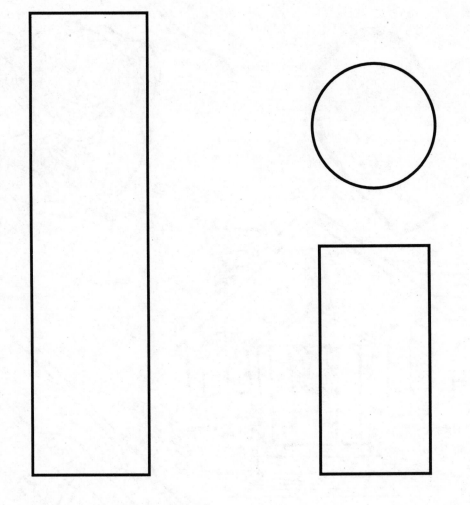

Ii

Finger Plays

Creative
Dramatics

Your students will have fun performing these finger plays together.

(The Familiar)
The Itsy, Bitsy Spider

The itsy, bitsy spider
Climbed up the water spout.
Down came the rain
And washed the spider out.
Out came the sun
And dried up all the rain.
And the itsy, bitsy spider
Climbed up the spout again.

(The Unfamiliar)
The Itty, Bitty Kitty

The itty, bitty kitty
Climbed up each counter drawer.
Down came the cans
Onto the kitchen floor.
Out came a butler
To pick up all the cans.
And the itty, bitty kitty
Climbed up the drawers again.

Intersecting Lines

Math

Objective: To observe the concepts of "intersecting lines" and "parallel lines"

Materials: four pieces of red licorice (cut the same size) per student

Directions:
1. Explain the terms "intersecting lines" and "parallel lines."
2. Give each child four pieces of licorice.
3. Have the children place the licorice on their desks after looking at the pattern you have drawn on the board.
   a. Make a tic-tac-toe board. The licorice pieces intersect.
   b. Make four parallel lines.

Inspecting Inchworms

Math

Objective: To estimate the number of objects in a jar

Materials: a large glass jar, Chinese noodles

Directions:
1. Place the Chinese noodles in a jar.
2. Let each child closely examine the jar and estimate the number of "inchworms" inside. List the numbers on the chalkboard.
3. Together, count the "inchworms."

Inch by Inchworms

Objective: To use a ruler to explore the concept of one inch

Materials: red licorice cut into 1" pieces, one ruler per student

Directions:
1. Give each child a handful of licorice.
2. Have them guess the number of "inchworms" (licorice pieces) needed to equal the length of the ruler.
3. Have them line up the "inchworms" along the ruler.
4. Survey the students to see how many "inchworms" they needed to reach the length of the ruler. (You may want to graph the results.)

Insect Pictures

Color these pictures.

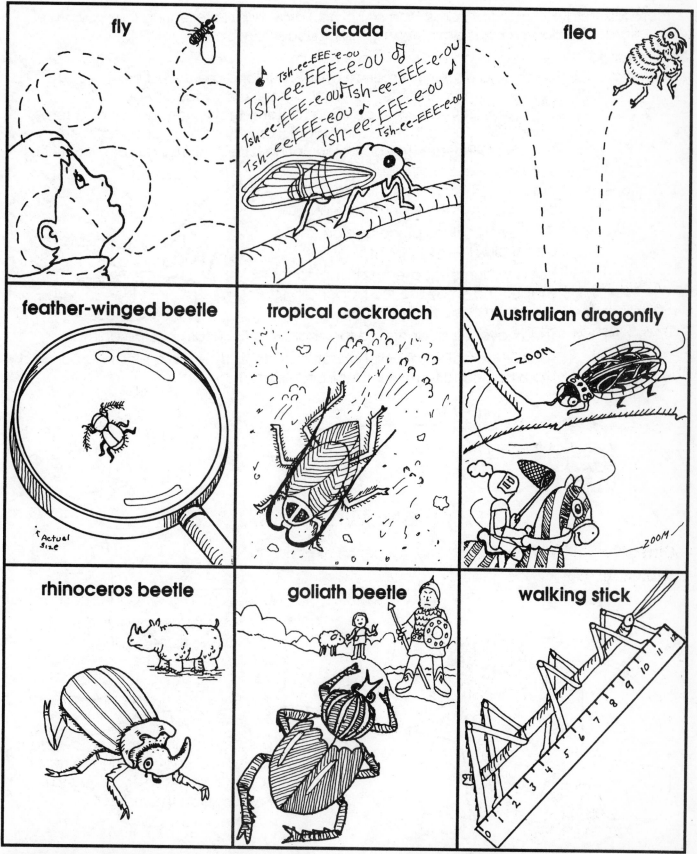

fly

cicada

flea

feather-winged beetle

*Actual size

tropical cockroach

Australian dragonfly

ZOOM

ZOOM

rhinoceros beetle

goliath beetle

walking stick

Inuit Art

Objective: To create sculptures that resemble Inuit art

Materials: clay, large paper clips (one per child), drawings representing Inuit sculptures (Some examples are below), plastic spoons, dry cloths

Background Information: Eskimos that live in North America and Greenland are called Inuit. About 25,000 Inuit live in North America. Their simple, yet gracefully beautiful sculptures are carved from soapstone (a stone that is both heavy and soft), bone and ivory (walrus tusks). The objects, usually animals or people, are carefully studied before the actual sculpting is begun. This art form continues to be used today.

Directions:
1. While the children carefully study the pictures, stress the simplicity of Inuit art.
2. Give each child a piece of clay and a paper clip.
3. Have students choose an animal to shape. They may use the paper clip to sculpt the basic shape of their animal.
4. Then have the students use their hands to finish forming the animal.
5. To give the objects a polished look, students may rub a plastic spoon or dry cloth back and forth or in small circular motions.

Imaginary Iguanas

Art

Objective: To create 3-D iguanas

Materials: one empty toilet paper or paper towel tube per student, construction paper, scissors, glue, iguana patterns (below), wiggle eyes (two per student), pencils, crayons, markers

Directions:

1. Trace the circles at the end of the tubes onto construction paper and draw four evenly-spaced tabs around each circle. Have students cut out the circles (around the tabs) and glue them onto the ends of the tube.

2. Students are to cover the rest of the tube with construction paper.

3. Enlarge the iguana patterns below and let students use them to cut out legs, a tail, a head and a crest (or precut these parts for the students). (The patterns themselves may be colored and used, or they may be traced onto construction paper and cut out.) Students should glue the patterns to the tube.

4. Students may cut out and glue a construction paper tongue to the front circle.

5. Help students glue on wiggle eyes.

6. Encourage students to decorate their iguana with stripes or spots. They may use crayons or markers or cut stripes or spots from construction paper and glue them on the iguana.

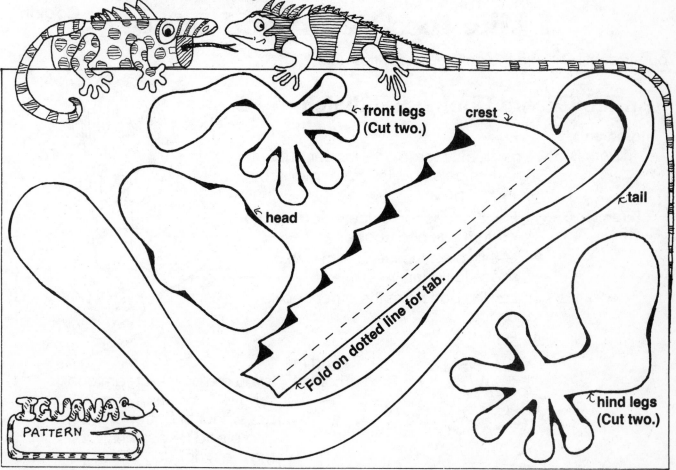

front legs
(Cut two.)

crest

head

tail

Fold on dotted line for tab.

hind legs
(Cut two.)

IGUANA
PATTERN

Ii

Cooking

I Like Ice Cream and Icing!

Your students will love the delicious activities below.

An Ice-Cream Cookie Sandwich

**Ingredients/
Materials:** two medium-to-large cookies per student
(Chocolate chip cookies are a favorite!),
ice cream, spoon

Directions:
1. Place one scoop of ice cream on the bottom side of a cookie.
2. Gently press the ice cream with a spoon to flatten it.
3. Lay the bottom of the other cookie on top.
4. Enjoy!

Food for Thought: If you ate an ice-cream cookie sandwich for lunch, should you have peanut butter and jelly and bread for dessert . . . or maybe a hot dog pickle split?

Poison Ivy

Science

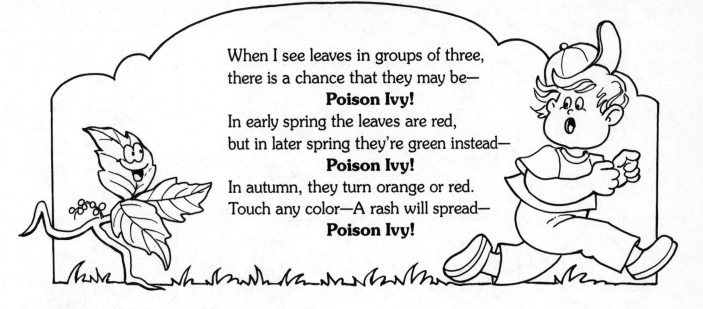

When I see leaves in groups of three,
there is a chance that they may be—
Poison Ivy!
In early spring the leaves are red,
but in later spring they're green instead—
Poison Ivy!
In autumn, they turn orange or red.
Touch any color—A rash will spread—
Poison Ivy!

Objective: To learn about poison ivy

Materials: drawing paper, crayons

Background Information: Poison ivy has leaves that are each made of three leaflets. These contain a poisonous oil that irritates the skin. At times, small greenish flowers and later, white berries grow on the main stem near the leaves. They, too, are poisonous, and even very tiny amounts will cause a rash.

Always wash your skin thoroughly with soap and water if you think that you have touched poison ivy. If red blisters develop, use calamine lotion, Epsom salts or bicarbonate of soda (baking soda).

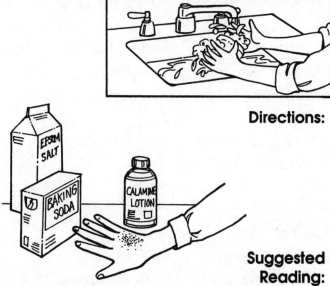

Directions:

1. Have students copy the poem on writing paper.
2. Discuss the background information with them.
3. Students draw pictures of poison ivy leaves at different times of the year to accompany the poem.

Suggested Reading: *Poisonous Plants* by Suzanne M. Coil

I Pictures for Miscellaneous Activities

Enlarge the pictures below to make flash cards or bulletin board characters. You could also hand one of the pictures out to students, have them paste it on paper and draw a scene around it.

Book List

Anno, M. (1988). *In Shadowland.* New York: Orchard Books.

Brown, M.K. (1986). *Let's Go Swimming with Mr. Sillypants.* New York: Crown Publishers.

Browne, A. (1984). *Willy the Wimp.* New York: Knopf.

Daughtry, D. (1984). *What's Inside?* New York: Knopf.

Domanska, J., illus. (1971). *If All the Seas Were One Sea.* New York: Macmillan.

Guthrie, D. (1985). *The Witch Who Lives Down the Hall.* Florida: Harcourt Brace Jovanovich.

Gwynne, F. (1989). *The King Who Rained.* New York: Simon and Schuster.

Gwynne, F. (1980). *A Chocolate Moose for Dinner.* New York: Windmill Books.

Gwynne, F. (1988). *A Little Pigeon Toad.* New York: Simon and Schuster.

Hoban, T. (1984). *Is It Rough? Is It Smooth? Is It Shiny?* New York: Greenwillow Books.

Lionni, L. (1986). *It's Mine!* New York: Knopf.

Lloyd, M. (1983). *Chicken Tricks.* New York: Harper and Row.

McCully, E. (1988). *The Christmas Gift.* New York: Harper and Row.

McCully, E. (1984). *Picnic.* New York: Harper and Row.

Numeroff, L. (1985). *If You Give a Mouse a Cookie.* New York: Harper and Row.

Shaw, C. (1947). *It Looked Like Spilt Milk.* New York: Harper and Row.

Stevenson, J. (1968). *If I Owned a Candy Factory.* Boston, MA: Little, Brown.

Williams, V. (1988). *Stringbean's Trip to the Shining Sea.* New York: Greenwillow Books.

Yolen, J. (1988). *Picnic with Piggins.* San Diego, CA: Harcourt Brace Jovanovich.

More I Pictures for Miscellaneous Activities

Enlarge the pictures below to make flash cards, bulletin board characters or characters that can be used in a story.

Book List

Agee, J. (1991). *Go Hang a Salami! I'm a Lasagna Hog!* New York: Farrar Strauss Giroux.

Carlstrom, N.W. (1987). *Wild, Wild Sunflower Child Anna.* New York: Macmillan.

Coil, S. (1991). *Poisonous Plants.* New York: Franklin Watts.

Cooney, B. (1988). *Island Boy.* New York: Viking Kestrel.

Goodman, L. (1989). *Ida's Doll.* New York: Harper and Row.

Hoban, T. (1983). *I Read Signs.* New York: Greenwillow Books.

Howe, J. (1987). *I Wish I Were a Butterfly.* San Diego, CA: Harcourt Brace Jovanovich.

Kellogg, S. (1973). *Island of the Skog.* New York: Dial Press.

Laurencin, G. (1987). *I Wish I Were.* New York: Putnam.

Low, J. (1980). *Mice Twice.* New York: Atheneum.

Martin, C.E. (1985). *Island Rescue.* New York: Greenwillow Books.

Minarik, E.H. (1958). *No Fighting, No Biting!* New York: Harper and Row.

Seibert, P. (1992). *Mush!* Brookfield, CT: Millbrook Press.

Yolen, J. (1980). *Mice on Ice.* New York: E.P. Dutton.

Jj

JUMBO

JAM

Jazzy Jazzercise

Physical Education

Take a short break. Play a record or tape that has a good, lively beat. Do simple exercises to the beat of the music.

A Jewel of a Jewelbox

Art

Provide students with small boxes with lids or ask the students to bring boxes. Provide an assortment of pasta (macaroni, shells, spaghetti, bows, etc.) and dried beans. Students decorate the lid and sides of the boxes by gluing on the pieces of pasta and beans. When completed, the student paints the box and lid using tempera paint. After the paint has dried, the teacher or an adult helper may spray the box with a fixative to prevent the paint from rubbing off. Students may store their jewels (items important to them) in their jewelboxes.

IF8661 The Alphabet

Jungle Scene

Art

Objective: To create a jungle scene using crayon resistance

Materials: construction paper, crayons, green paint, white paint, water, paintbrushes

Directions: Using white paper, have the children draw a jungle scene with crayons. It is important that they press down heavily as they draw.

Mix a little water, white paint and green paint to thin it to make a light green "wash."

Quickly, with light sweeping strokes, paint over the entire drawing with the green "wash." Like magic, the drawing will reappear.

Explain to the children that the paint rolls off the waxy crayon surface.

Suggested Reading:

The Trek by Ann Jonas
Sitting in My Box by Dee Lillegard
A Wise Monkey Tale by Betsy and Giulio Maestro

(See Poetry page 114.)

Jiggling Jellyfish

Science

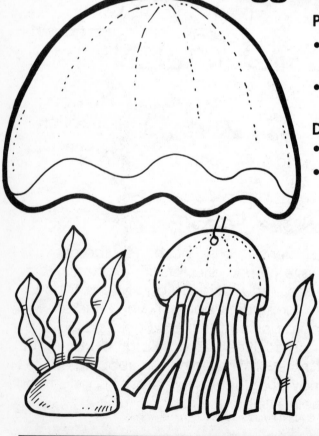

Preparation:

• Enlarge and copy the jellyfish body pattern on assorted colors of construction paper.

• Cut 8 to 10 strips of tissue paper or crêpe paper for each student.

Directions:

• Cut the jellyfish body along the solid outer line.

• Glue the strips of tissue or crêpe paper to the jellyfish body. Glue one end of each strip just at the line on the body. Display the completed jellyfish on a bulletin board that is covered with blue butcher paper. Have the students use scrap green construction paper to cut out plants and gray construction paper to cut out rock shapes to add to the bulletin board. Add the title "Jiggling Jellyfish." Or, punch a hole in the top of each completed jellyfish. Attach a piece of yarn or string and hang the jellyfish from the ceiling or lights.

 IF8661 The Alphabet

Jack-O'-Lanterns
Art

Objective: To make a Jack-O'-Lantern

Materials: Precut pumpkins from 9" x 12" sheets of orange construction paper; assorted colors of construction paper precut into eyes, noses, mouths, and stems; markers; paste or glue

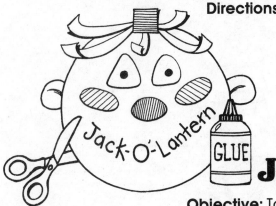

Directions: • Students paste together pieces you provide to make their own jack-o'-lanterns. Encourage creativity. The eyes do not have to match. More than one shape can be used for each feature. Students can add ears, hair, cheeks and eyelashes with markers.

Junk Food
Health/Science

Objective: To talk about the meaning of the phrase junk food

Materials: pictures of food, sheets of construction paper, glue

Directions: Cut out pictures of all kinds of food—healthy food and junk food. Make certain there are enough pictures for each child to have several from each category. Give each child a sheet of construction paper. Write the categories of food on the chalkboard. Have the children fold their papers in half. They then paste their pictures in the proper column. Let them share their papers and tell why they think some food is healthy and other food is called junk food.

Jumping Jacks and Jumping Rope

Teach the children to do jumping jacks. Then, teach them to jump to the rhythm and tempo of music. Using a piano or guitar, vary the rhythm and tempo. You could have the children say 1 J, 2 J's, 3 J's, 4 J's, etc., as they jump.

Children love to jump rope. Find some fun jump rope jingles and do them outside during recess. Encourage the children to teach the class jumping jingles that they know.

Judging Jams

Materials: several different jams and jellies, crackers

Preparation: Make a large graph with fruit pictures of each jam/jelly showing the category. Make fruit markers which students will use to mark their favorite jam/jelly on the graph. When everyone has had a turn, discuss the results of the graph.

Extension: Make a "Second Choice" graph.

Book List

Aliki. (1986). *Jack and Jake.* New York: Greenwillow Books.

Berenstain, S. and Berenstain, J. (1985). *The Berenstain Bears and Too Much Junk Food.* New York: Random House.

Galdone, P. (1982). *Jack and the Beanstalk.* Ticknor and Fields.

Hoban, R. (1964). *Bread for Jam and Frances.* New York: Harper and Row.

Keats, E.J. (1966). *Jenny's Hat.* New York: Harper and Row.

Schulman, J. (1977). *Jack the Bum and Haunted House.* Greenwillow Books.

Tresselt, A. (1948). *Johnny Maple Leaf.* New York: Lothrop, Lee and Shepard.

Van Allsburg, C. (1981). *Jumanji.* New York: Houghton Mifflin.

Jointed Jaguar

Science

Display pictures of jaguars. Locate on a large world map where jaguars can be found (Central America, South America, and Mexico in the tropical forest). Talk about jaguars. (See encyclopedia.) Make one copy of the jaguar pattern on yellow construction paper for each student. Students color and cut out the pieces. Use brads to attach the legs to the body.

Jack-O'-Lantern Worksheet

Color this and display.

Jumping - Jack Be Nimble

Games

Objective: To learn a nursery rhyme and practice repeating it

Materials: cylinder block or unbreakable candlestick

Directions: Have the children sit in a circle. Place a cylinder block or candlestick in the center of the circle. Review the nursery rhyme below.

> Jack be nimble.
> Jack be quick.
> Jack jump over
> the candlestick.

Replace the name "Jack" with the children's names to indicate when it is their turn to jump over the block in the center of the circle.

> Mary be nimble
> Mary be quick.
> Mary jump over
> the candlestick.

Jack in the Box

Objective: To provide an additional opportunity to learn a "J" sound poem

Directions:
> Jack in the box
> Jack in the box
> Curled up small
> Open the lid
> And he jumps up tall.

Say this poem together a couple of times. Ask the children what actions they could do to the poem. Children could "curl up small" and when the lid opens, they could "jump up tall!"

Cooking

Juice

Discuss the importance of oranges (Vitamin C) in the diet. Ask the children how they think orange juice, from a container, is made. Use several oranges to make enough juice to have a juice-tasting party.

Jellybeans

There are jellybeans in the closet.
There are jellybeans on the floor.
There are jellybeans in my pocket.
There are jellybeans near the door.

I like jellybeans in the north.
I like jellybeans in the south.
But the place I like jellybeans best
Is in my mouth!

by Ada Frischer

Poetry

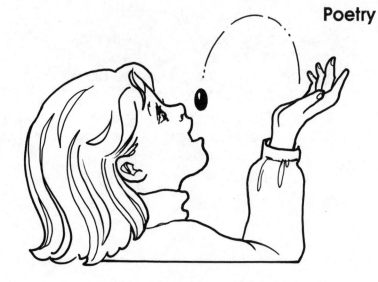

The Jungle

I went to the jungle
And what did I see?
All the animals were roaming free.
The tigers and parrots and monkeys too.
Living in the jungle - not in the zoo.

IF8661 The Alphabet

J Pictures for Miscellaneous Activities

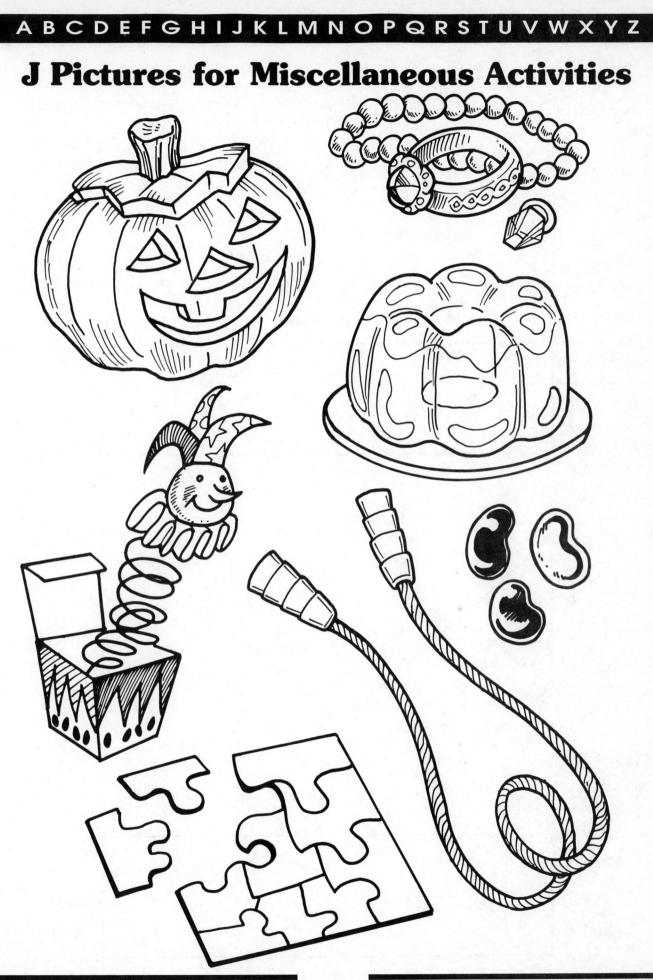

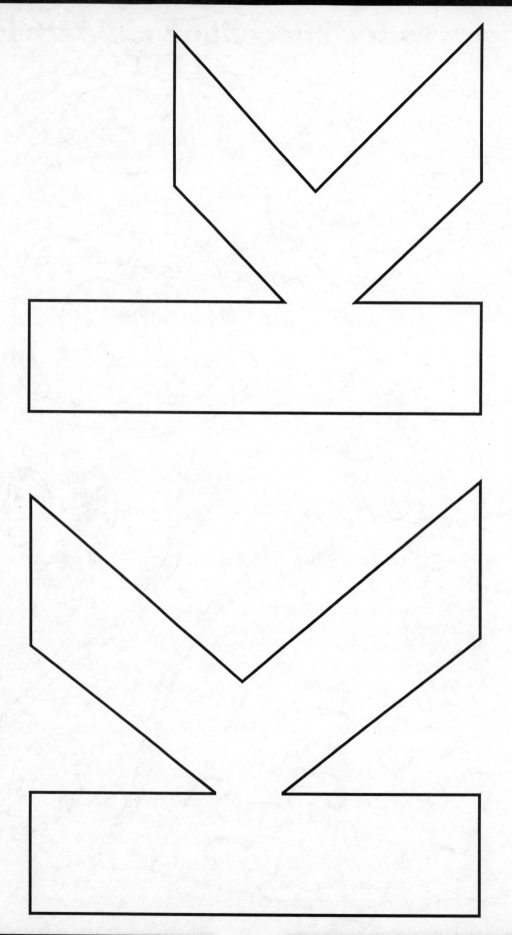

Kk

Kiwi Kabobs

Cooking

Preparation:
- Peel and cut kiwi into thin slices.
- Peel and slice bananas into ¾" slices.
- Drain juice from a can of pineapple chunks.
- Wash and hull whole strawberries.
- Place each fruit in a separate bowl or on separate plates.
- Provide toothpicks or cut bamboo skewers into shorter lengths.

Students create their own kabobs by placing pieces of the fruits on the toothpicks or skewers.

Kiwi Cookie Treats

Preparation:
- Peel and cut kiwi into thin slices.
- Soften strawberry cream cheese.
- Place vanilla-flavored wafer cookies in a basket.

Students spread softened strawberry cream cheese on a wafer cookie. Place a slice of kiwi on top of the cream cheese. Top this with another vanilla wafer cookie. Enjoy!

My Kitten

My kitten's name is Katie.
Her fur is soft as silk.
Her basket's in my kitchen.
That's where she drinks her milk.

by Ada Frischer

Katy Koo

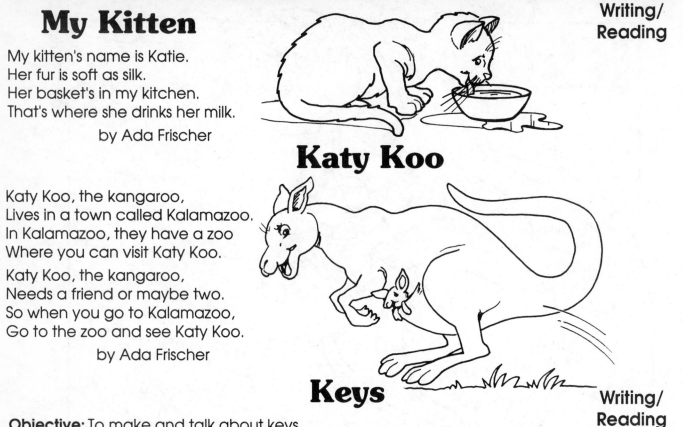

Katy Koo, the kangaroo,
Lives in a town called Kalamazoo.
In Kalamazoo, they have a zoo
Where you can visit Katy Koo.

Katy Koo, the kangaroo,
Needs a friend or maybe two.
So when you go to Kalamazoo,
Go to the zoo and see Katy Koo.

by Ada Frischer

Keys

Objective: To make and talk about keys

Materials: a copy of the silver key below, silver or gold crayons or glue and glitter

Directions: Talk about keys. What are keys for? Do your parents have keys? What kinds of things do keys turn on? Pass out copies of the key below and have the student decorate it with gold or silver crayons, or with glue and glitter.

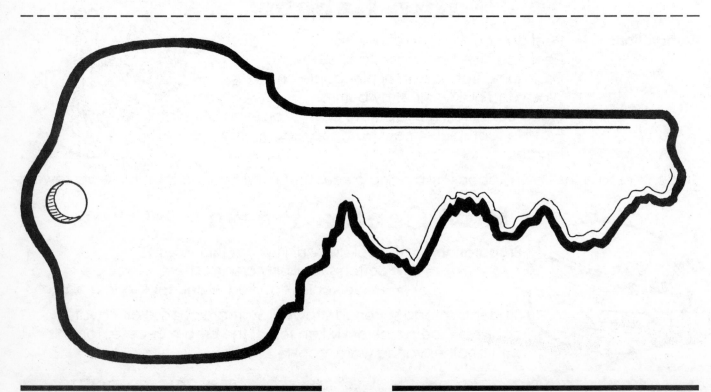

IF8661 The Alphabet

Write a Cinquain Poem About Koalas

Poetry

Display pictures of koala bears or even a stuffed toy koala. Locate where koalas live on a large world map. Write a class cinquain poem about koalas. The format for the poem is as follows:

Line 1: title (1 word)

Line 2: words that describe the title (2 words)

Line 3: action words (3 words)

Line 4: words that tell how you feel about the subject (4 words)

Line 5: a synonym or another word for the title (1 word)

Example: Koala,

Cuddly, cute,

Climbing, holding, scampering,

I giggle watching you,

Marsupial.

Make a Koala Bag Puppet

Art

Enlarge and copy the koala pattern on gray construction paper for each student. Student cuts out the pieces. Glue the head to the bottom of a small paper bag. Glue the body to the front panel of the bag below the head. Use the koala puppets when reciting the class poem about koalas for parents or another class.

Kool Kites

Social
Studies

Talk about kites. (Kites originated in China in 1200 B.C. and were used to send coded messages. At one time kites were used to gather information about weather. Today they are used as toys throughout the world.)

Make a kite. Copy the kite and bow patterns on brightly colored construction paper. Students color and cut out the kite and bows. Punch holes where indicated (●). Attach a length of yarn or string through the bottom hole. Glue the bows to the string. Attach a string through the top hole. Suspend the completed kites from the ceiling or lights.

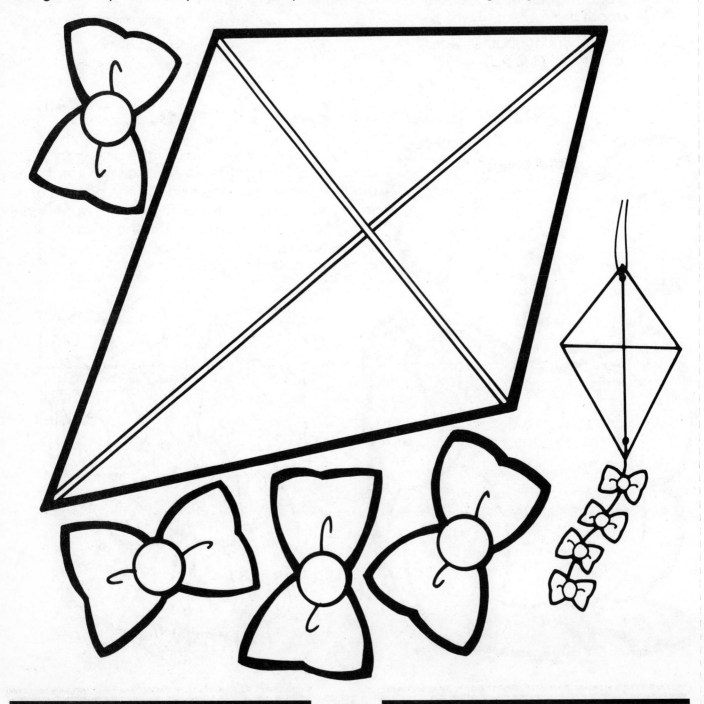

If I Were a King

Writing/ Reading

Objective: To discuss how students would rule their kingdom if they were kings

Materials: white paper and crayons, pencils, marker

Directions: Ask the students what kind of rules they would make if they were kings. How would their lives be different from how they are now? Where would they live? How would they travel?

Extension Activity:

Provide each student with a king's crown to wear during this activity. Use the pattern below to make a crown for each student. Have the students decorate the crowns.

Suggested Reading:

The King, The Mice and The Cheese by Nancy and Eric Gurney

Copy three times, then tape together.

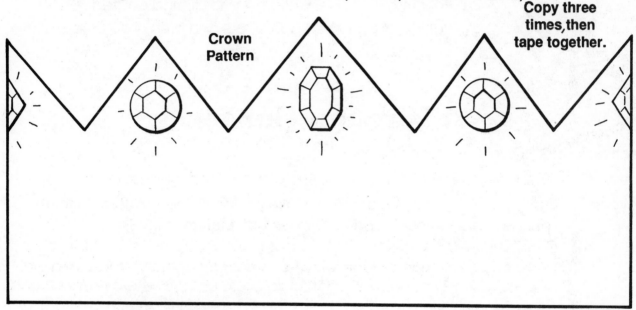

Crown Pattern

Kindness

Social Studies

Objective: To create a definition for kindness and create a list of ways students can be kind

Materials: large chart paper, markers

Directions: Ask students what it means when someone is kind. Write the word "kindness" on the chart paper. Next, write the students' definitions. Make a list of ways students feel they can be kind to each other.

Kazoo

Music

If you can, obtain several kazoos, form a kazoo band and parade around the room, or the playground if it is too noisy!

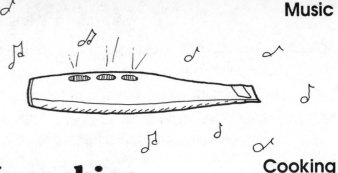

Krispy Krunchies

Cooking

1. Cook one cup dark brown corn syrup until it forms a firm ball in cold water. Stir occasionally. Add one teaspoon vinegar.

2. Mix 5 cups of dry, crisp cereal such as rice crisps, corn flakes, bran flakes, etc., and 1/2 cup salted peanuts in a greased bowl.

   Pour mixture 1 over mixture 2 and stir until coated.

   Pack into a greased pan. Cool and break into pieces.

A Kitchen Corner

Objective: To identify various kitchen items

Materials: various kitchen items, pictures of kitchen items, oaktag, glue, scissors

Directions: 1. Gather old magazines that will most likely have kitchen pictures in them.
2. Let children go through and cut out kitchen pictures they like.
3. Give children 2 pieces of oaktag to paste kitchen items on.
4. Make a large kitchen collage with the remainder of the pictures on a big piece of butcher paper. Let each child paste his/hers where he/she wants.

Suggested Trip

Fly a kite in the playground.

Book List

Keats, E. (1974). *Kitten for a Day.* New York: Macmillan.

Mayer, M. (1987). *What Do You Do With a Kangaroo?* New York: Scholastic.

Patterson, F. *Koko's Kitten.* New York: Scholastic.

Payne, E. (1985). *Katy No-Pocket.* New York: Houghton Mifflin.

Selsam, M. (1975). *How Kittens Grow.* New York: Four Winds Press.

Sendak, M. (1973). *In the Night Kitchen.* New York: Harper and Row.

K Is for Kangaroo

Writing/ Reading

Objective: To determine which picture cards begin with the sound for "K" as in "Kangaroo"

Materials: a child-size apron and a large piece of felt, white paper, marker, oaktag

Note: you could make an apron with a pouch on it. Just cut a piece of felt and glue it to the apron to represent a kangaroo's pouch. With a marker, write the letter "K" on the pouch.

Directions: Enlarge and cut out the pictures below. Some begin with the "K" sound and some do not. Glue them on oaktag to create cards. Place the apron on a student who is now a kangaroo! Seat students in a circle with the "kangaroo" standing in the front. Place the cards in a pile. Ask individuals to come up, pick a card and place it in the pouch if it begins with "K."

Suggested Reading:

Katy No-Pocket by Emmy Payne
What Do You Do With a Kangaroo? by Mercer Mayer
A First Look at Kangaroos by Millicent Selsam

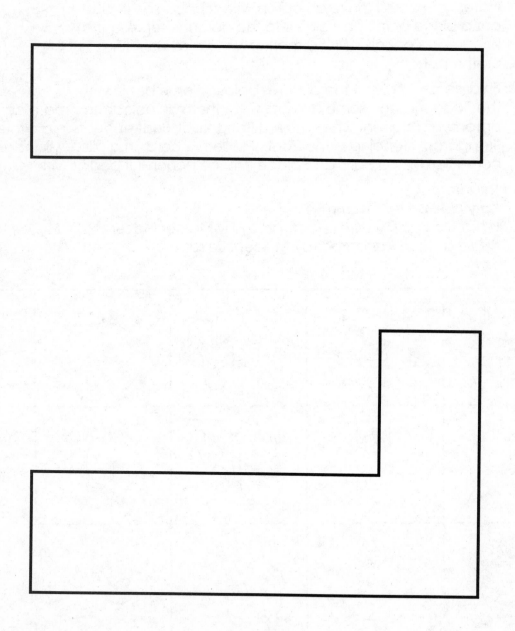

Lamb Patterns

Make name tags for your students using these little lambs. Have students decorate them.

Log Cabin

Art

Objective: To create a log cabin

Materials: Each child will need the following: 5 tongue depressors, 2 ice cream sticks, white glue, one sheet 9" x 12" construction paper, crayons

Directions: Children will count out the correct number of tongue depressors and ice cream sticks that they need.

They will glue the tongue depressors horizontally starting at the bottom of the construction paper to resemble logs. The ice cream sticks will form a peaked roof.

They will use the crayons to add a door, windows, grass, trees, and sky.

Writing/Reading

Library

Objective: To begin your classroom lending library

Materials: books students have written, books donated by students' families, library cards and pockets

Directions: In a corner of your room, set up a table or shelves on which to place books. Paste pockets and insert cards inside book covers. Explain to your students what a library is. Set limitations for your library (i.e., for how long a book will be loaned, how to care for books, how they should be transported to and from school, the procedure for borrowing a book).

Lists

Writing/Reading

Objective: To learn what a list is used for and to create one of their own

Materials: paper and pencils

Directions: Ask students if they have ever seen a list. What is a list used for? Next, create a list with the students. You may use one of the following suggestions:

a list of "L" words
a homework list
a list of favorite books
a class list of names
a list of class birthdays
a list of things to do in school today
a list of jobs
a list of family members

MY JOBS
clean my room
feed the dog
do homework

Leaf Rubbing

Science

Objective: To select a variety of leaves and create a leaf print

Materials: 8" x 11" white construction paper, 9" x 12" colored construction paper, an assortment of small pieces of crayon with the paper covering removed

Directions: Take a class walk around the school grounds. Have each child find 3 different kinds of leaves to bring back to the classroom. If you are in an area where the leaves turn colors and fall off trees in autumn, fall is a good time of year for this project.

Tape the leaves, vein side down, to the paper.

Turn the paper over. Use the sides of crayons to rub over the leaves. Use several colors over the leaves to create a blended look. (Red, brown, yellow, orange and green make a good autumn mixture.) Remove the leaves and mount the rubbing on a piece of contrasting colored construction paper to form a frame.

Liquid

Objective: To experiment with water and other liquids, to encourage observation and to introduce the scientific terms "liquid" and "solid"

Materials: paper cup, water, Jell-O, bowl, spoon, kettle, burner or stove, measuring cup

Directions: Talk about the characteristics of a liquid. It is something you cannot pick up with your fingers.

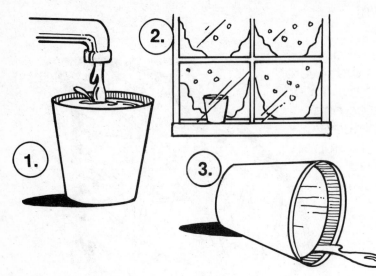

Experiment #1
On a cold day, put some water in a paper cup and put it outdoors. Check it regularly. (If you do not have cold days, put it in a freezer.) What happens to it? After it turns into a solid, bring it back into the classroom to check it. What happens now?

Experiment #2
Make Jell-O. Watch the liquid change to a solid. Then eat your "Experiment."

Light

Science

Objective: To experiment to find out how light travels and what happens to light when it is blocked and when it is reflected

Materials: flashlight, baby powder, mirror, chalkboard, overhead projector

Directions: Discuss with students what light is and what our light sources are. (See Suggested Reading below.)

Experiment #1:

On the chalkboard, draw a curved line, a straight line and a zig-zag line. Have students predict in which fashion light travels. Turn out the lights. Standing approximately six feet from the students, hold the baby powder in an upright position and squeeze the container allowing a small amount of powder to enter the air. Next, shine the flashlight in the direction of the powder. Students should be able to see the line the light creates.

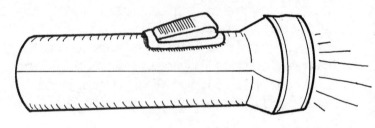

Experiment #2:

To find out what happens when light is blocked, simply shine the flashlight in the direction of your hand, a student's head or a book. Explain that light cannot pass through your hand as it does through a window. When light is blocked, a shadow is created. Use an overhead projector to let the students take turns making shadows.

Experiment #3:

To find out what happens when light is reflected, hold a mirror. Ask a student to shine the flashlight on the mirror.

Ask the class:

1. to locate the object the light is shining on
2. to name objects for you to reflect the light upon
3. what happens to light when it is reflected, when it is bent

Suggested Reading:

Light by Donald Crews
Shadows and Reflections by Tana Hoban
Shadows, Here, There and Everywhere by Ron and Nancy Goor
Mother, Mother, I Feel Sick by Remy Charlip

Lion Puppet

Art

Objective: To reinforce the "L" sound and to learn about the expression "March comes in like a lion."

Materials: lunch-size paper bags, 9" x 12" sheets of yellow and brown construction paper, crayons, markers, scissors, glue

Directions: Tell the children the expression, "March comes in like a lion . . ." Ask them how they think a lion would come in (i.e., with a roar, loudly, fiercely). Ask them how that might apply to weather. Ask them to give examples of lionlike weather. Then, make the lion below with them. Have each student bring in a lunch-size paper bag. Give each student a piece of brown and yellow construction paper. Then, work through each step with the class.

1. With the bag folded flat, glue 9" x 12" yellow construction paper to top back of paper bag. Be sure to center the paper and line it up with the flap of the bag. (See illustration.)

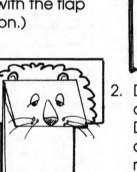

2. Draw a "mane" around the paper bag. Cut out the "mane" with the paper bag attached. Draw eyes, a nose and whiskers with a black crayon or marker. (Another way to create a mane would be to glue strips of yellow and brown paper to bag. Wrap paper strips around a pencil and curl strips toward front.)

3. Next, fold a 9" x 12" sheet of brown paper in half. To make paws, have children draw two "trees," one larger than the other. When the trees are cut, the children will have two sets of paws. (See illustration.)

4. Open the brown paper and find space to draw a "broom." This will become the tail! Have the children cut fringe for the tail hair.

5. Turn the paper bag and mane over and glue the paws and the tail on from the back. (See illustration.)

Lollipop Counting Book

Math

Objective: To create a lollipop counting book

Materials: construction paper, crayons, markers, stapler or notebook rings and hole punch

Directions: Give each child a number (from 1 to the number of students in your class) and a piece of construction paper. Using a marker, have the children write their numeral in the lower right corner of their papers. Then, using crayons, have children draw and color the correct number of lollipops to match their numerals. (See illustration.)

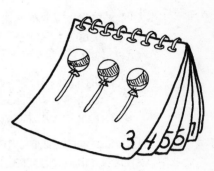

The books may be as long as you and the children want them to be! When finished, have the children put the pages in numerical order for you to staple.

Lollipop Graph

Objective: To help children estimate and graph the flavors of lollipops in a bag

Materials: a bag of lollipops, copies of the graph paper below, markers

Directions: Show the class the bag of lollipops. Ask the children to estimate the number of lollipops in the bag. Ask the children if they think there will be enough for the class to share. Record the children's estimations. Count the lollipops with the class.

Prepare a graph of lollipop flavors. Give each student a copy of the graph below. Students will color each lollipop a different color and then color a square for each lollipop above its flavor.

Count and tabulate the flavors. Write a math story with the class noting which flavor had the most lollipops, the least and if there were any ties.

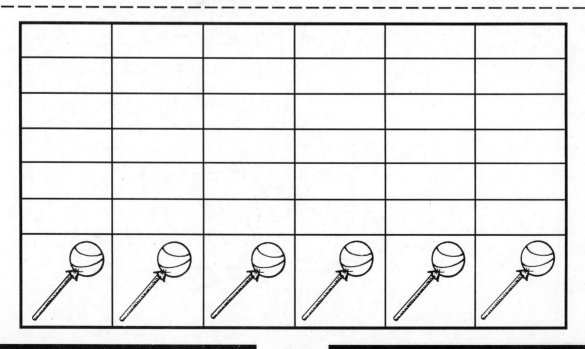

Living/Non-Living

Science

Objective: To distinguish between living and non-living things

Directions: Ask the children to name things that are living. Lead the discussion to animals, people, insects, fish and plants.

Discuss how living things need proper food, shelter and protection. They reproduce their own kind.

    A pumpkin seed will grow a pumpkin,
    A monkey will have a monkey baby,
    A human will have a human baby, etc.

Discuss non-living things. Have the children name things that are non-living: stove, sink, car, refrigerator, balloon, light bulb, TV, computer, doll, truck, bicycle, skates, water, etc.

How do these things differ from living things? (They cannot reproduce. A stove will not have a baby stove, skates will not have baby skates for your little brother or sister, etc.)

Prepare two books with several blank pages in each. Label one book **Living** and one **Non-Living**. Out of old magazines, have the children cut or tear out pictures. The children should be able to tell if their picture is a living or non-living object and why. Have the children paste their pictures in the appropriate book.

IF8661 The Alphabet

Conversation With a Lion

Poetry

I talked to a little lion
He was living at the zoo.
He roared and roared and roared again
So I answered, "How do you do?"

He answered with another roar.
And I am happy to say,
We had a polite conversation
In the zoo that lovely day.

by Ada Frischer

Lollipop

Lucy had a lollipop
She gave it to her sister
Her sister ate the lollipop
Then Lucy kissed her.

Lucy had a lollipop
She gave it to her brother
Her brother ate the lollipop
So Lucy got another.

Lucy had a lollipop
She didn't give it away
Lucy ate the lollipop
On another day.

by Ada Frischer

Things I Like

I like to laugh
I like to play
Laughing makes a happy day.
I like to learn
I learn in school
In school I learn the Golden Rule.

by Ada Frischer

Looby Loo

Children stand in a circle. Holding hands, they walk or skip in the circle singing the chorus:

> Here we go Looby Loo
> Here we go Looby Light
> Here we go Looby Loo
> All on a Saturday night.

Everyone stands in the circle. All drop hands and sing and do:

> I put my right hand in
> I put my right hand out
> I give my right hand a shake, shake, shake
> And turn myself about.

Repeat chorus walking or skipping in the circle. Then, sing and do the next verse:

> I put my left hand in, etc.

Continue song using the following verses:

> I put my right foot in.
> I put my left foot in.
> I put my whole self in.

End with the chorus.

Music

Suggested Trips

Your local library

Book List

Beim, J. (1955). *The Boy on Lincoln's Lap.* New York: Morrow.

Burton, V. (1942). *The Little House.* New York: Houghton Mifflin.

Giff, P.R. (1987). *Lazy Lions, Lucky Lambs.* Delacorte.

Guarino, D. (1989). *Is Your Mama a Llama?.* New York: Scholastic.

Hoban, T. (1981). *Take Another Look.* New York: Greenwillow Books.

Kay, H. (1956). *One Mitten Lewis.* New York: Lothrop, Lee and Shepard.

Keats, E.J. (1968). *A Letter to Amy.* New York: Harper and Row.

Kraus, R. (1971). *Leo the Late Bloomer.* New York: Windmill Books.

Lionni, L. (1959). *Little Blue and Little Yellow.* McDowell, Obolensky.

Lobel, A. (1964). *Lucille.* New York: Harper and Row.

McCloskey, R. (1914). *Lentil.* New York: Viking Press.

Moncure, J.B. (1981). *Love.* Chicago, IL: Childrens Press.

Piper, W. (1976). *The Little Engine That Could.* New York: Platt and Munk.

Rice, E. (1987). *Oh, Lewis!* New York: Macmillan.

Rockwell, A. (1977). *I Like the Library.* E.P. Dutton.

Skorpen, L.M. (1970). *All the Lassies.* New York: Dial Press.

Waber, B. (1965). *Lyle Lyle Crocodile.* Boston, MA: Houghton Mifflin.

Waber, B. (1969). *Lovable Lyle.* Boston, MA: Houghton Mifflin.

Zemach, M. (1983). *The Little Red Hen.* Farrar.

L Pictures for Miscellaneous Activities

Mm

Cooking

Macaroni

Objective: To observe how cooking alters the volume of objects

Directions: Measure an amount of dry macaroni in a measuring cup. Cook macaroni and observe what changes take place. Measure it again to see if the volume is different.

1) It changes from hard to soft.
2) It "grows."

Have a macaroni snack either as a salad or with sauce.

Milk Shake

1. Milk and chocolate syrup
2. Milk and frozen strawberries
3. Milk and banana

Put one of the above combinations in a blender with 2 or 3 ice cubes and enjoy a special treat.

Magnets

Science

Objective: To learn some of the properties of magnets through experimentation

Materials: magnets (both bar and horseshoe if possible), paper plates, small objects made of iron, plastic and paper (paper clips, bottle caps, spoons, bottle openers, egg beaters, whisks, screwdrivers, paper fasteners, pencils, erasers, crayons)

Directions: Discuss with students what magnets are and how they can be used. (See Suggested Reading below.) Have students work in groups. Supply each group with a paper plate and several small objects. Have students predict which objects are magnetic and which are not. (They can place what they feel is magnetic on the paper plate.) Next, supply students with magnets so that they may test their predictions.

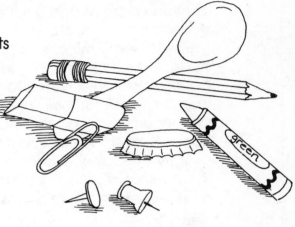

Suggested Reading:
Mickey's Magnet by Franklyn M. Branley

Marble Painting

Art

Materials: several marbles, assorted colors of paint in shallow containers, several spoons, white paper, gift boxes or cartons no deeper than 4", tape

Directions: Tape paper to the bottom of various boxes or cartons. Using a spoon, let each student dip a marble in a container of paint and then place the marble on the paper. The student holds the box or carton with both hands, tilting it to make the marble roll from side to side over the paper, leaving a track, or design, on the paper. Continue the procedure, using several marbles and colors until every student has had an opportunity to paint.

Suggested Reading:
Playing Marbles by Julie Brinckloe

Mittens

Art

Materials: white construction paper, yarn, pencils, water colors, paintbrushes, scissors, a mitten, a glove, newspaper

Directions: Recite the nursery rhyme "Three Little Kittens" below. Enlarge the mitten below and display it. Discuss the similarities and differences between a glove and a mitten. Show students one of each. Next, tell students that they will create mittens on paper. Have students place their hand on a white sheet of paper with their fingers together and their thumb away from their fingers. Have a partner draw around their hand to create a mitten. Repeat using the opposite hand. Help students cut out the mittens. Decorate mittens by painting them using water colors. Attach mittens by punching a hole in each mitten and tying them with yarn. If desired, display mittens in your classroom by hanging them over a piece of yarn strung across the room.

Suggested Reading:
Runaway Mittens by Jean Rogers

The Three Little Kittens

The three little kittens lost their mittens
and they began to cry.
Oh! Mother dear, we very much fear
That we have lost our mittens.
Lost your mittens! You naughty kittens!
Then you shall have no pie.
Mee-ow, mee-ow, mee-ow, mee-ow.
No, you shall have no pie.
Mee-ow, mee-ow, mee-ow.

 IF8661 The Alphabet

Masks

Art

Objective: To create a mask using a paper plate and a tongue depressor

Materials: paper plate, crayons, scissors, yarn, construction paper, tongue depressors

Directions: Discuss with the children how different kinds of masks can look funny, silly, scary, happy, sad, excited, etc. Each child should decide what "look" his/her mask will have. Then, distribute the paper plates and have each child draw a face on the plate. You may cut out the eyes if you wish, but it is not necessary because this mask will not be worn on the face covering the eyes. It will be attached to a tongue depressor and held up to the face so that it can be easily moved.

Use the yarn to make hair - long, short, braided, etc. Have each child design a hat to attach to the mask. Earrings can also be added.

Attach the paper plate mask to a tongue depressor and hold it up to, but not against, the face.

Mountain Mural

Objective: To create a mural

Materials: mural paper, crayons

Directions:
1. Explain to the children that a mural is a picture painted on a wall. Further explain that since we cannot always paint on a wall, we can create the feeling of a mural.

2. Measure the size of the wall or bulletin board you want to "paint." Cut mural paper from the roll to fit your area.

3. Plan with the children what their mountain mural might look like. What would they like to include in the mural? Examples: a mountain, the sun, clouds, snow, grass, trees.

4. Tape the mural paper to the floor. Recruit volunteers to draw specific things.

5. Staple the mural to the bulletin board or tape it on the wall.

Monster Book

Objective: To stimulate imagination using creative thinking and creative drawing and to create a class book

Materials: construction paper, crayons, paper punch, yarn,
books: *Millicent the Monster* by Mary Lystad
Where the Wild Things Are by Maurice Sendak
The Fourteenth Dragon by James E. Seidelman

Directions: Read the above books and discuss the fun and fiction aspects of monsters. Since monsters are not real, there is no special way a monster should look. Monsters can be happy or sad, funny or scary, big or little, fat or thin. Everyone can create his or her own monster.

Discuss with the children how they want their monsters to look.

Then give each child a piece of construction paper and crayons and encourage each child to "create" a monster.

Have each child dictate something about his/her monster such as how it looks, what it likes, what it does, where it lives, etc. Write it on the page.

Assemble the book. Design a cover. Include a dedication page and have each child sign the author page.

The Moon

Science

Objective: To learn about the moon

Materials: a sheet of black construction paper for each student, a white moon shape for each student (approximately 4" in diameter), glue, gold stars

Directions: Talk about how the moon's shape seems to change. Then have the students create a night scene with the materials listed above.

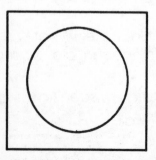

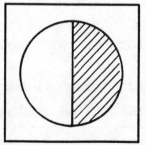
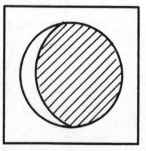

My Mom Book

This is a good activity and project for Mother's Day.

Objective: To write a book about Mom as a personal Mother's Day gift
(This activity should take a week or so to complete.)

Materials: copies of the pages below and on page 142, construction paper, crayons, pencils, stapler or notebook rings

Directions: 1. Read *Are You My Mother?* by P.D. Eastman. Discuss the ways in which children resemble their parents. Follow up with questions such as:

How are you like your mom?
How is your mom different from you?
What are some things your mom does?

2. Copy the boxes below and on page 142 for your class. Give students construction paper to make their covers. Write " MY MOM" on the front cover (emphasize the M's) and then have students draw a picture of their mother on it.

3. Discuss each page as you present it. Do one every day until the book is complete. Take dictation from the children to complete the sentences and then have the children illustrate the pages.

4. Assemble all pages. Staple, bind or put them together with notebook rings.

My Mom is _____ .

My Mom likes _____ .

My Mom likes to _____

_____.

My Mom's favorite food is ___

_____.

My Mom loves me because

_____.

I love my mom because ____

_____.

Moths

Science

Objective: To learn about the life cycle of moths

Materials: metamorphosis worksheet (p. 144), crayons and scissors for each child, stapler, white construction paper for cover

Directions: Discuss the life cycle of a moth with the class. Tell the children that although a moth and a butterfly undergo a similar metamorphosis, the adult bodies are different. This is a good time to read *The Very Hungry Caterpillar* by Eric Carle or other books about moths or butterflies as they develop from eggs. Your children would also find it fascinating to watch the caterpillars emerge from the egg, spin their cocoons, and then become moths or butterflies. Perhaps you could try this in your classroom.

Distribute copies of the metamorphosis worksheet on page 144. Have children color the different life stages of the moth. Have children cut the worksheet into four pieces and then reassemble them in correct sequence into book form for you to staple together. Add a cover sheet from construction paper. Cut to fit. Let the children decorate their covers.

Review the concept of metamorphosis: from egg to caterpillar to cocoon to adult. Below is an explanation of the metamorphosis of a moth.

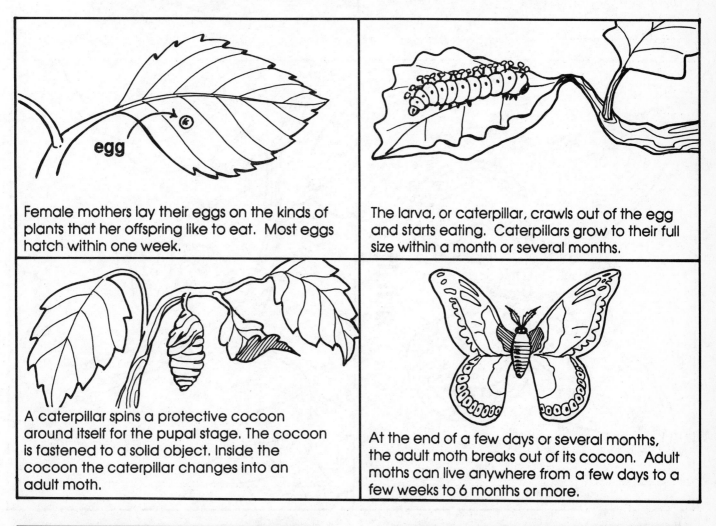

egg

Female mothers lay their eggs on the kinds of plants that her offspring like to eat. Most eggs hatch within one week.

The larva, or caterpillar, crawls out of the egg and starts eating. Caterpillars grow to their full size within a month or several months.

A caterpillar spins a protective cocoon around itself for the pupal stage. The cocoon is fastened to a solid object. Inside the cocoon the caterpillar changes into an adult moth.

At the end of a few days or several months, the adult moth breaks out of its cocoon. Adult moths can live anywhere from a few days to a few weeks to 6 months or more.

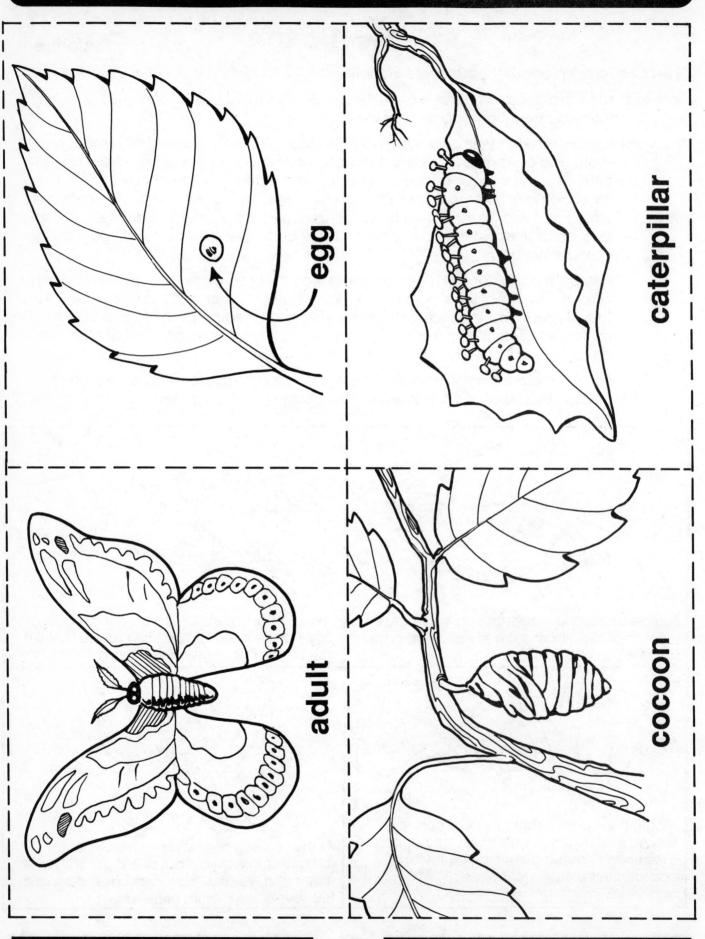

egg

caterpillar

adult

cocoon

M & M Graph

Math

Objective: To use a graph to show the number of different colored M & M's in a bag

Materials: M & M's of various colors for each child, one graph for each child, crayons

Directions: Have each child color the rows of the graph below each a different color according to M & M colors. After they open their bags, they will sort their M & M's by placing the candies on their graph in the appropriately colored row.

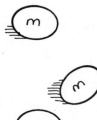

Color	M & M's				
(red→)					
(brown →)					
(yellow →)					
(green →)					

Money Game

Objective: To help children practice matching and to learn the name and size of a penny, a nickel and a dime

Materials: assortment of real coins: pennies, nickels and dimes

Directions: Put some coins on a table. Gather the children close to you so that they can see the coins clearly. Say the name of each coin before the game starts. Set aside a coin. Have a child find a coin that is "the same" as that one. Choose another coin. Have another student find a matching coin, and so on.

Musical Chairs

Play the old favorite game of musical chairs. Put enough chairs in a circle for every child less one. Children march around the circle to music. When the music stops, everyone must find a chair. The child who cannot find a chair is out. Continue this until only one chair and two children are left. The final child in the chair is the winner.

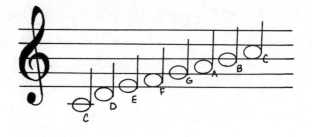

March

Using a piano, record or tape, play any of the John Philip Sousa marches to have a parade in the classroom.

Explain to the children that John Philip Sousa is also known as the "March King" because he wrote so many marches, and he conducted a marching band.

Making Music

Show the children a staff of music. Explain to them about lines, spaces and the letter names. Show them the different kinds of notes (whole note, half note, quarter note, etc.). Explain in a simple way how you count notes.

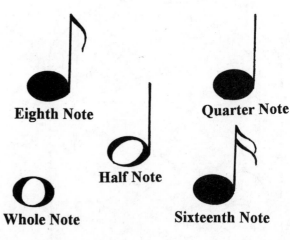

Eighth Note

Quarter Note

Half Note

Whole Note

Sixteenth Note

Book List

Asch, F. (1988). *Mooncake*. New York: Little Simon.

Barrett, J. (1985). *Cloudy With a Chance of Meatballs*. New York: Macmillan.

Bonsall, C. (1973). *Mine's the Best*. New York: Harper and Row.

Branley, F. (1956). *Mickey's Magnet*. New York: Crowell.

Branley, F. (1987). *The Moon Seems to Change*. New York: Crowell.

Brown, M.W. (1947). *Goodnight Moon*. New York: Harper and Row.

Burton, V. (1977). *Mike Mulligan and His Steam Shovel*. New York: Houghton Mifflin.

Duncan, L. *Birthday Moon*. New York: Viking Kestrel.

Eastman, P.D. (1960). *Are You My Mother?* New York: Beginner Books.

Hankin, R. (1984). *I Can Be a Musician*. Chicago, IL: Childrens Press.

Holl, A. (1969). *Moon Mouse*. New York: Random House.

Langley, A. (1987). *The Moon*. New York: Watts.

Lionni, L. (1986). *It's Mine!* New York: Knopf.

Numeroff, L.J. (1985). *If You Give a Mouse a Cookie*. New York: Harper and Row.

Simon, N. (1974). *I Was So Mad!* Chicago, IL: A. Whitman.

Tresselt, A. (1964). *The Mitten*. New York: Lothrop, Lee and Shepard.

VerDorn, B. (1990). *Moon Glows*. New York: Arcade Publications.

Wheat, J.K. (1977). *Let's Go to the Moon*. Books for Young Explorers, National Geographic Society.

M Pictures for Miscellaneous Activities

Enlarge the cards to make flash cards for use during the study of the "M" sound.

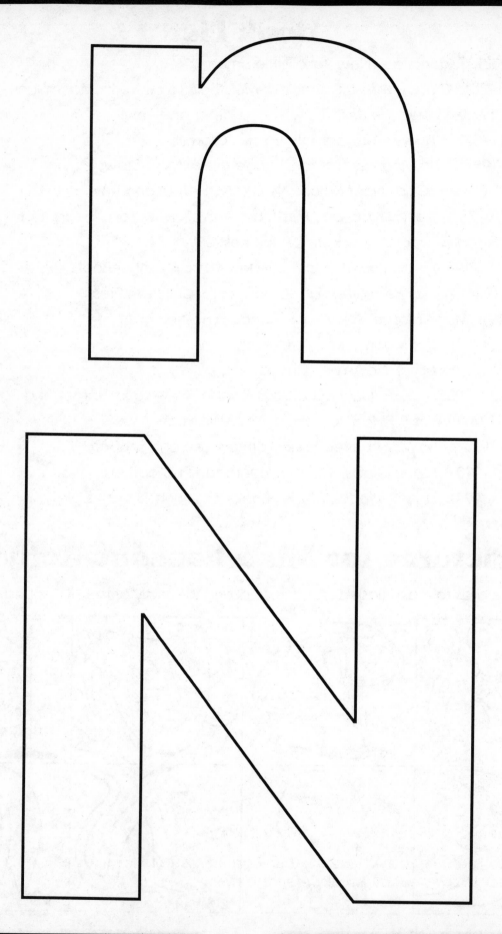

Nn

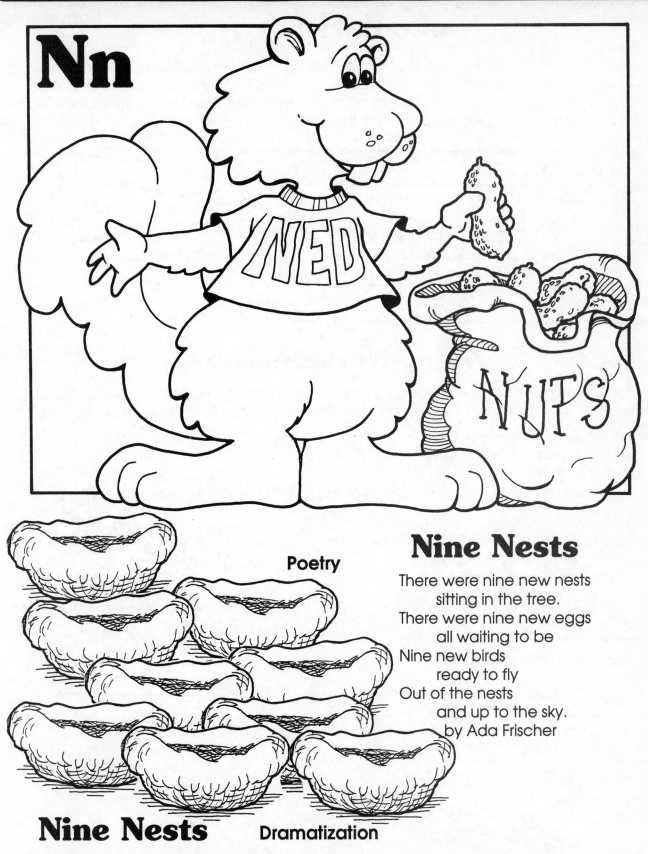

Nine Nests

Poetry

There were nine new nests
sitting in the tree.
There were nine new eggs
all waiting to be
Nine new birds
ready to fly
Out of the nests
and up to the sky.
by Ada Frischer

Nine Nests **Dramatization**

Select nine children to curl up small like an egg. The rest of the class recites the poem, and the nine new birds fly out at the appropriate time.

Nameplates

Handwriting

Give each student a 3-x-10-inch strip of white construction paper. Draw appropriately spaced lines through the middle of the strip. The student is to write his/her name on the line. When finished, glue the name strip to a piece of colorful construction paper, 6-x-12-inches. Students may color a design along the border. Tape the completed nameplates to the students' desks.

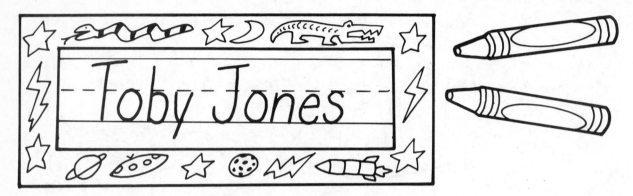

Noisy Noisemakers

Science

Talk about sound. Discuss how sounds are made and the different kinds of sounds (music, scary sounds, sirens and alarms, loud sounds, soft sounds, etc.) Then make noisemakers.

Materials: (for each student) 1 bathroom tissue roll
1 strip of crêpe paper—9-x-7-inches
2 twist ties
assorted dried beans, popcorn kernels (unpopped), pebbles, etc.

Directions:

1. Place tissue roll in the center of the crêpe paper.

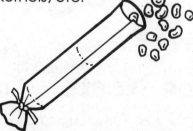

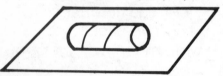

2. Wrap crêpe paper around the tissue roll and glue.

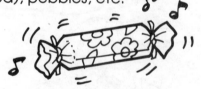

3. Gather one end and secure with a twist tie.

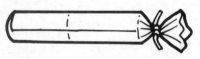

4. Fill about 1/4 to 1/3 with dried beans, kernels, etc.

5. Gather the other end and secure with a twist tie.

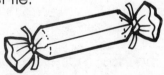

Students may decorate the outside of the noisemaker with crayons or cut and paste decorations cut from scrap construction paper.

Navigate the Way

Objective: To practice directional words: right, left, over, under, around, on, behind, etc.

Preparation: Set up a simple obstacle course that requires the students to go over, around, behind, under, etc.

Directions: Line up the students, either as a whole class or in small groups depending on the space and obstacle course to be "navigated."

Teacher then gives oral directions to help the students "navigate" or go through the obstacle course. (Example: Go *right* to the large table. Crawl *under* the table. Turn *left* and step over the balance beam.)

Then, let the students take turns giving directions to "navigate" the class through the obstacle course.

Number Nine

Math

Number nine,
in a line.
number nine,
ever so fine!

Nine little toys,
in a neat row.
nine little toys,
each one I like so!

Read the poems about the number nine. Have the students write the numeral nine. Use counters to make sets of nine objects. Help the students to learn to recite the poems. Give each student a sheet of white drawing paper on which to draw and color 9 pictures of something they would like to have (9 ice-cream cones, 9 kittens, etc.) When completed, have the students share their pictures with the class.

151

Night Picture

Art

Objective: To talk freely about night in hopes of making children more comfortable with the dark at night

Materials: heavy yellow construction paper, black crayons, wooden sticks such as Popsicle sticks

Directions: Cover construction paper with a heavy coating of black crayon. Be sure children press down hard and cover the entire paper to make the paper resemble the night sky. When the paper is completely covered with black, have children scratch a drawing using a hard object, such as a Popsicle stick or their fingernail.

This project works best if the children choose an outdoor scene to draw.

Extension Activity:

Before doing the above activity, read a book about nighttime. Talk about nighttime. Encourage the children to talk about any fears of the night they might have. Talk about why things seem scary at night.

Nurse

Social Studies

Objective: To alleviate fear of nurses and other medical personnel

Materials: Band-Aids, 11" x 18" drawing paper, crayons

Directions: To help young children view the school nurse as a friend and helper, visit a

doctor's office or your school nurse's office as early as possible in the school year. When this is done as a class activity, it often helps alleviate some of the fears young children may have about nurses and other medical personnel.

Have children draw and color large self-portraits in the classroom. While visiting the doctor's or nurse's office, give a Band-Aid to each child. Have the children place their Band-Aids on their drawings - on "their" arms or knees - as a reminder that a nurse is a friend and helper.

Needle and Thread

Games

Objective: To have fun cooperatively

Materials: happy children

Directions: Line students up, side by side, facing you. Tell students that you are a sewing needle and that they are the thread. Ask the students to join hands. The individual at the other end of the line is the knot. The teacher then leads the line toward the last two students. They hold up their arms and the teacher leads all the students under their arms. After everyone has passed under, one student will be forced to turn his/her body in the opposite direction. He/she will be "sewed up" tight!

Lead the line to its original position and then continue, this time ducking under the next two students' arms at the other end. The game is complete when all students have been "sewn up!"

As the students are being "sewn," you can chant the following:

> The thread follows the needle
> The thread follows the needle
> Round and round the needle goes
> As we sew the hole in my clothes!

Suggestion:

Have half the class watch and the other half participate when working with large groups.

Before playing the game, emphasize the importance of not dropping hands because that breaks the thread!

Noodle Dessert

Cook 1/2 pound broad noodles
according to directions.

Add: 1/2 pint sour cream
    1/2 pound cottage cheese
    1 teaspoon salt
    2 tablespoons sugar
    1/2 teaspoon cinnamon
    1/2 cup raisins

Noodle Numbers

Materials: noodles, pan, water, cookie sheet, food coloring, crayons, paper

Macaroni noodles can be softened and dyed. When softened, pasta will stay
pliable for a few hours. Dyeing pasta will also cause it to become soft. Soft
pasta may be shaped, left to harden and then used at a later time.

Follow the directions below to soften and dye pasta. Then, have the students
form the pasta into the shape of the numeral 9 and glue it to a piece of
construction paper when it is dry.

To soften pasta:

1. Put pasta in boiling water.
2. Boil until ready for eating. (Time
   directions are on package.)
3. Pour into strainer to drain.
4. Spread out on tray, cookie sheet
   or waxed paper to cool. Pieces
   should not touch one another.

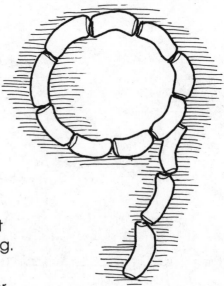

To dye pasta:

1. Put pasta in boiling water.
2. Add a teaspoon of food coloring. If pasta does not
   take on the color within a minute, add more coloring.
3. Boil 5 minutes and then pour into strainer.
5. When drained, spread out on a tray, cookie sheet or
   waxed paper so the pieces are not touching.

Nickels

Math

Objective: To help children become familiar with a nickel and what it is made up of

Materials: lots of nickels and pennies, newsprint

Directions: Show the children a clear container of pennies and a clear container of nickels. Ask them which they think is worth more, a penny or a nickel. Ask if anyone knows how many pennies it takes to make a nickel.

Give each student a nickel and various numbers of pennies, making certain each one has at least five. Say and count together, "One nickel is equal to five pennies - one, two, three, four, five." Have students write on their papers, "One nickel is equal to five pennies." Write it on the board. Then, have them draw the coins under the sentences.

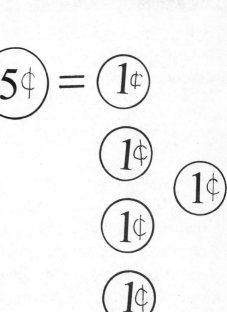

Number Game

Games

Select a leader. Have him/her think of a number.

The leader says, "I am thinking of a number from 1 to 10." He/she will then select someone to guess the number. If the number guessed is incorrect, the leader has to indicate if his/her number is higher or lower. Then, he/she selects another child to guess. When the correct number is chosen, that child becomes the new leader.

As the children's knowledge of numbers increases, the span of number selection can increase accordingly, i.e., 1 to 15, 1 to 20.

Number BINGO

Objective: To improve listening skills

Materials: copies of Bingo grids, pieces of construction paper to use as markers

Preparation:

Make Bingo card grids as shown. Randomly write numbers on the Bingo cards so there is one for each student. Use as high a number as you think your students can identify.

Directions: Give a Bingo card to each student along with enough squares of construction paper to cover their cards. Randomly say a number and write it on the chalkboard. The first person to cover his/her card wins.

Suggested Trips

Nature walk
Nurse's office
Nursery
Neighborhood walk

WELCOME to Your Nurse's Office!

First Aid

Book List

Brown, M.W. (1939). *Noisy Book.* New York: Harper and Row.

Brown, M.W. (1951). *The Summer Noisy Book.* New York: Harper and Row.

Brown, M.W. (1947). *The Winter Noisy Book.* New York: W.R. Scott.

Guilfoile, E. (1957). *Nobody Listens to Andrew.* Chicago, IL: Follett Publishing Company.

Hughes, S. (1985). *Noisy.* New York: Lothrop, Lee and Shepard.

Kuskin, K. (1962). *All Sizes of Noise.* New York: Harper and Row.

Mayer, M. (1986). *There's a Nightmare in My Closet.* Dial Books.

McGovern, A. (1967). *Too Much Noise.* Boston, MA: Houghton Mifflin.

Raskin, E. (1977). *Nothing Ever Happens on My Block.* New York: Macmillan.

Wood, A. and Wood, D. (1984). *The Napping House.* New York: Harcourt Brace Jovanovich.

Zion, G. (1958). *No Roses for Harry.* New York: Harper and Row.

N Pictures for Miscellaneous Activities

Enlarge the cards to make flash cards for use during the study of the "N" sound.

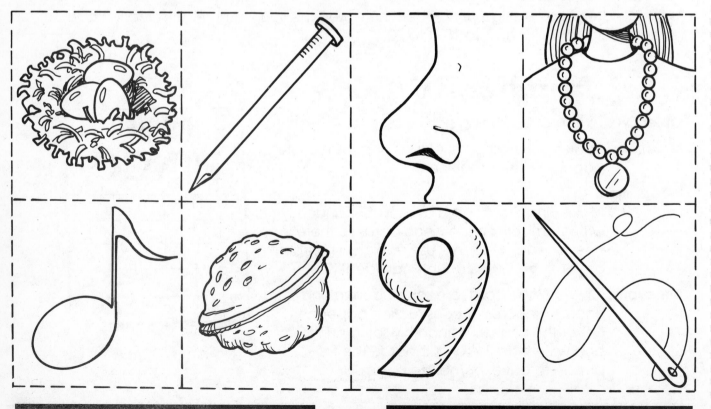

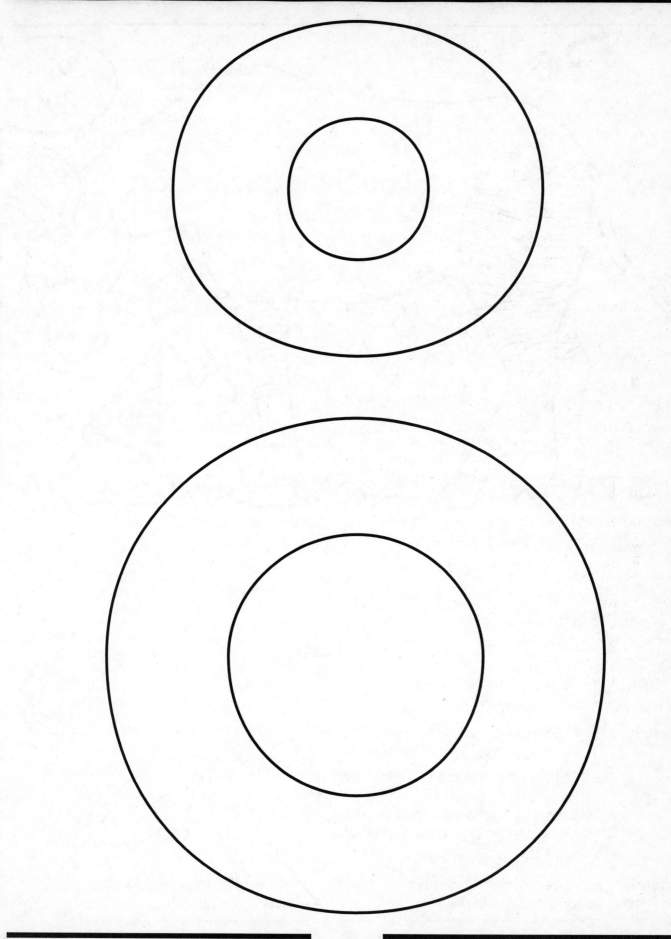

Oo

"O" Race

Game

Objective: To run a race using the letter "O"

Materials: Cheerios or Froot Loops, 4 spoons

Directions: 1. Divide the class into four teams, each in a line, in the gym or outside.

2. First student in each line runs with an "O" (a piece of cereal) balanced on the spoon to a spot you have marked and back. Then the next person goes.

3. First team to finish wins.

Extension: Have team members balance the "O" on the end of their finger instead of the spoon.

Old Glory

Objective: To study the U.S. Flag

Materials: flag pattern (below), red, white, and blue crayons, white paper

**Background
Information:** The U.S. flag has changed its appearance many times since the 1770's when it was first flown. No one knows who actually designed the first flag, though several people claimed that honor. The flag finally appeared as it does today in 1960.

No record shows why red, white and blue were chosen for the flag's colors. But, in 1872, these same colors were chosen for the Great Seal of the U.S. and given meanings. Red is for hardiness and courage. White is for purity and innocence and blue for vigilance, perseverance and justice. The stars represent our 50 states. The U.S. flag has been given several names, including the Stars ad Stripes, the Star-Spangled Banner and Old Glory.

Directions:
1. Discuss the background and significance of our U.S. flag with students.
2. Say the Pledge of Allegiance and sing a patriotic song such as "America the Beautiful."
3. Give each child the flag pattern.
4. Have students color the flag.

Octopus

Options

Dear Mr. Salesman,
    How can I choose
When you have so many
    Wonderful shoes?

Some shoes are flat.
    Others have high heels.
Some help you jog
    Or glide smoothly on wheels.

Some are for dancing.
    Others are for walking.
With all of these tongues
    They might begin talking!

So many choices
    And each one a "peach" . . .
I've decided to take
    At least one of each!

Overtures

Music

Objective: To learn the meaning of "overture" and to listen to overtures of musicals/movies familiar to children

Definition: An "overture" is an instrumental introduction to a larger musical work.

Directions: Find a tape or movie that contains and opening overture. Walt Disney animated movies and movies such as "The Wizard of Oz" often have an overture. Listen to the total overture and then see if the children can point out the songs contained in the overture.

Open Your Olfactories

Science

" . . . The better to smell with, my dear!" said the wolf.

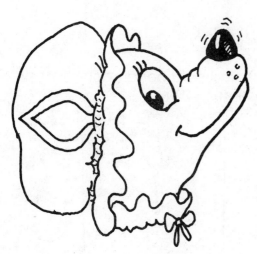

Objective: To demonstrate the importance of one's sense of smell

Materials: hard potato, hard apple, hard pear, knife, 3 bowls, toothpicks, blindfold

Background Information: The sense of taste is affected by the way food smells. For example, when you have a cold and a stuffy nose, some foods probably taste alike. People usually taste and smell food at approximately the same time. When the sense of smell is greatly diminished, the sense of taste may be affected, too.

Directions:

1. Dice the potato, apple and pear into small cubes.
2. Place the food in three different bowls.
3. Blindfold a student.
4. While the child pinches his/her nostrils shut, have him/her taste each item and try to identify it. (Since the food items have similar textures, this task will be difficult!)
5. Repeat with other student volunteers.
6. Determine the percentage of correct responses.

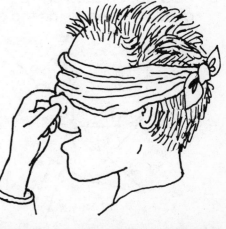

Oxygen

Science

Objective: To learn about oxygen and to make a pinwheel and see how it operates

Materials: 6" squares of paper, scissors, thin wooden dowels or sticks or pencils, pushpins

Background Information: Oxygen is a gas. Even though we cannot see, taste or smell it, we need oxygen to live. We breathe in oxygen from the air. Our blood carries it from our lungs to our muscles to make energy. Oxygen makes up about $1/5$ of the air. When we inhale, oxygen enters our bodies, but when we exhale, carbon dioxide leaves our bodies.

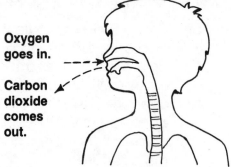

Oxygen goes in.

Carbon dioxide comes out.

Directions:

1. Give each student a 6" square of paper.

2. Have students fold the square diagonally.

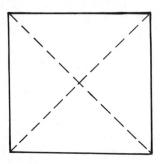

3. Show students how to cut on the folds almost to the center of the square, but not entirely there.

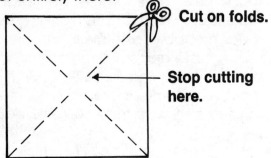

Cut on folds.

Stop cutting here.

4. Students should bend each corner into the center.

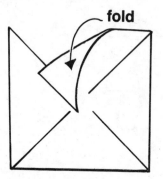

fold

5. Help students use one pushpin to attach all four corners to the top of the stick.

6. Instruct students to blow softly and then hard, noting the various speeds of the pinwheel.

Operator, Operator

Science

Objective: To make simple telephones and demonstrate how sound travels

Materials: two yogurt (or similar) containers, 12'-15' piece of string, small leather punch
(per pairs (or pointed tool), paper clips
of students)

Directions:
1. Students work in pairs to make telephones. Help them punch a hole in the center of the bottom of each container. Students should secure the string to the inside of each container by tying it to a paper clip. (See diagram.)
2. Encourage students to experiment to see how sound travels best through the string. (The best way is with the string pulled tight.)

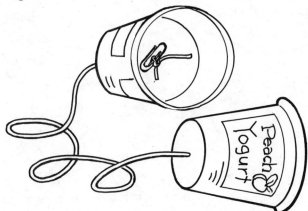

Olive Owl Treats

Cooking

Ingredients: round crackers
soft cream cheese
sliced black olives
pineapple slices cut into triangles

Directions:
1. Spread cream cheese onto a cracker.
2. Place two olive slices for the owl's eyes.
3. Add the pineapple for the beak.

**For Dining
Enjoyment:** Sing these words to the tune of "She'll Be Comin' Round the Mountain."

Owl be goin' down the hatch sometime soon.
Owl be goin' down the hatch sometime soon.
Owl be goin' down the hatch,
And then they'll make another batch . . .
Owl be goin' down the hatch sometime soon!
(Yell) Oh, no!

Finding an Oasis

Art

Objective: To write and illustrate a story about an oasis

Materials: writing paper, pencils, sheets of sandpaper, green construction paper, scissors,
(per pairs glue, construction paper scraps, crayons, markers
of students)

Directions: 1. Tell students the following story:

*You and your trusty camel, Camelia, have been
traveling for three weeks in the hot, dry and dusty Sahara
Desert. Your food and water are almost gone. Both you and
Camelia are so thirsty and hungry that your strength is
zapped, and you are both crawling slowly through the sand.
You begin to lose hope until you spot an oasis in the
distance. You carefully stand and begin to drag Camelia to
that special place ...*

2. Have students imagine what they find at their amazing oasis. Stress creativity!

3. Instruct students to illustrate their oasis. Some things they might include:
   a palace
   a McDonald's restaurant
   a soda fountain
   a hotel
   a lake with fish
   a lemonade stand
   a large fan and soda pop machine
   a swimming pool

Oceanography

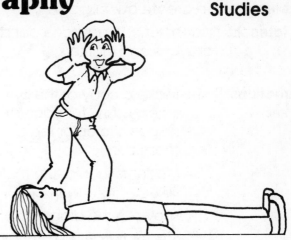

Objective: to dramatize different objects (living and nonliving) in the ocean

Materials: index cards, marker

Background Information: Oceanographers are scientists who study everything about the ocean, including its land, its tides (and their effect on weather) and sea creatures. They use research vessels or ships and tools and instruments such as echo sounders to measure the ocean's depth and to map its bottom.

Directions:
1. On index cards, draw pictures of anything that may be found in the ocean (one picture per card). Examples:

   octopus   sunken ship
   tides   seaweed
   diver   treasure chest
   shark   lobster
   sea horse   porpoise

2. Group students in pairs.
   Give each group a card and allow approximately five minutes so that students can practice "becoming" what is stated on the card.

3. Have each pair dramatize its word for the class. See who can guess the word.

Suggested Reading: *I Can Be an Oceanographer* by Paul P. Sipiera

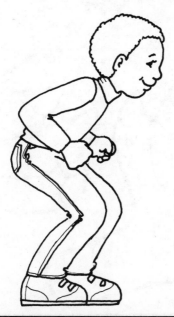

Olympics

Objective: To dramatize various Olympic events

Directions:
1. Instruct each student to choose an Olympic event. It can be part of the summer or winter games.

2. Students will take turns dramatizing their event and letting the others guess what it is.

3. Whoever guesses correctly gets to dramatize his/her event next.

Owl Puppets

Art

Objective: To create owl puppets

Materials: paper lunch bags (one per student), owl pattern pieces (below), scissors, glue, crayons and markers

Directions:
1. Make a copy of the patterns below, enlarging if necessary, for each student. Instruct students to color the pattern pieces and cut them out.
2. Students should turn their bag upside-down.
3. Have students glue the pieces to the bag as shown in the diagram.
4. Students can use markers or crayons to draw feathers on the bag.

Just for Laughs: What did the owl say as he fell asleep at noon? "Owl see you tonight!"

Extension: Use with poem on page 167, "Too Close for Comfort."

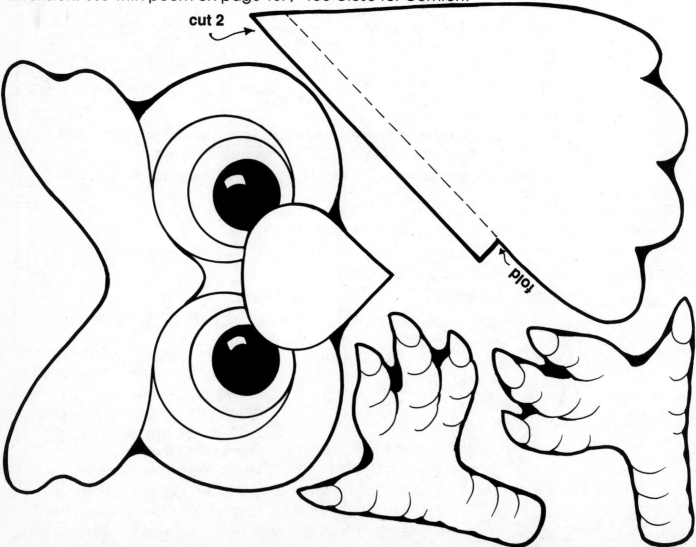

cut 2

fold

Little Owls

Finger Play/ Creative Dramatics

Your students will have lots of fun performing the finger play below. You could also have groups of students act out the poem for each other.

Too Close for Comfort

Five little owls sitting in a tree
    Whooooo — all belong to one family.
A sixth little owl sits close by.
    "**Whooooo** — are you?" they all reply.
"Why, I'm your cousin Malachi!"
    "**Ohhhhh!**"

Six little owls sitting in a tree
    Whooooo — all belong to one family.
A seventh little owl lands to rest.
    "**Whooooo** — are you?" they all request.
"Why, I'm your Great Auntie Celeste!"
    "**Ohhhhh!**"

Seven little owls sitting in a tree
    Whooooo — all belong to one family.
An eighth little owl takes a seat.
    "**Whooooo** — are you?" they all repeat.
"Why, I'm your mother's brother Pete!"
    "**Ohhhhh!**"

Eight little owls sitting in a tree
    Whooooo — all belong to one family.
A ninth little owl sits close beside.
    "**Whooooo** — are you?" they can't decide.
"Why, I'm your cousin Adelaide!"
    "**Ohhhhh!**"

Nine little owls sitting in a tree
    Whooooo — all belong to one family.
A tenth little owl joins them all.
    "**Whooooo** — are you?" they try to call.
But the branch cracks in half, and they start to fall.
    "**Ohhhhh!**"
"**Whooooo — are you?**" they say from the ground.
    "I'm your long lost Gramps, but now I'm found!"
And on that note, they found a new tree
    With a branch to fit the whole family!
    "**Ohhhhh well. Owls well that ends well!**"

Old MacDonald

Music

Directions: Sing "Old MacDonald Had a Farm" but make a few changes:

Old MacDonald had a zoo—
   Yabba, Dabba, Doo!
And in his zoo he had a _____ .
   Yabba, Dabba, Doo . . .

Have the children substitute any zoo animal and its sound. Encourage creativity and fun!

O Field Trips/Speakers and Follow-Up Activities

Objective: To use field trips/speakers as motivation for science, writing and art activities

Possibilities: an observatory
ophthalmologist
optometrist
parents for "Occupation Day"

Observing Constellations

After visiting an observatory, make large stars. Use adhesive putty to put them on the classroom ceiling to form famous constellations such as the Big Dipper.

Occupations

Students could make booklets containing pages depicting different occupations. On each page, help students write a few sentences about an occupation at the bottom. Then, have students illustrate the sentences.

O Pictures for Miscellaneous Activities

Enlarge the pictures to make flash cards or bulletin board characters. You could also give one picture to each student, have him/her paste it on paper and draw a scene around it.

ostrich	ocelot	ox	octopus

owl	octagon	osprey	otter

Book List

Benchley, N. (1966). *Oscar Otter*. New York: Harper and Row.

Gantschev, I. (1985). *Otto the Bear*. Boston, MA: Little, Brown.

Kellogg, S. (1984). *Paul Bunyan, a Tall Tale*. New York: William Morrow and Company.

Maestro, B. and Maestro, G. (1981). *Traffic: A Book of Opposites*. New York: Crown Publishers.

Miller, M. (1985). *Oscar Mouse Finds a Home*. New York: Dial Books.

Peppé, R. (1974). *Odd One Out*. Minneapolis, MN: Viking Press.

Piatti, C. (1964). *The Happy Owls*. New York: Atheneum.

Seuss, Dr. (1955). *On Beyond Zebra*. New York: Random House.

Smith, W.J. (1918). *Ho for a Hat!* Boston, MA: Joy Street Books.

Spier, P. (1971). *Gobble, Growl, Grunt*. New York: Doubleday.

Tejima, K. (1987). *Owl Lake*. New York: Philomel Books.

Yolen, J. (1987). *Owl Moon*. New York: Philomel Books.

video—*Paul Bunyan*. Walt Disney Educational Media Company. (1980). Northbrook, Illinois.

More O Pictures for Miscellaneous Activities

Enlarge the pictures below to make flash cards, bulletin board characters or characters that can be used in a story.

Book List

Asch, F. (1988). *Oats and Wild Apples.* New York: Holiday House.

Degen, B. (1980). *The Little Witch and the Riddle.* New York: Harper and Row .

Kellogg, S. (1991). *Jack and the Beanstalk.* New York: Morrow Junior Books.

Langstaff, J. (1972). *Over in the Meadow.* New York: Harcourt Brace Jovanovich.

Schwartz, A. (1987). *Oma and Bobo.* New York: Bradbury Press.

Sipiera, P. (1987). *I Can Be an Oceanographer.* Chicago, IL: Children's Press.

Solotareff, G. (1988). *The Ogre and the Frog King.* New York: Greenwillow.

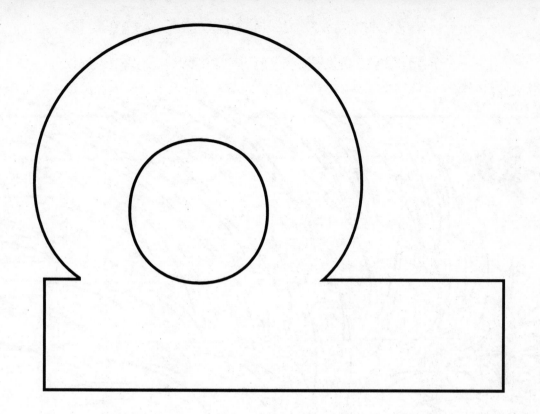

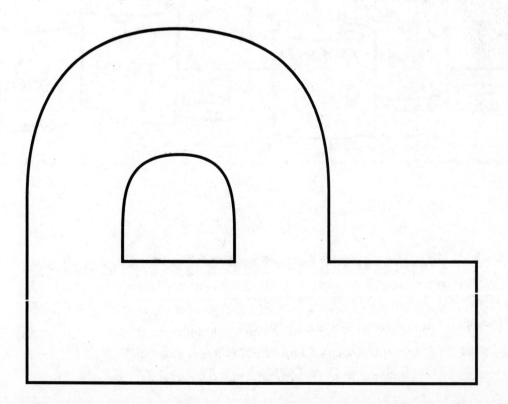

red
green
blue
yellow

Art/
Science

Peanut Butter Bird Feeder

Objective: To make a peanut butter bird feeder

Materials: peanut butter, pine cones, birdseed

Directions: Roll a pine cone in peanut butter and then in birdseed to make a treat for birds. Use string to hang the pine cones from tree branches.

IF8661 The Alphabet

Place Mats

Art

Objective: To make place mats to use at a special treat time

Materials: one sheet of 9" x 12" construction paper per student, scrap construction paper, scissors, stapler or tape or glue

Directions: Have students decorate their placemats by gluing various pieces of cut or torn paper onto the construction paper.

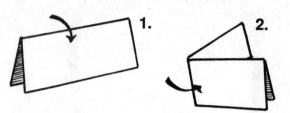
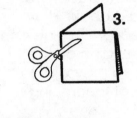
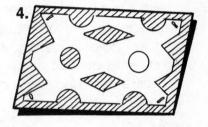

Puzzle

Materials: white paper, crayons, scissors, ruler, black marker, cup

Directions:

Have students draw a picture, filling the page. Divide the picture into simple pieces using a ruler and a marker. Then cut the pieces. Put in bag. Students may trade with each other.

Suggestion: You can tie this activity in with another area of study by directing students to draw or color a specific type of picture, such as a plant for science, a police officer for safety lessons, etc.

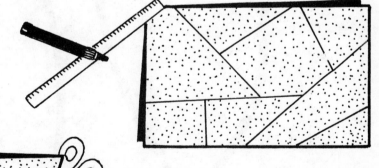

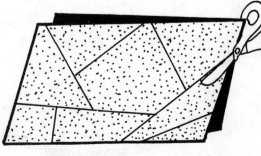

Penguins

Art

Materials: 18" x 12" sheets of white paper, 9" x 12" sheets of black paper, 4" x 6" sheets of yellow paper, white crayons, patterns, glue, 18" x 12" sheets of oaktag (for pattern), 9" x 12" sheets of oaktag (for pattern), crayons or markers

Directions: Trace and cut the "bowling pin " pattern below which becomes the penguin's body. Trace with white crayon and cut the wing pattern on folded black paper and cut two wings at once. On the yellow paper, trace and cut penguin feet and a beak. Have students assemble the pieces with glue and then color in details. (Depending on the abilities of your students, you may wish to have them do some or all of the tracing and cutting.)

Extension Activity:
See **Penguins** page 175.

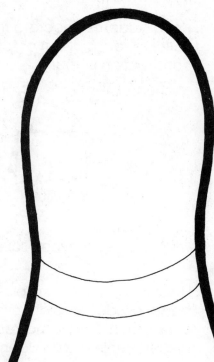

Penguins

Science

Objective: To learn about some of the characteristics of penguins

Materials: chart paper and marker

Directions: Ask students to tell you anything they know about penguins. Write or draw the characteristics they come up with on your chart paper. Use the list of information below to help guide your discussion. Keep students active in the discussion by asking them to make predictions, or take a "best guess."

- Penguins are birds that do not fly. They can swim skillfully, and they walk and slide on their bellies across ice.
- Penguins' feathers are short and thick.
- The daddy penguin keeps the eggs warm by placing them on top of his feet and covering it with the rolls of fat on the lower part of his belly.
- Penguins live only south of the equator.
- Penguins eat fish.

Pictograph

Math

Objective: To create a pictograph of their preference - peanuts or popcorn

Materials: large graph or plain white paper, paper cutouts of peanuts, paper cutouts of popcorn, glue, marker

Preparation: Use the patterns below to cut out a stack of peanuts and popcorn.

Directions: To set up the graph, create two sections, one for peanuts and one for popcorn. Label each section. Next, create boxes in each section large enough to fit your popcorn/peanut cutouts. Ask students to state their preference, peanuts or popcorn. As they choose, give each student the corresponding cutout. Next, have each child glue his/her popcorn or peanut cutout on the graph in the appropriate section. Tally and compare the results.

popcorn			peanuts		
🍿	🍿	🍿	🥜	🥜	🥜
🍿	🍿	🍿	🥜		
🍿					

Patterns

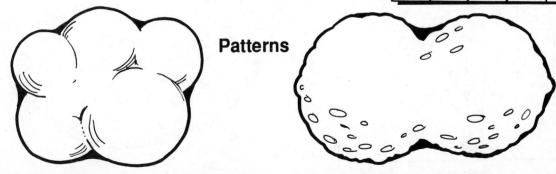

Pussy Willow Scroll

Art

Objective: To celebrate spring by having children make a pussy willow scroll wall hanging

Materials: 12" x 24" white construction paper, yarn, crayons without paper covering, brown paint, paintbrushes, cotton balls, glue, stapler

Directions:

Fold.

1. Fold back the top 4 inches of the white paper. Have the children color a background for the pussy willow branch by using the side of a large crayon without a paper cover. Encourage them to press lightly and use long, curved strokes, like a rainbow.

2. Next, have the children paint a branch using the brown paint. (See illustration.)

Brown

3. After the paint has dried, add drops of glue and tiny pieces of cotton balls to the branch.

GLUE

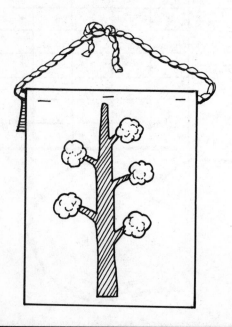

4. Tie a length of yarn in a knot to form a circle. Slip the yarn under the folded flap and staple the flap closed. The scroll is now ready for hanging.

Plants from "Seeds"

Science

Objective: To note shapes of various "seeds" and to observe differences of plants when the seeds grow

Materials: various seeds such as an unroasted peanut, pumpkin and potato "eye," paper cups, soil, tray or dish for draining, sunny windowsill

Directions: Discuss plant needs (soil, sun, water). Tell the children that one of the ways plants reproduce is by producing seeds. Show them the seeds that you have collected: several pumpkin seeds, some peanuts (remove shells), and a potato. Cut a section of the potato containing an "eye." Compare these seeds and plant them in paper cups. Put holes in the bottom of the cups first. Label the cups and place them on a tray or dish for draining. Put them in a sunny window, water them and wait!

Note which seeds grow first and any differences between the plants.

Pollution

Objective: To become aware of oil spill disasters

Materials: brownie or lasagna pan, water, cooking oil, sponge, paper towel, a piece of nylon, a coffee filter

Directions: Oil spills have been disastrous for our environment. To demonstrate why, fill a brownie or lasagna pan with water. Next, pour a small amount of cooking oil in the water. The cooking oil will act in the same manner as the crude oil. Observe what happens. Then, ask several students to try to remove the oil from the water. (Supply them with the materials listed above.)

Suggested Reading:
Pollution and Wildlife by Michael Bright
Water Pollution by Darlene Stille
It Was Just a Dream by Chris Van Allsburg

Extension Activity:
Observe the properties of a bird's feather. Pour water on a feather. The feather remains dry. What happens when cooking oil is placed on the feather?

Puzzles

Games

Objective: To set up a workable system for sharing classroom puzzles

Materials: puzzles (in as many shapes, sizes and forms as you can find), markers (to color-code the backs of all the pieces before you introduce the puzzles to the class)

Directions: Have a class discussion about puzzles. Talk about the many different types of puzzles (wooden, floor, shape, double-sided). Be sure your rules for the puzzles are clear to the children. A good rule is to finish one puzzle and put it back before starting another one! Talk about the importance of coding the backs of puzzles. Share your "code system" with the children.

Lastly, give the children some ideas about how to work the puzzle. Encourage children to tell the class how they begin a puzzle and how they figure out clues from the shapes and colors of the pieces. Be sure to talk about the need for cooperation, sharing and responsibility.

Hot Potato

Objective: To play an old, time-honored game

Materials: a potato, timer

Directions: Seat students in a circle. Give one student the potato. Set the timer for a short amount of time (30 to 90 seconds). When the timer is set, students pass the "hot" potato around the circle as quickly as possible. When the timer rings, the student holding the potato is "out." The game ends when there is only one student remaining.

Note: Students who are "out" can still participate by:
1. running a timer.
2. becoming a counter by recording the number of students remaining on the chalkboard.
3. becoming a "judge" by judging who had possession of the potato when the timer sounded.
4. becoming a potato "catcher" by retrieving the potato if it is dropped.

Poll

Social Studies

Objective: To conduct a poll to obtain information

Materials: poll sheet

Directions: Discuss with students how a poll is used to obtain information. Conduct a popularity poll in your classroom by asking each student their favorite song, television show, and book. Design a large poll sheet, using rebus pictures. Record the results while the class watches.

Extension Activity:
Graph the results of the poll.

Police

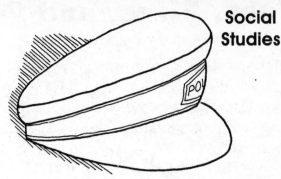

Objective: To become familiar with how police officers can help us

Directions: Discuss with students what they should do if they're lost or need help. Explain how police officers help. Discuss the components and colors of a police officer's uniform.

Suggested Reading:

Let's Find Out About Policemen by Charles and Martha Schapp

I Can Be a Police Officer by Ray Broekel

Police Officers, A to Z by Jean Johnson

Popcorn

Use this as a science experiment as well as a cooking experiment.

Observe the corn kernel.

How does it feel?
What color is it?
What size is it?

What happens when you add heat?

Observations:

It changes size.
It changes color.
It changes texture.
It becomes edible and chewable.

Potato Puffs

Ingredients: potatoes, one egg, salt, pepper, butter, a little milk, crushed corn flakes

Directions: Peel and boil potatoes. Mash with a little milk, butter, salt and pepper to taste. Roll into little balls.

Beat egg diluted with two tablespoons water.

Dip the potato balls in the egg and then roll in the corn flake crumbs.

Bake on a greased cookie sheet at 375 degrees for about 20 minutes.

It's fun to make your own corn flake crumbs by using a rolling pin and crushing the corn flakes in a plastic bag. However, you can also buy corn flake crumbs.

Peas, Pizza, and Peanut Butter

Cooking

Peas

Ask the children where they think peas come from. Explain to the children that peas do not grow in a box or can. Have them shell peas and taste them raw. Then, cook them in boiling water.

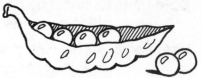

Extension: See poem in middle of this page.

Pizza

Toast English muffin halves, top with pizza sauce or a similar tomato sauce. Add oregano, Parmesan and mozzarella cheese and put them in the oven, or toaster oven, to melt the cheese. Enjoy!

Peanut Butter

Put roasted, shelled peanuts through a food processor and enjoy "pure" peanut butter on crackers.

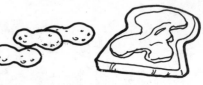

Pass the Peas, Please!

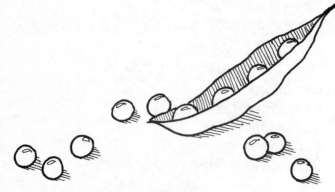

Please, please, pass the peas.
Not the potatoes, not the cheese.
When I'm hungry, I must have these.
So please, please, pass the peas.

There are no peas?
Well what a squeeze.
I am so hungry, that I may sneeze.
There really are no more peas?
Then, go ahead and pass the pizza, please.

by Ada Frischer

People

Objective: To identify people doing different activities

Materials: magazines, Popsicle sticks, scissors

Directions: Let children cut or tear out people from magazines who are engaged in different activities or careers. Have them mount their people on Popsicle sticks to make puppets. Let each child show off his/her puppets.

Dramatization

Suggested Trips

Post office   Police station
Pizza parlor   A play
Park   A picnic
Planetarium   Pumpkin patch

IF8661 The Alphabet

Book List

Anderson, H.C. (1978). *The Princess and the Pea.* New York: Seabury Press.

Behrens, J. (1985). *I Can Be a Pilot.* Chicago, IL: Childrens Press.

Bond, M. (1973). *Paddington.* New York: Random House.

Carle, E. (1970). *Pancakes, Pancakes!* New York: Knopf.

Collidi, C. (1988). *Pinnochio.* New York: Knopf.

de Paola, T. (1978). *The Popcorn Book.* New York: Holiday House.

Freeman, D. (1978). *A Pocket for Corduroy.* New York: Penguin Books.

Goodall, J. (1980). *Paddy's New Hat.* Atheneum.

Hoban, (1972). *Push Pull Empty Full.* New York: Macmillan.

Keats, E.J. (1967). *Peter's Chair.* New York: Harper and Row.

Matthias, C. (1984). *I Can Be a Police Officer.* Chicago, IL: Childrens Press.

Potter, B. (1955). *Peter Rabbit.* New York: Grosset and Dunlap.

Steig, W. (1980). *Sylvester and the Magic Pebble.* New York: Simon and Schuster.

Van Allsburg, C. (1985). *The Polar Express.* New York: Houghton Mifflin.

P Pictures for Miscellaneous Activities

Enlarge the cards to make flash cards for use throughout the study of the "P" sound.

Qq

Creative Quartets

Music

Learn a favorite familiar song. Then, divide the class into groups of four (quartets). Have each quartet sing the song for the class.

Quadruplets

Math

Explain to the students that a quadruplet is a set of four things that are the same. Have the students name things that come in sets of four. Divide your class into cooperative groups. Give each group assorted objects, at least four of each object. Ask the groups to sort the objects into "quadruplets," or sets of four. When all groups have finished sorting, have each group tell the class about their "quadruplets."

Quilt

Art

Objective: Turn a bulletin board into a class quilt!

Materials one 6" x 6" square of white construction paper for each child, markers, enough colored strips to cover the perimeter of the quilt to form a border

Directions: During colonial times, quilters frequently quilted together at social gatherings called quilting bees. Tell the class you will be having a quilting bee. Discuss the history of quilt making and the many different types of quilts that are made. Some are used as blankets and bed coverings, and some are used as wall hangings. Tell the children that the class will work together to make a "wall hanging" quilt using a classroom bulletin board. You may want to present one theme for the "quilt" beforehand, or you may want to name the "quilt" after the children are finished drawing. Have the children design, draw and sign their squares. Arrange the squares on the bulletin board in a quilt pattern. Some children may have to make two squares to even the sides of the quilt to make a large square or rectangle. Staple a border of colored strips around the perimeter. Draw on stitches.

Extension Activity:

Read *The Josefine Story Quilt* by Eleanor Coerr. Ask the children to inquire if they have a special quilt at home that was made by a family member or has a story attached to it.

"Q-tip" Painting

Objective: To paint with cotton swabs and paintbrushes

Materials: 9" x 12" sheet of blue or black construction paper

Directions: Using brown or green paint, have children paint a tree on the construction paper. When dry, introduce painting with cotton swabs. Provide white paint for snow. Have children dip cotton swabs into the white paint and paint dots to show snow sitting on branches, on the ground or blowing in the wind.

Q Words

Objective: To identify words begining with the "Q" sound

Materials: copies of the Q below and the pictures on page 189, glue

Directions: Go over each picture with the children and let them identify it. Then, let them cut and paste the pictures around the large Q.

It's Quarter Time!

Math

Objective: To become familiar with a quarter

Materials: a quarter for every child, crayons, newsprint

Directions: Give every child a quarter. Discuss how a coin is identified by having a "heads" side and a "tails" side. Ask if anyone knows who is on the heads side (George Washington). Talk about the word "Liberty" and ask if anyone knows what it means. Then, read the motto, "In God We Trust." Explain that the year the coin was made is always on the heads side.

Then, turn the quarter over and ask if anyone can identify the bird (the eagle, our national bird). Tell them the name of our country is written there as is the term "QUARTER DOLLAR." Then, show them how to make rubbings of their quarter using different-colored crayons.

IF8661 The Alphabet

Q Is for Question Mark

Art

Objective: To become familiar with a question mark

Materials: copies of the question mark below, magazines and newspapers, scissors, glue

Directions: Draw a large question mark on the chalkboard. Ask the children if anyone knows what it is and what it is used for. Explain that it is used at the end of a written question. Write several simple questions on the board. Let different children draw a question mark at the end.

Then, give them copies of the question mark below. Let them cut out different question marks from old magazines and glue them on the question marks.

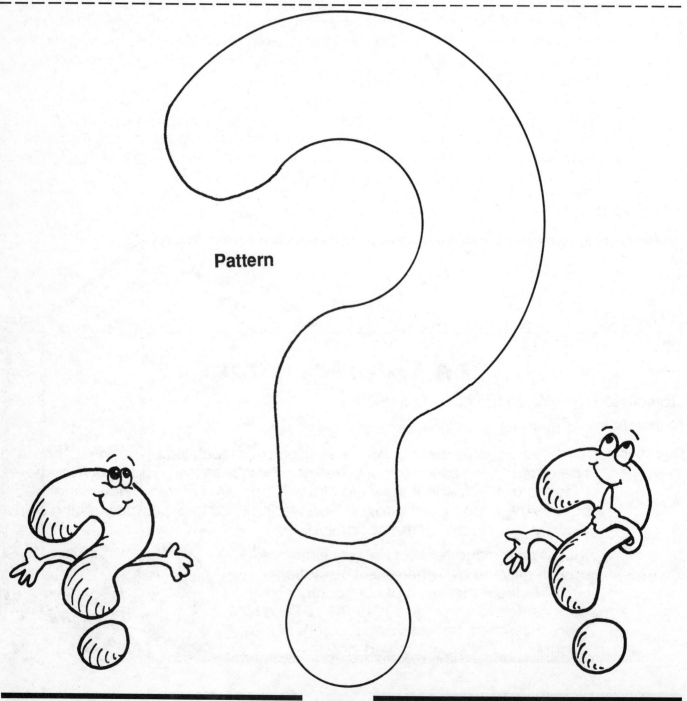

Pattern

Quart Size Please!

Math

Materials: 2 pint containers
4 quart containers
1 gallon container
1 large dishpan
water
1 copy of the quart pattern for each student

Directions: Display an empty quart container of milk, bottle or carton. Talk about different beverages and foods that are sold by the quart. Use water to demonstrate how it takes 2 pints to fill the quart container and 4 quarts to fill a gallon container. Place the dishpan on a large table. Fill the containers and pour one into the other. Start with the pints to fill the quart. Then fill the quarts with water to pour into the gallon. You may then reverse the procedure. Fill the gallon container and pour it into the quart containers. Then pour the water in one of the quarts into the two pint containers.

Give each student a copy of the quart pattern. The students cut out the quart. Then they may either draw and color pictures of items sold by the quart or they may use magazines and newspaper inserts to find and cut out pictures of items sold by the quart to glue on their quart patterns. Allow time for the students to share their "Quart Size" pictures with the class.

Quart Pattern

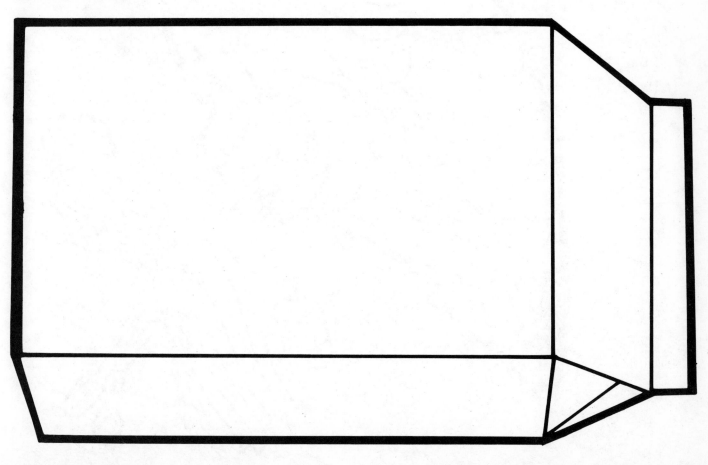

Catch Sight of a Quetzal

Science

Display a picture of a quetzal. (See encyclopedia.) Locate on a map where quetzals can be found. (Central and South America) Discuss how this bird is different from other birds. Make a copy of the quetzal on white construction paper for each student. Students are to color the picture and cut it out. Then give each student five 12-x-1-inch strips of green crêpe paper to use to make the long tail. Students glue the strips below the bird's tail feather. Then the students may taper the loose end of each feather and cut slits along the sides to create a fringed feathery look. Display the completed pictures on a wall.

Quiet, Quiet

There's a new baby in my house.
Shh, Shh, Quiet, Quiet!
I go to school. We're ready to read.
Shh, Shh, Quiet, Quiet!
I'm at home ready for bed.
Shh, Shh, Quiet, Quiet!
I think I'm ready to make a riot!
Shh, Shh, Quiet, Quiet!

by Ada Frischer

Book List

Coerr, E. (1986). *The Josefina Story Quilt.* New York: Harper and Row.

Jonas, A. (1984). *The Quilt.* New York: Greenwillow.

Wood, A. and Wood, D. (1982). *Quick as a Cricket.* Playspaces.

Zolotow, C. (1963). *The Quarreling Book.* New York: Harper and Row.

Zolotow, C. (1989). *The Quiet Mother and the Noisy Little Boy.* New York: Harper and Row.

Q Pictures for Miscellaneous Activities

Enlarge the cards below to make flashcards for use throughout the study of the "Q" sound.

IF8661 The Alphabet

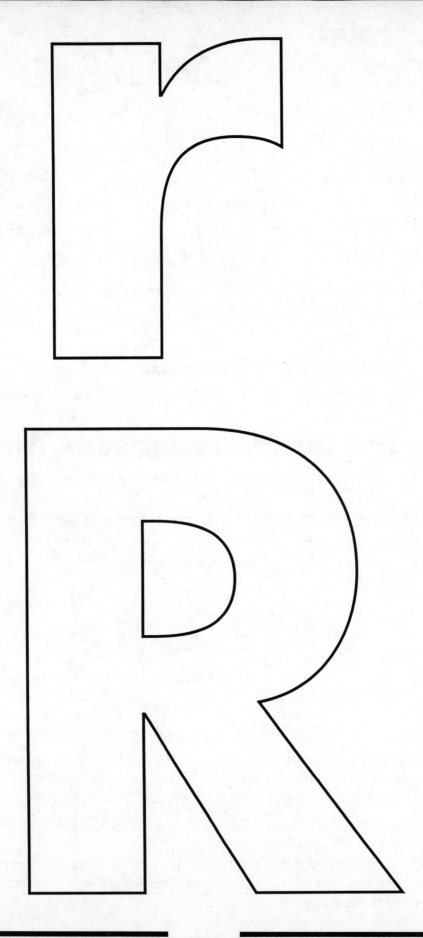

Rr

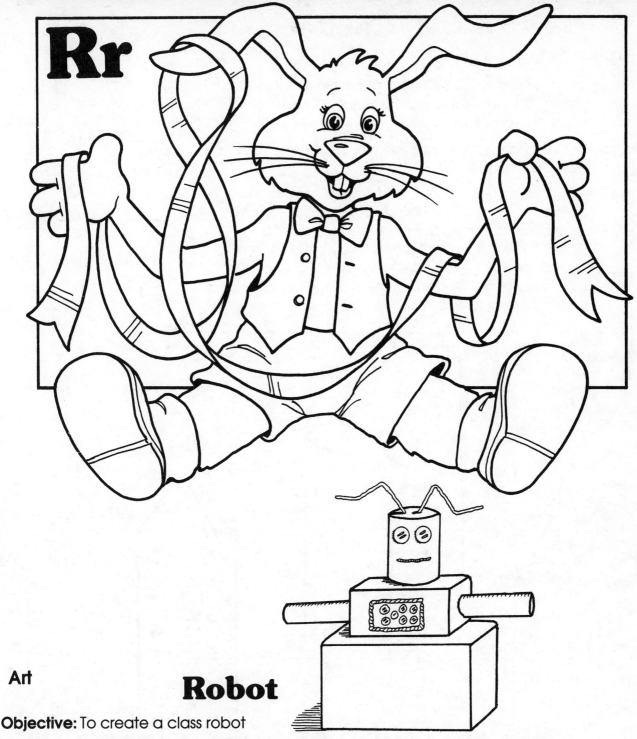

Art

Robot

Objective: To create a class robot

Materials: one large box or carton, one smaller carton, one cylinder-shaped box (such as a salt or oatmeal box), one paper towel roll, several assorted buttons, yarn, aluminum foil, glue, pipe cleaners

Directions: Cover the cartons, boxes and roll with aluminum foil and assemble as illustrated.

Glue on yarn to outline the control box and glue buttons in place for the controls. Use pipe cleaners for the antennae and buttons and yarn for the face.

Rocket

Art

Objective: To create rockets

Materials: for each child: 9" x 12" sheet of white construction paper, 6" blue circle, red crêpe paper cut in long strips, crayons, tape, glue

Directions: Have children decorate the 9" x 12" sheet of paper. (See illustration.)

Roll and tape the decorated paper vertically to form a long tube or cylinder. Cut a radius into the blue circle. Overlap the ends and tape to form a cone. Tape this to the top of the cylinder to form the cone of the rocket. Attach red crêpe paper streamers to the bottom of the cylinder to resemble exhaust flames.

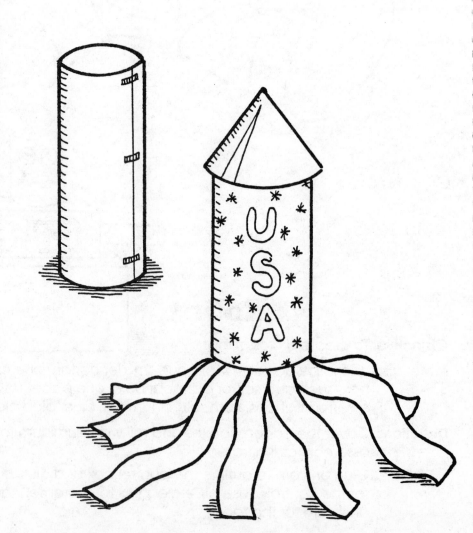

Rock Paperweight

Art

Objective: To design a rock paperweight

Materials: one small rock for each child, acrylic paints, one can of polyurethane spray, one small and one medium-sized paintbrush per child, marker

Directions: Collect rocks; wash and dry. Allow each child to select his/her own rock. With the marker, write the child's name and date on the bottom of the rock. Have the child select one color of the acrylic paint to paint the rock using a medium brush. When dry, using the smaller brush, have the child paint small dots of one or more colors all over the rock. When dry, spray rock outdoors with the polyurethane. Two or three coats of spray work fine. Allow rocks to dry before touching them.

R Is for Red!

Objective: To identify things that are red

Materials: 8 1/2" x 11" sheets of newsprint, 8 1/2" x 11" sheets of red construction paper, crayons, stapler, black marker

Directions: Brainstorm with the children a list of things that are often red, such as apples, strawberries, fire engines, stop signs, wagons, etc. Give each child two sheets of newsprint. Have the children fold the sheets of newsprint in half and draw pictures of things that are red on them. Give each child a sheet of construction paper to make the cover. On it, you should write **R Is for Red** using a black marker. Staple the pages together to make books.

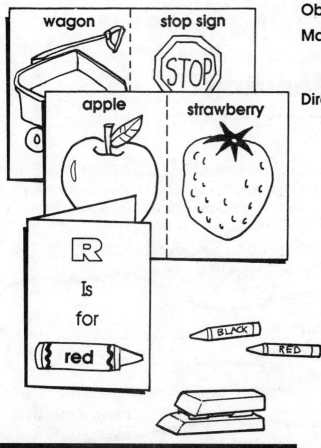

Rhymes - Complete the Rhyme

Reading

Objective: To help children become aware of rhyming

Directions: • Read the poems below using voice inflection to stress the rhyming words. Read several times, eventually pausing to let the children fill in the rhyming words.

Look at the bear.
He's sitting on a chair.

We drove far.
We drove in our car.

I had some cookies.
I ate four.
They were so good,
I wanted more.

It is night.
Turn on the light.

I like to run.
It is fun.

I have a kitten.
He plays with my mitten.

In the fall,
I play ball.

I ate the fish
On the dish.

I look in the mirror.
What do I see?
When I look in the mirror
I see me.

Look at my cat.
He is so fat.
He is sleeping on the mat.

R Is for Reading

Reading

Objective: To encourage reading by setting up a reading center

Materials: books, pillow, rug

Directions: Make a comfortable area in which the children can "read" books. Provide a rug and lots of big pillows. Let the children bring their favorite books from home to share during "R" week. Make certain they are properly identified so they can be taken home at the end of the week.

Have a reading race. Make copies of the footprint below on construction paper. Record each book read and attach the footprints to a wall.

Name_____
Book Title_____
Author_____

Rainbow

Science

Objective: To learn the colors of the rainbow in the correct order

Materials: 9" x 12" sheets of white construction paper, crayons, a prism

Directions: Help children discover a rainbow by shining light through a prism.

Have the children make their own rainbows using crayons and white paper.

Recycling

Science/Art

Objective: To use recycled materials to produce a creative work of art

Materials: any materials students would discard (e.g., milk containers, foil, ribbon, wrapping paper, juice and cereal boxes, straws, etc.), the top or bottom of a gift box for each student, glue, scissors

Directions: Ask students to bring in materials. Lay materials out on a table or floor. Demonstrate how the students can glue the materials to create a robot, a house, a rocket, an animal, or any masterpiece of modern art. Give students the top or bottom of a gift box to use as a base for their work. Paint if desired.

Suggested Reading: *50 Simple Things Kids Can Do To Save the Earth* by the Earthworks Group

Ruler Fun

Art

Objective: To give practice in drawing lines with a ruler

Materials: copies of the R from page 190, a ruler for each child, crayons

Directions: Give children copies of the large R, preferably on light-colored construction paper. Have them cut them out and use their rulers to draw lines on them using all different colors of crayons. Display them for "R" week.

Raisins and Stuff

Cooking

Raisins make a very good snack that can be mixed with many things:
- peanuts
- a dry cereal such as Cheerios or Rice Krispies
- grated carrots (add a little vanilla yogurt)
- peanut butter: spread on a cracker, stuff in celery, or spread on apple sections

Raspberry Rounds

¾ cup butter
1 ⅔ cups unsifted flour
1 ½ cups oatmeal
1 cup confectioners sugar
1 cup packed brown sugar
½ teaspoon baking soda
12 oz. raspberry preserves

Mix brown sugar and butter. Add baking soda, flour and oatmeal. Pack half the mixture in a greased 9" x 13" x 2" baking pan. Spread the raspberry preserves on top. Sprinkle the second half of mixture over the preserves. Bake 20-25 minutes at 400 degrees. When cool, use a round cookie cutter to cut into circles. Remove with spatula and sprinkle with confectioners sugar.

Rowing

Music

Have two children as partners sit on the floor facing each other with soles of the shoes touching. Partners should hold hands and "row" back and forth singing, "Row, Row, Row Your Boat."

Then, make up new versions of the song using "R" words and let the children come up with the actions. Examples:

Read, Read, Read Your Book
Run, Run, Run Around
Rain, Rain, Rain Comes Down
Reach, Reach, Reach the Sky
Ride, Ride, Ride Your Bike

Read, Read, Read Your Book.

clap . . . clap clap

Rhythm

Using any music (such as piano, guitar or tape) have children clap to the rhythm. A march is a good rhythm to start with. After children can clap out a rhythm, use other body movements such as marching, skipping, hopping or jumping to the beat of the music.

Book List

Bodecker, N.M. (1973). *It's Raining, Said John Twaining.* New York: Antheneum.

Brown, M.W. (1972). *The Runaway Bunny.* New York: Harper and Row.

Carle, E. (1987). *The Rooster's Off to See the World.* Picture Book.

Freeman, D. (1978). *A Rainbow of My Own.* New York: Penguin Books.

Galdone, P. (1985). *Rumpelstiltskin.* New York: Houghton Mifflin.

Ginsburg, M. (1974). *Mushroom in the Rain.* New York: Macmillan.

Hall, A. (1968). *The Remarkable Egg.* New York: Lothrop, Lee and Shepard.

Hoban, T. *Round and Round and Round and Round.*

Hutchins, P. (1967). *Rosie's Walk.* New York: Macmillan.

Kalan, R. (1978). *Rain.* New York: Greenwillow.

Lionni, L. (1982). *Let's Make Rabbits.* New York: Pantheon Books.

Lobel, A. (1984). *The Rose in My Garden.* New York: Greenwillow.

Potter, B. (1955). *Peter Rabbit.* New York: Grossett and Dunlap.

Spier, P. (1982). *Peter Spier's Rain.* Garden City, NJ: Doubleday.

Tresselt, A. (1946). *Rain Drop Splash.* New York: Lothrop, Lee and Shepard.

Williams, M. (1987). *The Velveteen Rabbit.* Avon Books.

R Pictures for Miscellaneous Activities

Enlarge the cards below to make flash cards for use throughout the study of the "R" sound.

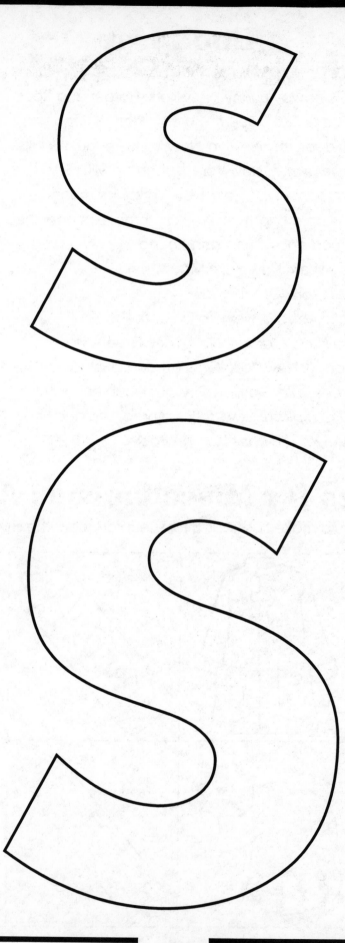

Ss

Cooking

School Supper
for Lunch

Pepare an "S" menu with the children for a supper in school at lunch time.

An ideal menu might be:
Soup
Sandwich (of choice)
Salad - grated carrots with raisins

Other foods to add might include strawberries, string beans, squash, spinach

❀ MENU ❀

Soup . . . .

Sandwich . . . . .

Salad . . . .

Soap Sailboats

Art

Objective: To create a sailboat that will float

Materials: Ivory soap, Popsicle or paste sticks, construction paper, toothpicks, pencils, scissors, knife (for adult use only)

Directions: Using the pencil, have the children draw the pointed bow of the sailboat on the soap. The teacher, aide, or parent volunteer cuts these corners off with a knife for the children. The children use the Popsicle sticks to smooth the sides and pointed edges of the "boat."

Using construction paper, have the children trace (you provide pattern) and cut out a small triangle-shaped sail. Stick the toothpick through the sail and into the boat (see example) and have a class regatta.

Stick figures secured with toothpicks can be put on the boats as well.

Adult cuts off corners.

Suggested Reading:
Mr. Bear's Boat by Thomas Graham

Writing/ Reading

Super Shapes

Objective: To become familiar with a circle, triangle, and square

Materials: colored construction paper cut into the shapes listed above, white 9" x 12" paper, marker

Directions: Show students the shapes you have cut out. Have children say the shape names. Next, students can use the shapes to design their own modern art. Use markers to add finishing touches.

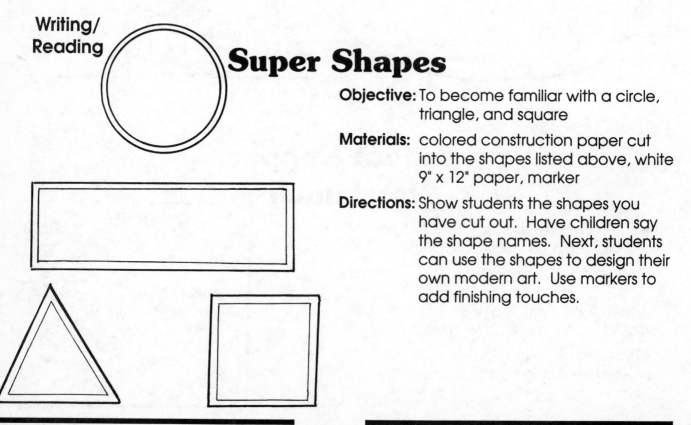

Sight

Objective: To introduce the children to the five senses in general and the sense of sight in particular

Directions: Explain to the children that there are five senses (seeing, hearing, smelling, touching, tasting). Ask them to name any they know. Talk about the fact that sometimes a person lacks one of the senses (e.g., a deaf person cannot hear and a blind person cannot see).

Explain that today you are going to concentrate on the sense of sight and the importance of the care of the eyes. This is a good opportunity to discuss playground safety as well. Ask the children to come up with some playground rules to protect the eyes such as: "Never throw rocks, pebbles, sticks, etc., at someone." "Never run with pencils, sticks, etc."

Sit with the children sitting in a circle. You are the game leader. Select an object in the room and then tell one thing about it saying, "I see something in the room that is (red)." Several children may try to guess what it is from this one clue. If they are unsuccessful, add another clue. "I see something in the room that is red and hanging." If no one guesses it, add a third clue, "I see something in the room that is red and is hanging and has two other colors." Answer: flag. The child who guesses is the winner.

Smell

Objective: To introduce the sense of smell

Materials: cotton balls, vinegar, vanilla extract, cologne, onion (cut), orange slices, flour, garlic clove (cut), 4 small plastic containers, aluminum foil

Directions: Discuss the sense of smell. Many things have distinctive aromas, and we can help identify objects by smelling.

Saturate one cotton ball with vinegar, one with vanilla extract and one with cologne. Put a cut onion, garlic, orange and flour in separate containers. Cover with foil and punch holes in the foil.

Have the children smell the cotton balls and the containers and try to identify the source of the smell. They should not put their noses too close to the objects. You may get answers such as salad, cookies, etc.

Stress that this experiment is a controlled school experiment. They should NEVER put their noses too close to any objects they are smelling. They should never do this experiment at home. Some things may be harmful to smell such as ammonia, bleach and other cleaning fluids or powders.

Seed Sort Game

Objective: To practice sorting seeds

Materials: several different kinds of seeds such as pumpkin, apple, grapefruit, watermelon, cantaloupe, lemon or orange, small containers to store the mixed seeds, egg timer

Directions: Spread out the small containers. The object of the game is to sort the seeds into containers before the time runs out. Turn over the egg timer and let the fun - and learning about classification - begin!

Extension Activity:
Have children bring in fruit. Remove and save the seeds. Make a salad.

Suggested Reading:
Seeds, and More Seeds by Millicent Selsam

Solar Energy

Science

Objective: To understand that the sun is, and can be used as, a source of heat energy

Materials: a sunny day, a wooden block, a metal spoon, a black or blue piece of material (such as a sock), a light piece of material, chart paper and marker

Directions: Discuss with students how the sun not only provides us with light, but also with heat. Ask students if they know how their classroom or home is heated when it is cold/cool outside. Explain that the sun could also heat our classroom or home, but we need to capture, or trap, the heat first. This heat from the sun is called "solar energy." Show students the materials listed above. Tell them that the class will conduct an experiment to find out which materials hold the sun's heat best. Place the items in a sunny location. After a couple of hours, have students test by feeling the objects to find out which items hold heat best. Which items feel warm? Which items feel cool? Make a class chart of your findings.

Note: This activity works best in spring or summer when the sun is strong.

Suggested Reading:
Solar Energy at Work by David Petersen

Sink/Float

Objective: To conduct an experiment to find out if various objects sink or float in water

Materials: a plastic bin or container of water; a box of various objects such as a wooden peg, bead, scissors, paper clip, ruler (wood and plastic), piece of string, pencil, crayon, straw, stone, paintbrush, etc.; a chart divided in half - one side labeled **Sink**, the other labeled **Float** (You may wish to illustrate the words.)

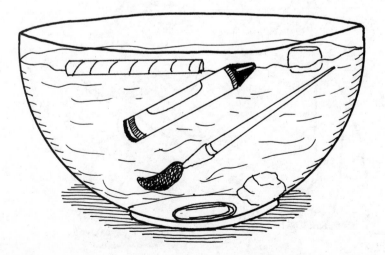

Directions:
Have children take turns selecting an object from the box and predicting whether it will sink or float. Check the prediction by putting it in a bin of water. Then, place the object on the appropriate side of the **Sink/Float** chart.

Steal the Snowman

Games

Materials: large open area, a plastic bowling pin or an empty plastic soda bottle

Directions:
- Divide the class into two teams. Line the students up at opposite ends of your play area facing each other.

- Give each player a number. (Each team should be given the same set of numbers so that two students, one on each team, have the same number.)

- Place the plastic pin or bottle in the center of the playing area between the two teams. The pin or bottle represents a snowman. You will then call out a number.

- The two students from opposite teams who share the number called, run out to the "snowman." The first student there picks it up and runs with it to "safety," which is back to his/her spot.

- If the student who picks up the bottle reaches his/her spot without being tagged, he/she scores a point for his/her team.

- The student who does not "steal the snowman" tries to tag the "thief." If successful, he/she scores a point for his/her team.

- The game ends when every player has had a turn, or as long as time or interest permits.

Other "S" Games: "Simon Says," "Soccer"

 IF8661 The Alphabet

Sand Soup

Games

Materials: bucket of sand, "bowls," "spoons," leaf bits, small twigs, pebbles, etc.

Directions: • Have students create their own crazy soups by adding various ingredients to a bowl or cup of sand. Stir and show off to the other cooks. You may wish to be outside and allow cooks to gather their own ingredients.

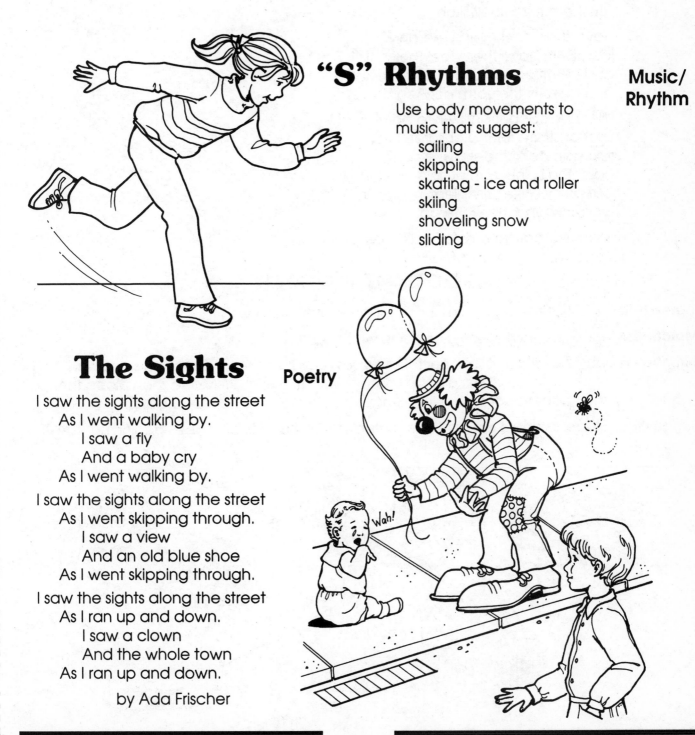

"S" Rhythms

Music/ Rhythm

Use body movements to music that suggest:
  sailing
  skipping
  skating - ice and roller
  skiing
  shoveling snow
  sliding

The Sights

Poetry

I saw the sights along the street
  As I went walking by.
    I saw a fly
    And a baby cry
  As I went walking by.

I saw the sights along the street
  As I went skipping through.
    I saw a view
    And an old blue shoe
  As I went skipping through.

I saw the sights along the street
  As I ran up and down.
    I saw a clown
    And the whole town
  As I ran up and down.

      by Ada Frischer

Skeletons

Objective: To paint a skeleton and to make the children aware that there is a skeleton inside their bodies

Materials: 12" x 18" black sheets of construction paper, white paint, paintbrushes, scissors

Directions: Have the children feel their head. Tell them this is their skull.

Have them feel their spine and identify it. Have them feel their ribs and identify them. Have them feel and identify their arm and leg bones.

Use black paper and white paint. Demonstrate for the children how you can paint the skull first. Then, paint the spine, ribs, arms and legs. Cut out the skeletons leaving some black around the white painting.

This is a great activity for Halloween.

Sponge Painting

Ingredients: To create sponge paintings of shapes beginning with the "S" sound

Materials: sponges, shallow trays of paint, white paper, scissors

Directions: Cut sponges into assorted "S" shapes such as sun, star, sailboat, snowman, snake, etc. Students dip the sponges into the paint tray and then place them on their paper to create prints. Students can create a scene or design.

Suggestion: Students could create their prints on large cutouts of shapes beginning with "S."

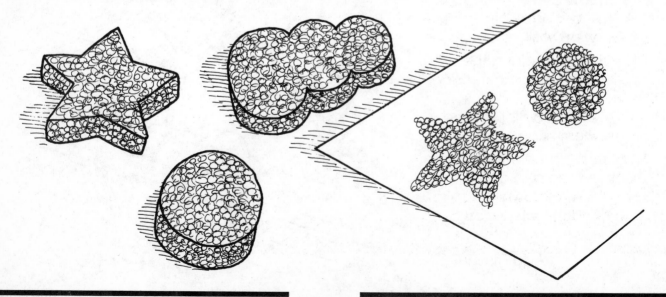

Book List

Ahlberg, J. and Ahlberg, A. (1988). *Starting School.* New York: Viking.

Briggs, R. (1978). *The Snowman.* New York: Random House.

Brown, M. (1947). *Stone Soup - An Old Tale.* New York: Scribner.

Bulla, C.R. (1962). *What Makes a Shadow?* New York: Crowell.

Carle, E. (1972). *Secret Birthday Message.* New York: Crowell.

Carle, E. (1984). *The Very Busy Spider.* New York: Philomel Books.

Charlip, R. (1966). *Mother, Mother, I Feel Sick.* Parents' Magazine Press.

De Paola, T. (1989). *Strega Nona.* New York: Simon and Schuster/Chardiet Unlimited.

Duvoisin, R. (1956). *The House of Four Seasons.* New York: Lothrop, Lee and Shepard.

Gag, W. (1938). *Snow White and the Seven Dwarfs.* Putnam Publishing Group.

Gibbons, G. (1983). *Sun Up, Sun Down.* Chicago, IL: Childrens Press.

Graham, M.B. (1978). *Be Nice to Spiders.* New York: Harcourt Brace Jovanovich.

Greene, C. (1983). *Shine, Sun!* Chicago, IL: Childrens Press.

Greene, C. (1982). *Snow Joe.* Chicago, IL: Childrens Press.

Hader, B. (1976). *The Big Snow.* New York: Macmillan.

Hoban, T. (1972). *Count and See.* New York: Macmillan.

Hoban, T. (1984). *I Read Signs.* New York: Greenwillow Books.

Hoban, T. (1983). *I Read Symbols.* New York: Greenwillow Books.

Hutchins, P. (1986). *Surprise Party.* New York: Macmillan.

Keats, E.J. (1962). *The Snowy Day.* New York: Viking Press.

Lionni, L. (1968). *Swimmy.* New York: Pantheon.

Mayer, M. (1986). *Just Me and My Little Sister.* Western Publishing.

Selsam, M. (1959). *Seeds and More Seeds.* New York: Harper.

Sendak, M. (1976). *Chicken Soup With Rice.* Weston, CT: Weston Woods.

Sendak, M. (1977). *Seven Little Monsters.* New York: Harper and Row.

Seuss, Dr. (1962). *Dr. Seuss's Sleep Book.* New York: Random House.

Seuss, Dr. (1953). *Scrambled Eggs Super!* New York: Random House.

Shaw, C.G. (1947). *It Looked Like Spilt Milk.* New York: Harper and Row.

Showers, P. (1974). *Sleep Is for Everyone.* New York: Harper and Row.

Steig, W. (1969). *Sylvester and the Magic Pebble.* New York: Windmill Books.

Tresselt, A. (1989). *White Snow, Bright Snow.* New York: Lothrop, Lee and Shepard.

Waber, B. (1972). *Ira Sleeps Over.* Boston, MA: Houghton Mifflin.

Zolotow, C. (1958). *The Sleepy Book.* New York: Lothrop, Lee and Shepard.

S Pictures for Miscellaneous Activities

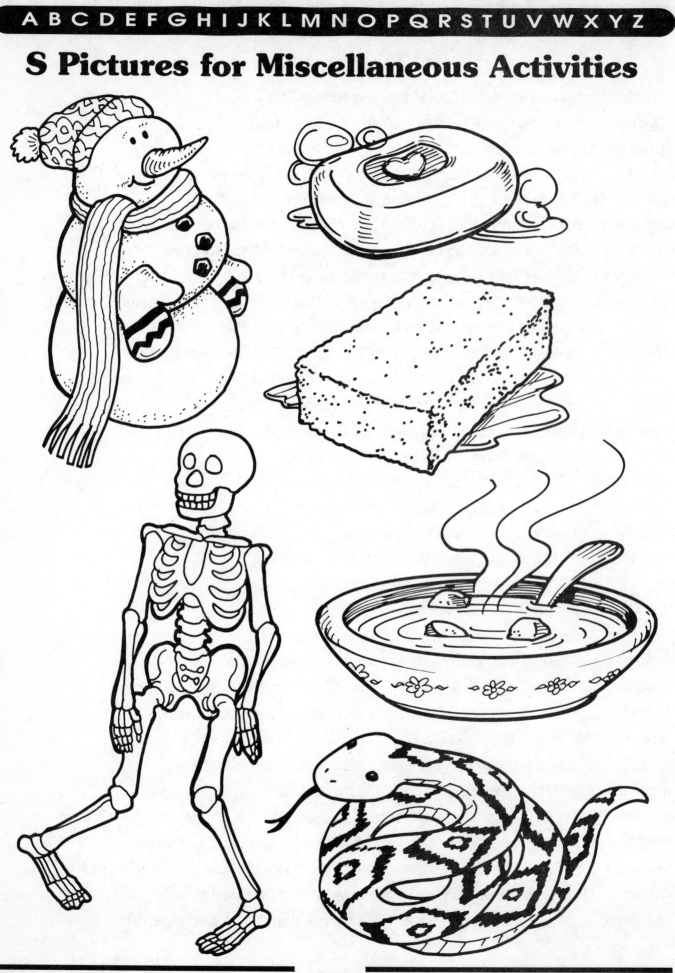

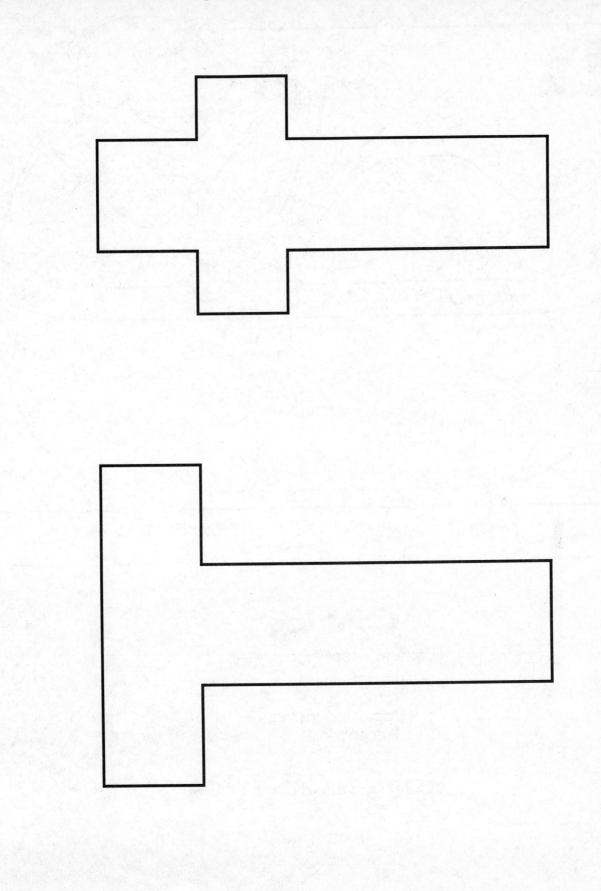

Cooking

Suggested cooking activities:

tomato salad
tomato sauce
tapioca pudding
French toast

Suggested Trips

Train ride

Tractor ride

Tepees

Art

Objective: To create a class tepee

Materials: two bed sheets (preferably yellow, white or beige), five 6' to 8' poles or sticks, 5' of rope, assorted colors of paint, paintbrushes, open area, masking tape or small rocks

Directions: To decorate your tepee, lay the sheets out on the floor, or on the ground outside. (Fasten them to the floor/ground with masking tape or small rocks.) Talk with your class about Native American tepees. Tell them how they were made of poles cut from trees and buffalo hides. Explain the care of putting them up and taking them down. Ask why that was important.

After the discussion, tell the class they are going to make a tepee. Let them decide how to decorate the tepee, and have students paint the sheets accordingly. Let sheets dry. Next, arrange the poles or sticks in tepee fashion (see illustration) leaving an open area for an entrance/exit. Have students hold poles/sticks in place. If working outdoors, you can push the ends of the poles/sticks into the ground. Wrap the rope around the poles/sticks where they join, and tie.

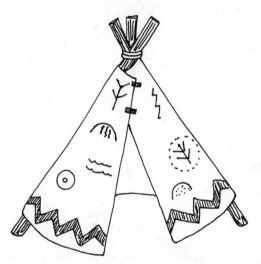

Last, drape the sheets around the outside of the sticks or poles, leaving a space for an entrance/exit. The sheets can be secured with peel and stick Velcro, but this will not be necessary unless there are strong winds in your area.

Indian Writing

You may wish to share some of these symbols with the students before they paint the tepee.

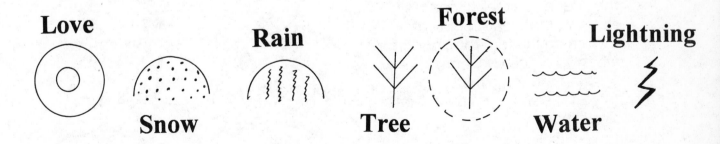

Love

Snow

Rain

Forest

Tree

Water

Lightning

Extension Activity:

Let the children play in the tepee pretending to be Native Americans of long ago.

Tom-Tom

Art

Objective: To further enhance the study of Native Americans

Materials: oatmeal box or salt box for each child, markers or paint, construction paper

Directions: Cover the cylinder box with construction paper. Have the children paint designs on the box. Do not paint the top or bottom of the container.

Tom-Tom Rhythms

Music

Objective: To repeat rhythms that a student/teacher plays on a tom-tom

Directions: Explain to students how a tom-tom is played. Next, instruct students to sit "Indian style" with their hands on their knees. Tell students that you will play a rhythm on the tom-tom, and that when you raise your hand, they will clap the same rhythm back to you. Keep the rhythms short and simple.

Clap, Clap . . .
Clap, Clap, Clap

Tissue Paper Trees

Art

Objective: To create a 3-dimensional tree

Materials: green tissue paper cut into 1" squares, green and brown crayons or paint, construction paper, flat top pencil with no eraser, paste or a small amount of white glue in a paste dish

Directions: Model for the children how to make a tree trunk using the brown crayon or paint, or provide them with a tree trunk cut out of brown construction paper. Using a green crayon, make a "cloud" sitting on the tree trunk. Cover the cloud completely with green "leaves."

To form the leaves, place the flat top of the pencil in the center of a square of green tissue paper. Wrap the square around the pencil. Dip just the flat part in the paste or glue and place it on the tree. Remove the pencil. The tissue leaf will remain on the paper.

Teeth

Science/Art

Ask a hygienist or dentist to give a demonstration on the proper way to brush teeth. Then have students bring in old toothbrushes. Provide thick tempera paint, paper and smocks. Students "paint" with the toothbrushes.

Taste Test

Science

Objective: To realize that different people prefer different tastes and to continue the study of the senses

Materials: two flavors of one type of food, for example, two flavors of Jell-O, two flavors of pudding, two different kinds of crackers; two spoons for each student; a blindfold if necessary

Directions: Provide each student with a copy of the form below. Explain that they will each take a turn taste-testing two food samples while blindfolded and decide which they enjoy the taste of more. Stress that you will be working with something that they are familiar with. Explain that you are working with something that is healthy, not harmful. Emphasize how children and adults should not put anything but healthy foods in their mouths. (See Extension Activity below.) Blindfold the child, spoon-feed him/her one flavor from one bowl and then, using a new spoon, spoon-feed him/her the second flavor. Next, the student marks his/her preference secretly on the form and washes his/her spoons. When everyone has had a turn, tally and compare results. Discuss the fact that we can all taste, but we all have taste preferences. **Note: Check student records for food allergies before doing any of the food activities.**

Extension Activity:
Now would be a good time to discuss alcohol, drugs and poison.

I prefer the taste of:

1. 2.

IF8661 The Alphabet

Tasting With Our Tongues

Science

Objective: To identify foods with different tastes: sweet, sour and salty

Materials: pictures of food, magazines, scissors, three sheets of 12" x 18" construction paper, paste

Directions: Discuss the functions of our tongues: speech, swallowing, taste. Explain to students that today, there will be more discussion of the sense of taste. Hold up pictures of several kinds of food (ice cream, orange juice, peanuts, chips, lemons, sour balls) and ask the students to describe the taste of each. Label each of the three sheets of construction paper with one of three tastes putting a picture next to the word to help students "read" the heading themselves. Next, have the students find pictures of food in magazines that have a sweet, sour or salty taste. Students can cut them out and paste them to the appropriately labeled sheet of construction paper to form a collage.

Optional Activity:

Have students sample the three tastes discussed. Supply each student with a piece of pretzel, a small cookie and a quarter of a lemon slice. (**Be sure to check student records for food allergies first**.) Discuss and record the tasting results.

Note: Be sure to discuss safety. Stress that children and adults should not put anything but healthy foods in their mouths.

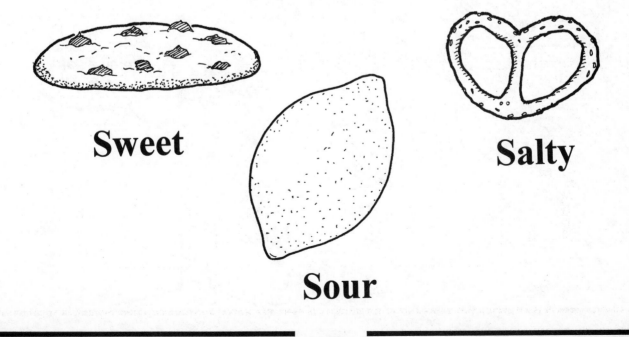

Sweet

Sour

Salty

Touch Box

Science

Objective: To explore the sense of touch as one of the five senses

Materials: a large box, a sock, glue, various objects to identify by touch

Directions: Cut a round hole large enough for a hand to fit into the side of the box . Cut the toe off the sock. Glue the sock to the outside of the box around the hole to form a sleeve. Now, push the "sock sleeve" into the hole. You have made a touch box!

Place an object in the touch box.

1. Have a child place his/her hand in the sock and then try to guess what is in the box.

2. Put part of an object in the box, such as the cap of a pen, and have children guess the whole object.

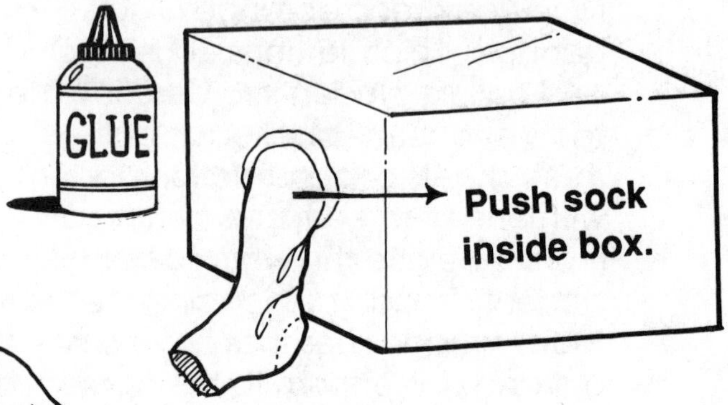

GLUE

Push sock inside box.

It's very slippery!

I found a pair of spoons!

Temperature

Science

Objective: To use a thermometer to measure temperature

Materials: 2 thermometers, 2 cups warm and cold water, red and white yarn, cardboard or oaktag, hole punch, marker

Directions: Ask students if they've ever been sick and had their temperature taken. Ask them what their mom or dad used to measure their temperature. Discuss what temperature is. Tell students that air and water also have a temperature, and that it is also measured with a thermometer. Using the teacher-made demonstrative thermometer (as described below), explain how a thermometer's mercury moves up as it gets warmer and down as it gets colder. Next, place a thermometer inside the classroom and one outside the classroom window. Compare the temperatures. Place a thermometer in cold water and one in warm water. Again, compare the temperatures. Make a chart of the temperatures.

Demonstrative Thermometer

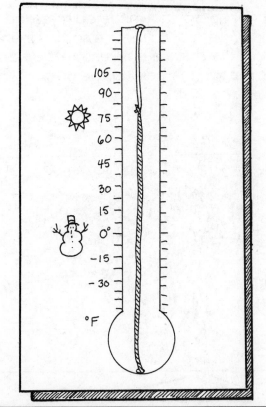

On oaktag or cardboard, draw a thermometer. Tie a piece of red and a piece of white yarn together at one end. Punch a hole at the top of the thermometer and at the bottom of the thermometer. String the red and white yarn through the holes, tying it in the back and cutting off the excess. Holding the yarn from the back, you can move the yarn up and down to demonstrate how a thermometer works. The red yarn represents mercury. To help students understand, draw pictures on the side of the thermometer to correspond with the degrees.

IF8661 The Alphabet

Triangle

Math

Objective: To make children aware of the triangle shape

Materials: paper, scissors, several triangle shapes

Directions: Show the children a triangle shape. Count the sides and the points. Place several triangle shapes of various sizes and colors on a table, two of each kind. Have the children match the triangles that are "the same."

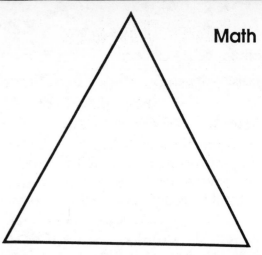

Telephone

Games

Objective: To help children understand how messages often get miscommunicated

Directions: Seat students in a circle. You become the telephone operator. Think of a message to be sent through the "telephone wire." The message is whispered from you to the student on your right and then on to the student next to him/her and so on in a counter-clockwise direction until it reaches the last student, seated to the left of you. This last student relates the message out loud. His/her message is then compared with the original message.

Note: If a student has not heard the whispered message, he/she may ask, "Operator?" The message is then repeated once. If the student is still unsure, he/she must relay the message the best he/she can.

Tag

Objective: To afford the class plenty of exercise

Materials: an open play area

Directions: Tag is a simple game. One child is "It" and chases the other children until he/she tags another child who then becomes "It."

Two Tigers

Poetry

Two big tigers
Were walking near a tree.
One's name was Rum Tum Tum.
The other was Ree Tee Tee.

Rum Tum Tum was hungry.
Ree Tee Tee was sad.
Neither one had had dinner
So, the two were very mad.

by Ada Frischer

Book List

Barton, B. (1986). *Trains.* New York: Harper and Row.

Barton, B. (1986). *Trucks.* New York: Harper and Row.

Beckman, B. (1985). *I Can Be a Teacher.* Chicago, IL: Childrens Press.

Brown, M. (1986). *Arthur's Teacher Trouble.* Little, Brown and Company.

Brown, M. (1986). *Arthur's Tooth.* Little, Brown and Company.

Galdone, P. (1986). *The Teeny-Tiny Woman.* Ticknor and Fields.

Gibbons, G. (1982). *Tool Book.* New York: Holiday House.

Gibbons, G. (1987). *Trains.* New York: Holiday House.

Gibbons, G. (1981). *Trucks.* New York: Holiday House.

Giff, P. (1984). *Today Was a Terrible Day.* New York: Penguin Books.

Lobel, A. (1976). *Frog and Toad.* New York: Harper and Row.

Mayer, M. (1981). *Terrible Troll.* Dial Books.

Parkinson, K. (1986). *The Enormous Turnip.* Niles, IL: A. Whitman.

Rockwell, A. (1974). *Toolbox.* New York: Macmillan.

Selsam. M. (1965). *Let's Get Turtles.* New York: Harper and Row.

Siebert, D. (1990). *The Train Song.* New York: T.Y. Crowell.

Silverstein, S. (1964). *The Giving Tree.* New York: Harper and Row.

Tresselt, A. (1969). *It's Time Now.* New York: Lothrop, Lee and Shepard.

Udry, J. (1956). *A Tree Is Nice.* New York: Harper and Row.

Ungerer, T. (1964). *One, Two, Where's My Shoe?* New York: Harper and Row.

Zolotow, C. (1963). *Tiger Called Thomas.* New York: Lothrop, Lee and Shepard.

Zolotow, C. (1986). *Timothy Too.* Oakland, CA: Parnassus Press.

T Pictures for Miscellaneous Activities

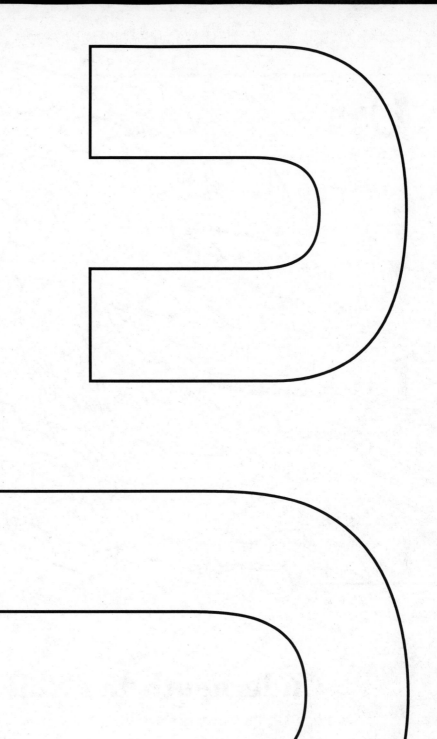

Uu

Underneath the Soil

Science

Objective: To observe how earthworms move in soil

Materials: glass jar, soil, earthworms, water

Directions:
1. Put a few earthworms on the bottom of the jar.
2. Add soil on top of them.
3. Slowly pour in water. (Add enough to soak the bottom.)
4. Observe how the earthworms move to the top.
5. Discuss why they go to the top. (As the water is soaked into the soil, the worms do not have air to breathe and must move to the surface.)

Up, Up and Away!

Art

Objective: To create hot air balloon mobiles

Materials: balloons, newspaper strips, wheat paste, tempera paint, paintbrushes, hot glue gun, glue sticks, soda pop can tabs, pint-sized fruit baskets, small stuffed animals or dolls, scissors, fish line, four 24" pieces of yarn per student

Directions:

1. Have students make papier-mâché balloons by wrapping newspaper strips covered with wheat paste around balloons. Let them dry completely.

2. Have students paint the balloons to create colorful patterns.

3. Have each student tie four 24" pieces of yarn to a soda pop can tab. Use the hot glue gun to secure each tab to the top of each balloon. Show students how to drape the yarn down the balloon, dividing it into fourths. About halfway down the balloon, secure each strip of yarn to the balloon with a drop of hot glue. Note: Be sure only you or other adults use the hot glue gun

4. Then, students tie the ends of the yarn to the basket and cut off excess yarn.

5. Have students place a stuffed animal or doll in their basket.

For the Record: The earliest recorded launch of a hot air balloon was a model flown indoors in 1709 in Portugal.

The Uvula

This is a fun little poem students can memorize to say when they have a sore throat.

> Poor, shy little uvula
> Alone and feeling blah,
> The doctor wants to see you and says
> "Open wide and say Ah."

U-Boats

Objective: To create a U-boat

Materials: butcher paper, pencils, crayons, markers, paint, paintbrushes

Background Information: During World War I, Germany showed the world how the submarine could be used as a deadly warship. The Germans called their submarines *Unterseebooten*, or U-boats. These boats became the most feared boats on the seas during the war.

Directions:
1. Show students pictures of submarines
2. Have each student design a submarine on butcher paper.
3. Be sure each student leaves enough room so that there is one window on the boat for his/her picture.
4. Have students draw or paste pictures of themselves in the windows.
5. Display the submarines on an undersea mural.

Humorous Humans

All children love to sing. Let your students enjoy this little song. Sing the verse below to the tune of "Frére Jacques." Then point to a student and have him/her try to make the class laugh by telling a joke, making a face or doing something funny. Repeat until everyone has had a chance to perform.

> Are you laughing,
> Are you laughing,
> Everyone,
> Everyone?
> I can make you smile.
> Watch a little while
> Have some fun!
> Have some fun!

Going Undercover

Science

Objective: To learn how animals use camouflage and to illustrate their disguises

Materials: pictures of "undercover animals" (page 226), 9" x 12" sheets of acetate, thin permanent markers, stapler, crayons

Background Information: Many animals use a form of disguise or camouflage to help them hide among their surroundings. This protects them from being eaten by other animals.

1. **Arctic foxes** are brown in summer (to blend in with trees and plants) and grow white fur coats in winter (to blend in with snow).

2. **Chameleons** have the largest range of color changes. Their skin color can change to black, brown, green, blue, yellow and red to match their surroundings. They change color when they are threatened, hot or cold—or when they want to attract a mate.

3. The **Asian horned frog** looks brown and leafy which allows it to blend in with plants in the forest.

4. The stripes of a **tiger** are hidden well in sunlit, tall grass. This helps it slowly sneak up on animals it wishes to catch.

5. Baby **zebras** have stripes even when they are born. They are protected when they hide in the middle of a herd where all the zebras' stripes blend together.

6. **Giraffes** have a long body that is disguised by a patchwork coat. This coat helps it blend well with Africa's tall trees.

7. The **stick insect** hides itself very well by blending in with twigs and branches. It can also stand perfectly still.

8. An **oystercatcher** nests on beaches. It lays brown and white speckled eggs among the same colors of rocks to protect the eggs.

9. A bird called a **potoo** protects itself by perching very stiffly on tree stumps.

Directions:
1. Give each child a copy of page 226, entitled "Undercover Animals."
2. Discuss how the animals look and let students color them.
3. Staple a piece of acetate to each animal page.
4. Read the description of each animal.
5. Let students use markers to draw what is needed on the acetate to show how the animal can go undercover.

Undercover Animals

Arctic Fox

Chameleon

Asian Horned Frog

Tiger

Zebra

Giraffe

Stick Insect

Oystercatcher

Potoo

IF8661 The Alphabet

Underside Up!

Creative Dramatics

Your students will have lots of fun dramatizing this poem. You may want to go all out and let students try it in a gym using mats!

The Upside-Down Catfish

Five little catfish
    Swimming down the stream—
The first flipped over
    And left the team.

The second did a back flip,
    The third a somersault,
The fourth did a back bend,
    But the fifth yelled, "Halt!"

"Why do you always want
    To swim upside-down?
You each look so silly—
    Just like a crazy clown!"

"Try it once," said the first,
    "And you will soon see—
On the leaves growing
    Lots of green algae!"

So the fifth flipped over
    And tried it awhile.
Then across his face
    Grew a very wide smile!

Five little catfish
    Swimming down the stream—
Turned upside-down, and
    Together made a team!

For the Record: When upside-down catfish are young (up to 10 weeks old), they swim right side up in the Congo River. However, they eventually choose to swim on their backs so they can eat the algae that grows on the underside of leaves.

Observing Our Universe

Science

Objective: To make a mini planetarium

Materials: a refrigerator box, Styrofoam balls, fluorescent paint, paintbrushes, fluorescent/ neon cardboard, glitter, scissors, glue, markers, flashlight, string, tape

Background Information: The universe is made up of matter, light and energy. It consists of everything that exists anywhere in space. It comprises everything in our solar system including planets, moons, stars/sun, meteors and comets.

1. Cut a large door in the refrigerator box. Cut a slot for the door handle. Students can paint the outside of the box to resemble the universe.

2. Assign groups of children different items to make:

   • planets—painted Styrofoam balls
   • stars/constellations—fluorescent cardboard
   • comets/meteors—fluorescent cardboard decorated with glitter
   • moons—fluorescent cardboard with craters drawn on them

3. Have students decorate the inside top half of the box with the items in the universe. Hang the planets and moons from the top with string. Glue comets, meteors and stars to the top and sides.

4. Let students take turns visiting the planetarium. Have them close the door and use a flashlight to look around.

5. Have students write a story about their trip to the planetarium.

U Pictures for Miscellaneous Activities

Enlarge the pictures to make flash cards or bulletin board items. You could also give one picture to each student, have them paste it on paper and draw a scene around it.

Book List

Abolafia, Y. (1985). *My Three Uncles*. New York: Greenwillow.

Anno, M. (1988). *Upside-Downers: Pictures to Stretch the Imagination*. New York: Philomel Books.

Churchill, E. (1989). *Paper Toys That Fly, Soar, Zoom and Whistle*. New York: Sterling Publishing Company.

Euvremer, T. (1987). *Sun's Up*. New York: Crown.

Linden, M. (1987). *Under the Blanket*. New York: Little, Brown.

Lyon, D. (1985). *The Runaway Duck*. New York: Lothrop, Lee and Shepard.

Marzollo, J. (1980). *Uproar on Hollercat Hill*. New York: Dial.

Monsell, M. (1988). *Underwear*. Morton Grove, IL: Whitman.

Pinkwater, D. (1984). *Ducks!* New York: Little, Brown.

Pinkwater, D. (1982). *Roger's Umbrella*. New York: Dutton.

Prelutsky, J. (1982). *The Baby Uggs Are Hatching*. New York: Greenwillow.

Ryder, J. (1989). *Under the Moon*. New York: Random House.

Seuss, Dr. (1982). *Hunches in Bunches*. New York: Random House.

Thorne, J. (1982). *My Uncle*. New York: Macmillan.

Titherington, J. (1986). *Pumpkin, Pumpkin*. New York: Greenwillow.

Zolotow, C. (1975). *The Unfriendly Book*. New York: Harper and Row.

More U Pictures for Miscellaneous Activities

Enlarge the pictures to make flash cards or bulletin board characters or characters that can be used in a story.

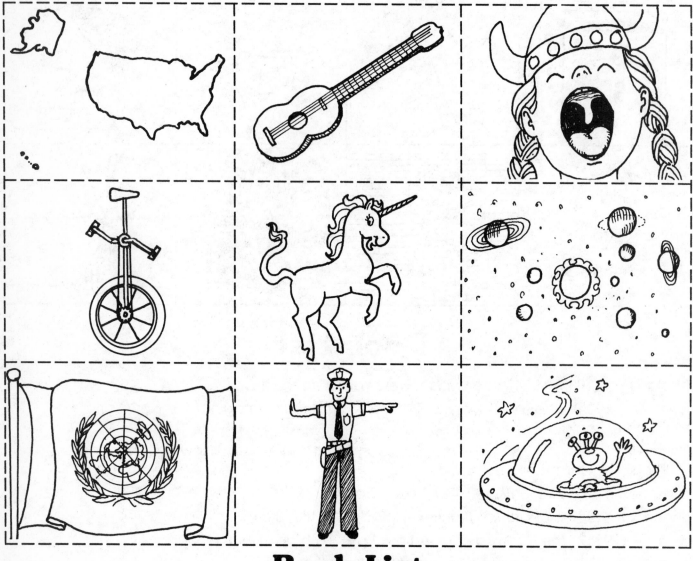

Book List

Allard, H. and Marshall, J. (1978). *The Stupids Have a Ball.* Boston, MA: Houghton Mifflin.

Birrer, C. and Birrer, W. (1987). *The Lady and the Unicorn.* New York: Lothrop, Lee and Shepard Books.

Greene, C. (1983). *A New True Book: United Nations.* Chicago, IL: Children's Press.

Luenn, N. (1987). *Unicorn Crossing.* New York: Atheneum.

Mayer, M. (1982). *The Unicorn and the Lake.* New York: Dial Press.

Parker, N. (1985). *The United Nations from A to Z.* New York: Dodd, Mead and Company.

Pinkwater, D. (1988). *Aunt Lulu.* New York: Macmillan.

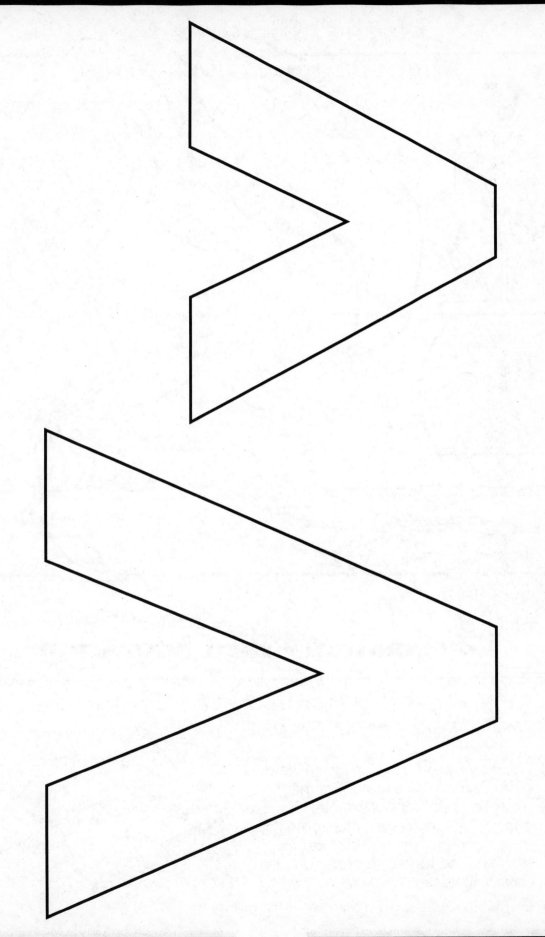

V-Formation - Bird Migration

Objective: To become familiar with the V-formation in which some birds migrate

Materials: masking tape, pictures of migrating birds (if available)

Directions: Discuss why some birds migrate. Show pictures (or draw a sketch) of the migrating flight formation. Next, create a large "V" across your classroom floor with masking tape. Have students stand on the tape and pretend to be migrating birds!

Science

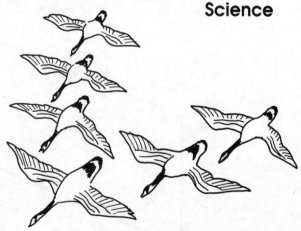

Video

Objective: To help students feel proud of their work by creating a class video.

Materials: quiet room/area, video camera and tape, tripod, students' work, music stand, masking tape, volunteer parents or staff

Directions: Set up the video camera on the tripod in a quiet area or in the cafeteria. Place the music stand facing the camera. Place an "X" with masking tape on the floor where you'd like each student to stand. Each student will take a turn presenting his/her work. One by one, have students leave the room to be taped. (The parent or staff volunteer can operate the camera.) The student says his name and shows something he/she has made. When everyone has had a turn, watch the tape and allow students to take the tape home to share with their families. **(Parental consent to videotape may be necessary in some districts.)**

Vegetable List

Objective: To review colors of vegetables and to use the vegetables for making a salad or soup

Materials: chart paper, markers

Directions: Discuss the importance of vegetables to good health. Hold up a vegetable or a picture of a vegetable and ask the class its color. Make vegetable lists on chart paper according to color. Discuss which vegetables might make a good soup or salad.

Vegetables

Green	Yellow	Other
broccoli	squash	beets
peas	pumpkin	cauliflower
string beans	corn	red pepper
lettuce		carrots
celery		mushrooms
peppers		onions
cucumber		

Extension Activities:

1. Make vegetable soup.
2. Make a vegetable salad. Use lettuce, small pieces of broccoli and cauliflower and sliced zucchini. Toss in a bowl with vinaigrette dressing.

   Vinaigrette dressing recipe
   1 tablespoon wine vinegar
   1 tablespoon Dijon mustard
   3 tablespoons olive oil

Use these proportions and increase as necessary.

Optional: Add parsley, basil, diced shallots.

Valentine Person

Art

Objective: To create unique valentines to hang up for Valentine's Day

Materials: pink, white and red construction paper, 12" x 1" strips of construction paper, 4" round paper doilies, pencil, crayons, scissors, paste, red yarn, paper fasteners

Directions: Each child will need construction paper for two large hearts for the body and head, four small hearts for the hands and feet, four strips for the arms and legs, and one doily. Mix and match the colors for each valentine person. Accordion fold the strips.

The children can either trace and cut, or cut pre-traced hearts. Attach the head, arms and legs to the body using paper fasteners. Paste the four small hearts to the arms and legs. (See illustration.)

Draw a face on the head. Teacher writes "I love you" on the body. Attach a doily behind the top of the head. Punch a hole near the top and attach a piece of red yarn to hang the Valentine People around the classroom.

Enrichment Activity:
Make a "Very Happy Valentine Town." Have children each bring in a container (milk cartons, yogurt containers, juice cartons). Provide red, white, pink and purple construction paper hearts or pretraced hearts and scraps to decorate their containers. Have them use the hearts for windows and doors.

IF8661 The Alphabet

V Vest

Art

Objective: To make a vest to reinforce the "V" sound

Materials: large grocery bags, scissors, markers

Directions:

1. Place a folded grocery bag flat in front of you, with the flap up.
2. Cut off the entire bottom of the bag at the fold end of the flap. (The bag will now be open at both ends.)
3. Next, to make the opening for the vest, cut straight up the center.
4. When you open the vest, the two sides will be folded in. Cut half circles into these folds for arm holes.
5. Form a V-neck at the front opening. Turn the bag inside out. Have students decorate vests with markers. Have a fashion show with the finished product.

1   **2**   **3**   **4 + 5**

Vase With Flowers

Objective: To make a vase of flowers to use to decorate the classroom

Materials: 8" x 11" sheets of white construction paper, pencils, black fine-line markers, crayons, 9" x 12" sheets of black construction paper for mounting and framing

Directions: Have children find the middle of the paper and draw a horizontal oval with a pencil. This is the "water." Next, children draw a rounded line from one end of the water to the other end to form a vase. (See illustration.)

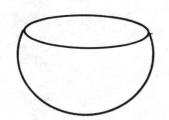

Working with a pencil, add many stems. All stems must dip into the water!

Now add a circle to every stem for the center of the flowers. Add petals, and finally, the leaves. (See illustration.)

When the drawing is completed, have the children trace every pencil line with a black fine-line marker. The final step is the coloring. Then, mount the drawings on black construction paper, display and admire.

          IF8661 The Alphabet

Violets

Poetry

Five purple violets in the flower store
I bought one and then there were four.
Four purple violets growing near a tree
I picked one and then there were three.
Three purple violets in the garden grew
I picked one and then there were two.
Two purple violets growing in the sun
I picked one and then there was one.
One purple violet growing all alone
I picked it and then there was none.
Those five purple violets met face to face.
They were all bunched together in my little vase.

by Ada Frischer

Volcano

Science

Objective: To make a "volcano"

Materials: clay, baking soda, vinegar, red food coloring, small dish or tray, small container

Directions: Draw a simple picture on the chalkboard that depicts the basic parts of a volcano or enlarge the diagram given below. Show it to the children, explaining the different parts and the concept of "eruption."

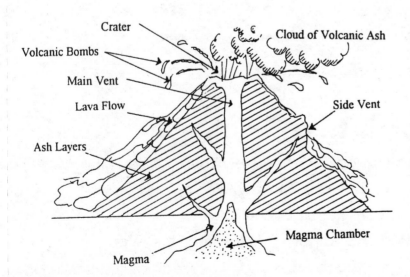

Crater
Volcanic Bombs
Main Vent
Lava Flow
Ash Layers
Cloud of Volcanic Ash
Side Vent
Magma Chamber
Magma

Then, help the children make a volcano shape with clay. Be sure the opening at the top is big enough to accommodate and support the small dish or tray. Put two spoonfuls of baking soda into the small dish through the opening of the volcano. In another small container, mix a little red food coloring with some vinegar. Pour the vinegar solution into the small dish with the baking soda and watch the "lava" overflow!

Be sure to explain that the composition of lava is not vinegar and baking soda!

Vibration

Objective: To see and feel vibration, and to demonstrate how vibrations cause sound

Materials: a plastic ruler, cymbals, a musical triangle, tuning fork, rubber bands of varying widths, shoe boxes

Directions: Seat students around a table or desk. Place a ruler on the edge of the table/desk, with approximately eight inches of the ruler hanging off. Holding the ruler securely on the table/desk, gently lift the other end of the ruler and release it, causing it to vibrate. Ask the students:

1. What do you see?
2. What do you hear?

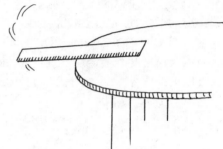

Repeat the process and this time ask a student to stop the ruler with his/her hand. Make observations.

Experiment with the cymbals, tuning fork, etc. Allow students to feel the vibrations.

Ask students to bring in shoe boxes from home. Create a rubber band "guitar" by placing rubber bands of various widths around the open boxes.

Extension Activity:

Invite a violinist to your classroom to both explain how a violin works and to perform.

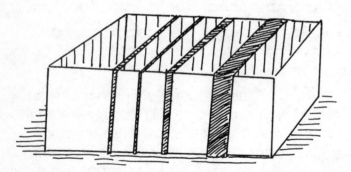

Book List

Faulkner, Mat. (1987). *The Amazing Voyage of Jackie Grace.* New York: Scholastic Inc.

Hutchins, Pat. (1985). *The Very Worst Monster.* New York: Morrow, William, and Co., Inc.

Sendak, Maurice. (1957). *Very Far Away.* New York: Harper and Row.

Storr, Catherine, reteller. (1984). *Rip Van Winkle.* Chatham, NJ: Raintree Steck-Vaughn Publishers.

Westcott, Nadine Bernard. (1981). *The Giant Vegetable Garden.* New York: Little, Brown and Company.

V Pictures for Miscellaneous Activities

What a W!

Make several oaktag patterns of a W from p. 240 to use for a variety of activities

Objective/Activity 1: To identify things that are white

Materials: black construction paper, white crayons or chalk

Directions: Have children trace around the W on black construction paper using white crayon or chalk and cut it out. Then, they draw things that are white on the W's. Brainstorm these items first (snow, milk, stars, polar bear, goose).

Objective/Activity 2: To identify things that begin with the "W" sound

Materials: light-colored construction paper, crayons

Directions: Have children trace around the W on construction paper and cut it out. Have children draw 20 items that begin with the "W" sound.

Objective/Activity 3: To understand the questions: Who? What? Where?

Materials: light blue construction paper, black crayons

Directions: Have children trace and cut out the W. Then, write Who? on the chalkboard for children to copy on their W. Do the same for What? and Where? Talk about W questions and have children illustrate them.

Weaving

Paper Weaving

Materials: one 9" x 12" sheet of construction paper, twelve 1" x 9" strips of construction paper of a contrasting color

Directions: Do the following activity with the children.

Fold the 9" x 12" paper in half the long way. From the folded end, cut straight lines one inch apart to 1/2 inch from the end.

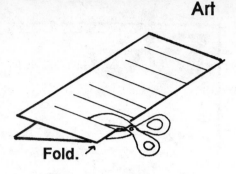

Fold. ↗

Open the paper. Weave the strips into the 9" x 12" paper going over and under the slits in a weaving fashion.

The first strip will go over and under.

The next strip will go under and over creating a waffle weave effect.

Wood Sculptures

Objective: To encourage imagination by creating wood sculptures

Materials: small pieces of wood, glue, paint, paintbrushes, cardboard

Directions: Using the pieces of wood and glue, model for the students how the wood could possibly be arranged on a cardboard base to create a sculpture. Creations could be completely abstract, or they could be models of an object such as a building or toy. Next, allow students to create sculptures. Let them dry overnight. Paint if desired.

Note: The size of the cardboard will depend on the size and number of wood pieces used.

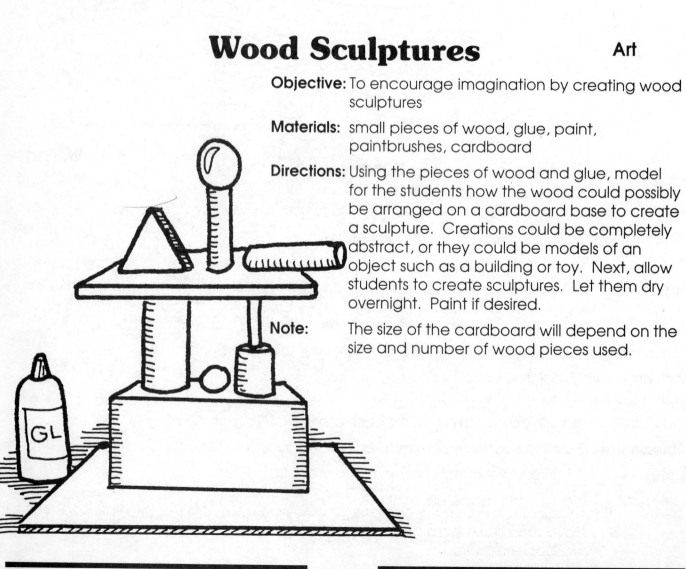

IF8661 The Alphabet

Wind and Water Experiment

Science

Objective: To conduct an experiment to see if wind has any effect on drying a wet area

Materials: chalkboard, wet sponge or cloth, book

Directions: Before you conduct the experiment, discuss with the children the fact that wind is moving air. Have them create a windy atmosphere by moving a hand quickly back and forth in front of their faces. Then, let them try it with a paper or book.

Tell the children that you are going to put two wet spots on the chalkboard. One will dry by itself, the other will have wind blowing on it. Have the children predict which spot will dry faster, or if they will dry at the same time. Tally the predictions.

To conduct the experiment, place two wet spots on the board at an arm's distance from each other. Fan one with a book. Observe the changes and draw conclusions.

Wallpaper

Art

Objective: To create a wallpaper mosaic

Materials: old wallpaper books, glue, large piece of butcher paper, tape

Directions: Gather old wallpaper books from wallpaper stores. Let the students look through the books until each one finds a pattern he/she likes. Let them cut out their pattern. Direct them to cut many shapes out of their pattern.

Then, tape the butcher paper to a wall low enough so the students can reach it. Have them take turns gluing their creations wherever they would like to create a wallpaper mosaic.

IF8661 The Alphabet

Save the Whales!

Art

Objective: To understand the term "endangered"

Materials: 12" x 18" sheets of construction paper, crayons, whale pattern

Directions: Explain to the children that sometimes there becomes too few of an animal left in the world. This leads to the fear that the animal may die out completely. When that fear arises about an animal, it is termed "endangered," which means it is in danger of becoming extinct like dinosaurs.

Explain that whales were hunted so much that they were endangered and people around the world fought to save them.

Provide children with a simple pattern of a whale. Have them trace the whale and then complete the picture.

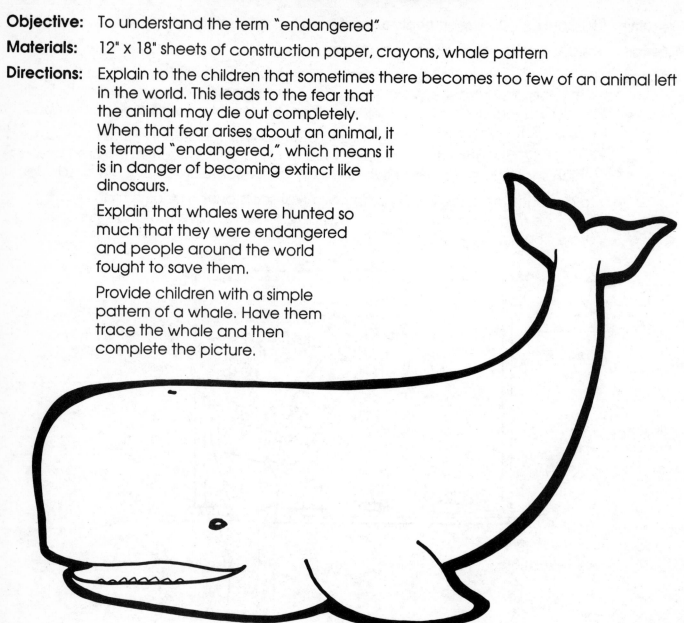

If I Had One Wish

Creative Thinking

Objective: To encourage creative thinking

Materials: construction paper, markers, crayons, books - *The Magic Feather Duster* by Will and Nicholas, *Sylvester and the Magic Pebble* by William Steig, *The Fish Who Could Wish* by John Bush, Korky Paul

Directions: Read one or all of the suggested books.
Ask the children to think about what they would wish for if they had one wish. Each child should illustrate the wish. Take dictation from each child, explaining the reason for the wish.

A Wonderful Witch

Art

Objective: To create a wonderful witch

Materials: 9" x 12" construction paper in assorted colors, a supply of smaller construction paper in various sizes and colors, glue, colored Sunday comics torn in strips, markers, scissors

Directions: Have the children fold a piece of 9" x 12" colored construction paper in half vertically. Cut on a diagonal across the top open end. Save these triangular pieces to use as shoes. Open the folded paper and glue the triangular shapes under the dress as shoes. (See illustration.)

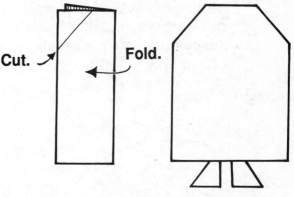

Cut. Fold.

Have children draw and cut a circle for the head and a triangle for the hat. Glue these together with the hat on the top of the head. Draw a face on the head with markers. Tear colored Sunday comics pages into strips for hair. Glue the strips to the back of the head. (See illustration.)

Curl the hair strips around a pencil or leave them straight. Attach the head to the body. Make a broom out of a rectangle and a square and glue it on an angle to the front of the dress. Fringe cut the bottom of the broom. (See illustration.)

My witch's name is Weirdie!

Extension Activity:

When the children have completed their witches, have them sit in a circle with their witches. Let them take turns naming and introducing their witches, telling something about them. For example:

"My witch's name is Susie, and she is a kind witch who loves children."

"My witch's name is Weirdie, and she likes to do weird things."

"My witch's name is Wanda, and she loves to wander all over the sky."

Weight

Science

Objective: To record students' weights

Materials: a pound scale, class list

Directions: Have students weigh themselves. Record the weights. Repeat the activity in several months. Compare individual and class results. Talk about how the children are growing.

Social Studies

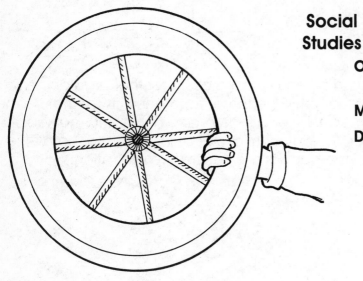

Wheels

Objective: To begin to understand the importance of the wheel

Materials: newsprint, crayons

Directions: Ask the children to name things that have wheels. Lead them into the realization that without wheels, we would have a difficult time moving things.

Have the children draw something that has wheels.

Watermelon

Art

Objective: To make "watermelon slices"

Materials: red construction paper, several patterns for watermelon slices, pre-cut green "rinds," glue, black crayons

Directions: Have children trace and cut watermelon slices from the red paper.

Have pre-cut green "rinds" available for gluing. Children will glue the rinds onto the red slices. (See Illustration.) Instruct them to draw seeds with the black crayon.

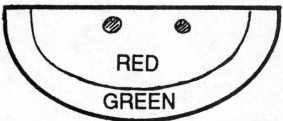

Poetry

Wishes

I wish it were winter
When the cold wind blows,
I like the way it tingles my nose.
I wish it were winter
When the white snow falls
I like to make white snowballs.
by Ada Frischer

Book List

Adams, A. (1985). *A Woggle of Witches.* New York: Macmillan.

Baker, J. (1991). *Window.* New York: Greenwillow Books.

Barton, B. (1972). *Where's Al?* New York: Seabury Press.

Barton, B. (1979). *Wheels.* New York: Harper and Row.

Graham. B. (1988). *Has Anyone Seen William?* London: Walker.

Hirschi, R. (1990). *Winter.* New York: Cobblehill Books.

Hutchins, P. (1967). *Rosie's Walk.* New York: Macmillan.

Hutchins, P. (1974). *The Wind Blew.* New York: Macmillan.

Keats, E.J. (1977). *Whistle for Willie.* New York: Puffin Books.

Kerber, K. (1985). *Walking Is Wild, Weird and Wacky.* Landmark Editions.

Martin, C. (1987). *I Can Be a Weather Forecaster.* Chicago, IL: Childrens Press.

Milne, A.A. (1952). *When We Were Very Young.* New York: Dutton.

Milne, A.A. (1961). *Winnie-the-Pooh.* New York: Dutton.

Pollock, P. (1985). *Water Is Wet.* Putnam Publishing Group.

Reese, B (1983). *Dale the Whale.* Chicago, IL: Childrens Press.

Rossetti, C.G. (1991). "Who Has Seen the Wind?" - *An Illustrated Collection of Poetry for Young People.* New York: Rizzoli.

Schenk de Regniers, B. (1961). *Going For a Walk.* New York: Harper and Row.

Sendak, M. (1984). *Where the Wild Things Are.* New York: Harper and Row.

Smith, K.B. (1987). *George Washington.* New York: J. Messner.

Stille, D. (1990). *Water Pollution.* Chicago, IL: Childrens Press.

Williams, S. (1990). *I Went Walking.* San Diego, CA: Harcourt Brace Jovanovich.

Wise, M.B. (1954). *Willie's Adventures.* New York: W.R. Scott.

Cooking

Waffles - 12 Waffles

3 ½ cups flour
4 teaspoons double-acting powder*
1 teaspoon salt
2 tablespoons sugar
6 egg yolks, 6 egg whites
8 tablespoons butter
3 cups milk

Mix the flour, double-acting powder, salt and sugar. Beat egg yolks well. Add the butter and milk to the yolks. When combined, add the liquid ingredients to the dry ingredients with a few quick strokes. Next, beat the egg whites until stiff. Fold them into the batter. For easy pouring, place batter in a pitcher. Fill waffle iron approximately 2/3 full. Close the iron and cook approximately 4 minutes. *In high altitude, 3 teaspoons.

W Pictures for Miscellaneous Activities

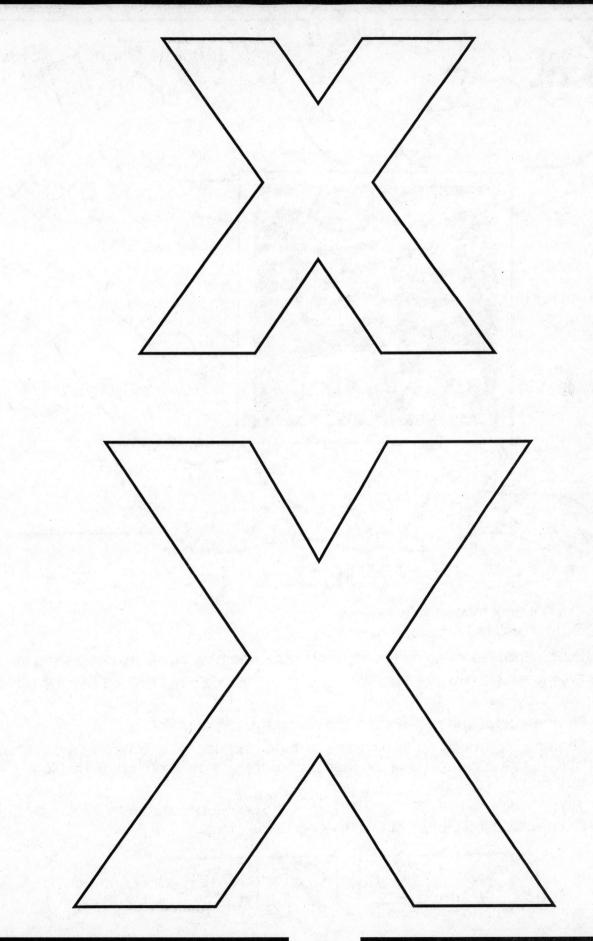

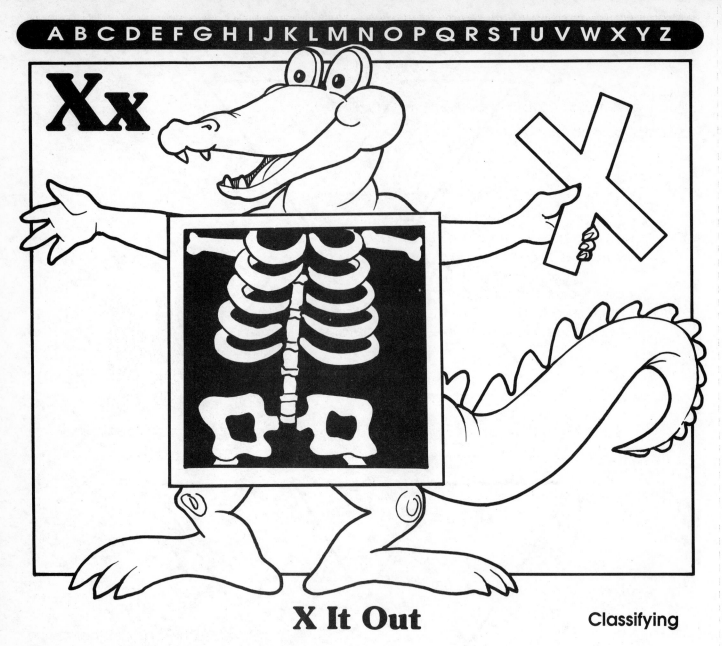

X x

X It Out

Classifying

Materials: Cut out an **X** for each student.
Gather assorted pictures that can be used for classifying.

Directions: Explain that the letter **X** is used to cross out something that does not belong.

Give each student 3 or 4 pictures, one of which would not belong with the others, and a cut out **X**.

Students place the pictures in a line across the top of their desks.

Students are to look carefully at the pictures and decide which picture does not belong to the group. He or she then places the cut out **X** on top of the picture that does not belong.

When everyone has completed the activity, have each student explain why he/she decided the picture did not belong to the group.

IF8661 The Alphabet

X-Ray

Science

Objective: To help children understand the purpose of an x-ray and what it shows

Materials: old x-rays

Directions: Borrow some old x-rays from a hospital or doctor's office. Show them to the children.

Talk about the purposes of x-rays (look for broken bones, diagnose diseases, check suitcases at airports). Explain that an x-ray takes a picture when it hits a solid mass. In our bodies, the x-ray goes through our skin and tissue and then hits the mass of the bones and takes pictures of our skeletons.

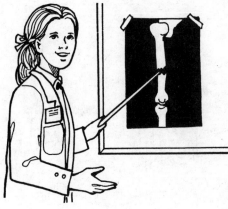

1. Have children feel their head. Explain that the inside bone is called a skull.

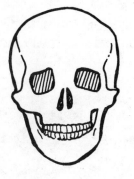

2. Have students feel the back of their neck. Explain that this is their vertebrae and that it extends all the way down to the end of their tailbone where they sit.

3. Next, have them feel their shoulder blades and collarbone.

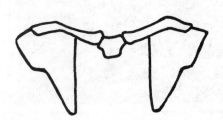

X-Ray continued

Science

4. Next, have students feel their ribs and breastbone.

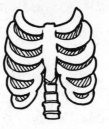

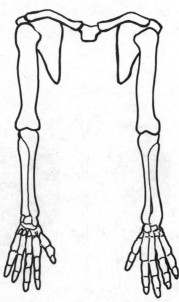

5. Have them feel the bones in their arms and arrive at the conclusion that the upper arm bones are larger than the lower arm bones.

6. Then, have students feel their hip bones.

7. Feel the upper and lower leg bones, the kneecap and the feet and toes.

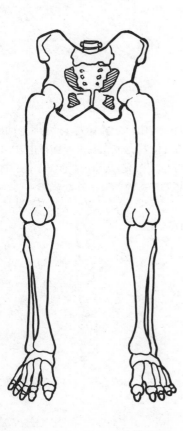

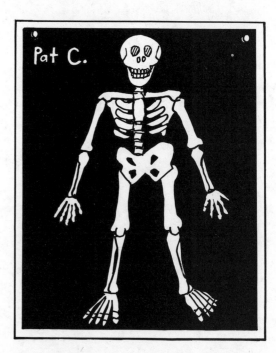

Pat C.

X Marks the Spot

Games

Objective: To participate in an "X Marks the Spot" treasure hunt

Materials: a sketched floor plan of the classroom, several small treasures such as stickers

Directions: Draw a floor plan of the classroom and make a copy for each child. Hide several treasures in various spots around the room. Mark one "X" on each floor plan to indicate where one treasure is hidden. Following "X Marks the Spot" directions, the children will search for the treasure indicated on their floor plan.

You can have a different location and treasure for each child, one treasure for the entire class to find, or one treasure for every 4 or 5 children to locate cooperatively.

X and O

Teach the children how to play tic-tac-toe. Emphasize how to make an O and X as well as how to take turns.

The children take turns putting an X or an O in an empty box. Three X's or three O's in a row wins the game.

Start with an "X" in the middle. Have children practice writing winning combinations.

Who Is Person X?

Language Arts

Materials: Make a large construction paper **X**. Tell the class that the **X** stands for the mystery person. The teacher begins by describing one person in the class, referring to him/her as Person **X**. Have the students listen to the clues. When a student thinks he/she knows the identity of Person **X**, he/she is to raise his/her hand. If the student guesses correctly, hand him/her the X. He/she then describes the next Person **X**.

Is Brand X Better?

Math/Graphing

Materials: two different brands of cereal or trail mix, butcher paper, two small cups for each student, paper for markers

Preparation:

1. Cover one of the boxes or packages with butcher paper so that the label is completely hidden. Write Brand X on the butcher paper.

2. Prepare a graph.

3. Prepare graph markers: Make plain squares for the known brand and **X**'s for Brand X. Make enough markers so that each student will have one of each marker. Mark half of the cups with **X**. Put **X** brand food in each of these cups and the other brand in the rest of the cups.

Directions: Give each student a sample of both brands to taste.

Tell the students to decide which brand they like best.

Call on one student at a time to paste or tape his/her marker (square or **X**) on the correct space of the graph to show his/her choice.

When everyone has had an opportunity to paste his/her choice on the graph, discuss the results. Talk about why one brand was better than the other.

X Pictures for Miscellaneous Activities

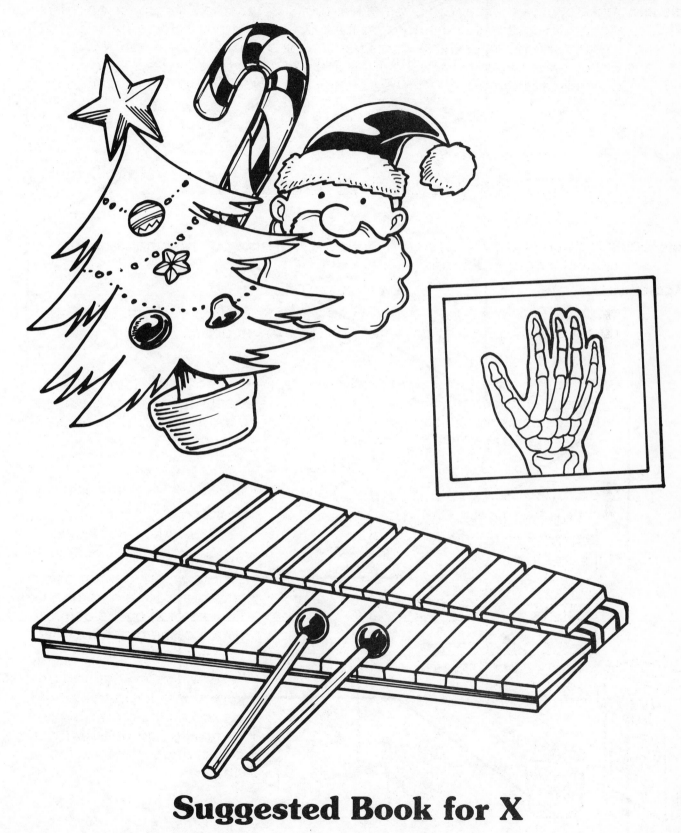

Suggested Book for X

Felder, E. (1972). *X Marks the Spot.* New York: Coward, McCann and Geoghan.

Yummy Yogurt Treats

Cooking

Let the students create their own yogurt snacks.

Materials: vanilla yogurt or frozen yogurt

bowls of washed and sliced fresh fruits (strawberries, raspberries, peaches, blueberries, bananas, pineapple chunks)

bowl of crunchy cereal

spoons

small plastic bowls

serving spoons for yogurt, fruits, and cereal

Directions: Place bowls of fruits and cereal on a large table. Teacher or adult should spoon the yogurt into the bowls. Then, the students may top their yogurt with the fruit of their choice and a spoonful of crunchy cereal.

Yellow

Objective: To make a book of things that are yellow

Materials: large sheets of yellow construction paper, old magazines and catalogs, glue, black markers or crayons, stapler

Directions: Give each child a large piece of yellow construction paper. Fold it three times to make 8 sections. (See example.)

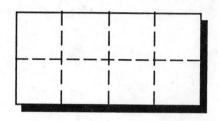

Have them use a black crayon or marker to divide their papers into sections. Hold a class discussion about things that are yellow (lemons, bananas, baby ducks, some raincoats, daffodils and daisies, some Popsicles, school buses, etc.). Write the list on the chalkboard. Then, make old magazines and catalogs available for the children to use to cut out things that are yellow. They are to glue one picture in each section.

Have the children cut their sections apart and staple them together to make their "Yellow" books. Or, leave their papers together and make a class book, "Our Big Book About Yellow."

Yellow Yarn Y's

Objective: To make a yarn Y

Materials: yellow construction paper, oaktag Y patterns, yellow yarn, glue, crayons

Directions:
• Enlarge the Y pattern shown and make several Y patterns out of oaktag.

• Have the children trace around a Y pattern on a large piece of construction paper.

• Then, have them trace around their Y with white glue. Before the glue dries, they should take their piece of yellow yarn and put it on the glue to make a yarn Y.

If You Want to Be

Music

A fun song for the class to write as a group is a take-off on "Clap Your Hands." Some examples are shown:

If you want to be a monkey,
   grow a tail.
If you want to be a monkey,
   grow a tail.
If you want to be a monkey
   and swing from the trees,
If you want to be a monkey,
   grow a tail.

If you want to be a rhino,
   grow a horn.
If you want to be a lion,
   learn to roar.
If you want to be a chimp,
   make a face.
If you want to be a giraffe,
   stretch your neck.

Yeast Rises

Cooking

Explain that yeast is an important ingredient used in baking bread. Use your favorite bread recipe and have the class make bread or use the dough to make rolls. This will allow each student to knead his/her own dough and watch it rise.

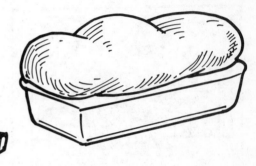

Yodeling

Music

Play records or tapes to listen to yodeling. Then have the students try to yodel.

What Was Yesterday?

Calendar

Practice the days of the week. Use a calendar to identify the days. Say the days in sequence. Then play a game. The teacher starts the game using the phrase "If today is ____ , then yesterday was ____ ." The student who says the correct day may then have a turn to say the phrase.

S	M	T	W	Th	F	S
		1	2	3	4	5
6	7	8	9	10	11	12
13	14	15	16	17	18	19

A Whole Year

Use a 12-month calendar to explain that a year contains twelve different months. Teach the names of the months in sequence to the students. Talk about special days that happen during each month of the year. This could also be an opportunity to talk about the seasons of the year. Have the students draw and color a picture of their favorite time of the year. Allow time for each student to share his/her picture with the class.

Social Studies

Your Own Yard

Have the students describe their yards at home and tell what they like to do in their yards. Then, give each student a sheet of white drawing paper on which to draw and color a picture of his/her yard. On a separate sheet of writing paper have the student dictate one or two sentences, as an adult writes, telling why his/her yard is special and how he/she has fun in the yard. Display the pictures and writing sheets on a bulletin board or wall.

By the Yard

Math

Introduce the yardstick ruler. Compare it to a 12-inch ruler. Explain and demonstrate that three feet make a yard. Point out several objects and ask the students which measuring tool would be better to use. (Examples: a pencil, door, chalkboard, book, shoe, bookcase) Talk about when it is more practical to use a yardstick rather than a twelve-inch ruler. Demonstrate how to use a yardstick to measure. Divide your class into cooperative groups and have them do some measuring.

Yikes! It's a Yellow Jacket!

Science

Discuss yellow jackets. They are not bees. They are related to hornets. Have the students relate any experiences they have had with yellow jackets. If possible, show the children a dead, preserved yellow jacket nest. Explain that it is made of paper. Yellow jackets chew wood and fibers from plants to make the paper for the nest. Yellow jackets are helpful in that they eat other insects such as flies and caterpillars. Some kinds like to eat sweet things like fruit. You may also want to discuss first aid for a sting. Mix baking soda and water to make a paste to put on the sting. Display a picture of a yellow jacket. Make a copy of the yellow jacket on white paper for each student. Have the students use yellow and black crayons to color the picture. The wings are transparent, so they do not need to be colored.

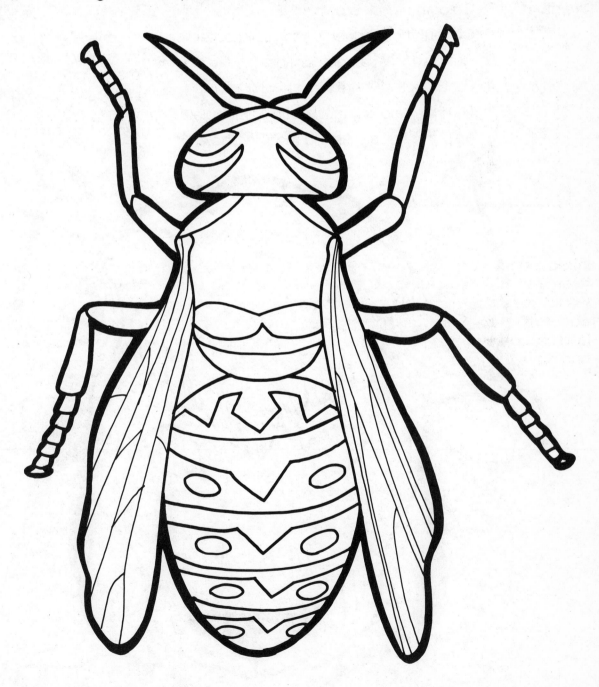

What's a Yak?

Science

Display a picture of a yak. Locate on a large wall map where yaks can be found (plateaus of Tibet). Talk about yaks. Have the students name other animals that resemble a yak. Make a yak mask.

Materials: 1 copy of the yak mask on white construction paper for each student
crayons
scissors
hole punch
2 pieces of string about 10 inches long for each student

Directions: 1. Color the mask brown.

2. Cut out the mask along the solid outer line.

3. Cut out the eye hole sections.

4. Punch holes where indicated (•).

5. Tie a piece of string through each hole.

6. Help the student tie the mask in back.

Book List for Y

Aruego, J., and Dewey, A. (1979). *We Hide, You Seek.* New York: Greenwillow Books.

Bang, M. (1991). *Yellow Ball.* New York: Morrow Junior Books.

Carlstrom, N. (1986). *Jesse Bear, What Will You Wear?* New York: Macmillan Publishing Company.

Joslin, S. (1958). *What Do You Say, Dear?* New York: Harper Trophy .

Kraus, R. (1970). *Whose Mouse Are You?* New York: Macmillan Publishing Company.

Lionni, L. (1959). *Little Blue and Little Yellow.* New York: Ivan Oblensky Inc.

Lionni, L. (1987). *Nicolas, Where Have You Been?* New York: Alfred A. Knopf.

Martin, Jr., Bill. (1991). *Polar Bear, Polar Bear, What do You Hear?* New York: Henry Holt and Company.

Price, M. (1986). *Do You See What I See?* New York: Harper & Row, Publishers.

Raschka, C. (1993). *Yo! Yes!* New York: Orchard Books.

Testa, F. (1982). *If You Take a Pencil.* New York: Dial Press.

Waber, B. (1980). *You're a Little Kid With a Big Heart.* Boston: Houghton Mifflin Company.

Y Pictures for Miscellaneous Activities

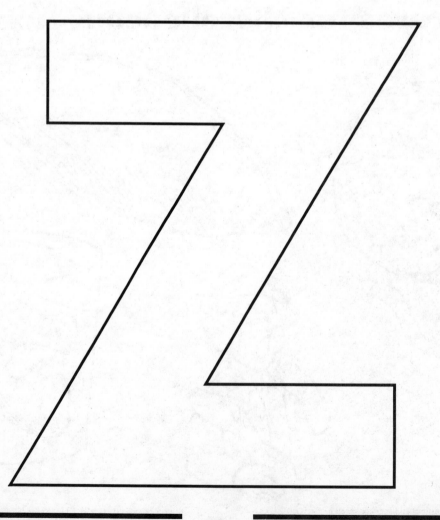

E-Z Zebra

Objective: To make zebras for classroom display

Materials: 12" x 18" white construction paper, newspaper cut in strips, markers, glue, black yarn

Directions: Have the children trace a large zebra without stripes on the 12" x 18" white construction paper using a pattern you supply. Show them how to measure and glue newspaper strips on their zebra for stripes, tearing them to the right length. Add some black yarn for a mane and finish the picture with markers.

The Zoo

Poetry

Zoo, zoo, zoo!
I went to the zoo.
I saw lions and tigers
And zebras too.

I liked the seals.
I liked the bears.
I liked the zebras.
That stood in pairs.

Zoo, zoo, zoo!
I went to the zoo.
I saw monkeys and elephants
And zebras too.

by Ada Frischer

Act it out!

Zippy Zoos

Drama

Objective: To give students the opportunity to dramatize being different zoo animals

Materials: a copy of the phrases below, a paper bag

Directions: Children love to act. They are wonderfully uninhibited at this age. For a fun activity that can be repeated again and again, copy and cut out the phrases below. Put them in a paper bag for children to choose and act out. If it would be easier for the children, you could let them work together in pairs.

zippy zebras	crying camels	sneaky snakes	angry anteaters	slippery seals
grumpy giraffes	happy hippos	preening peacocks	tiptoeing turtles	pesky parrots
bouncing bears	kicking kangaroos	terrible tigers	magical monkeys	leaping leopards
elegant elephants	lonely lions	dancing deer	crabby crocodiles	running rhinos

IF8661 The Alphabet

Math

Zilch! Zero!

Discuss the value of the number zero. Divide your class into cooperative learning groups. Cut large zeros out of butcher paper, one for each group. The students are to draw and color pictures on the large zero to illustrate items they do not want. (Examples: I want zero rattlesnakes, inoculations, broken bikes, etc.) Have each group share their Zilch! Zero! with the class.

Reading

Zip Up Those Z's

Make a copy of the zipper pattern on white or assorted colors of construction paper for each student. Provide magazines, newspapers, newspaper inserts, and catalogs for the students to find and cut out as many **Z** letters as they can. Students cut out the zipper. Write their names on the back. Glue the **Z** letters that they find to the zipper.

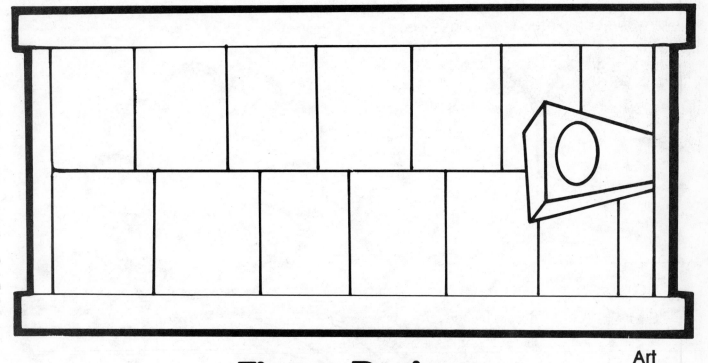

Art

Zigzag Designs

Begin the lesson by having the students actually experience a zigzag line. Set up cones to form a zigzag path.

Have the students stand in a line, placing their hands on the shoulders of the person in front of them. The first person in the line leads the way from cone to cone in a zigzag pattern. Then, demonstrate on the chalkboard how to draw zigzag lines. Give each student a sheet of white drawing paper on which to create a zigzag design, or you may wish to copy a zigzag pattern on the paper and have the students color it.

Science

Zany Zinnias

Discuss what plants need to grow. Talk about the different kinds of plants. Have the students plant zinnia seeds and watch them grow. They can be planted in a class flower bed or individual containers such as large plastic cups.

Students can make paper zinnias while they wait for their flowers to bloom.

Materials:

For each student: 1 copy of the zinnia pattern on white, pink, red, orange, or yellow construction paper, 1 copy of the leaf patterns on green construction paper, scissors, glue, 1 pipe cleaner

Directions:

1. Cut out the flower and leaf patterns.
2. Glue the flower petal sections together, layering from the largest to the smallest.
3. Glue one end of the pipe cleaner to the back of the flower.
4. Poke a hole in the end of the leaf and slide it up the pipe cleaner stem.
5. Display the completed flowers in a vase.

Book List

Bridges, W. (1968). *The Bronx Zoo Book of Wild Animals.* New York: New York Zoological Society.

Gibbons, G. (1987). *Zoo.* New York: T.Y. Crowell.

Hoban, T. (1987). *A Children's Zoo.* New York: Mulberry Books.

Lopshire, R. (1960). *Put Me in the Zoo.* New York: Random House.

Seuss, Dr. (1950). *If I Ran the Zoo.* New York: Random House.

Van Allsburg, C. (1987). *The Z Was Zapped.* Boston, Massachusetts: Houghton Mifflin.

Zoo Animal Patterns

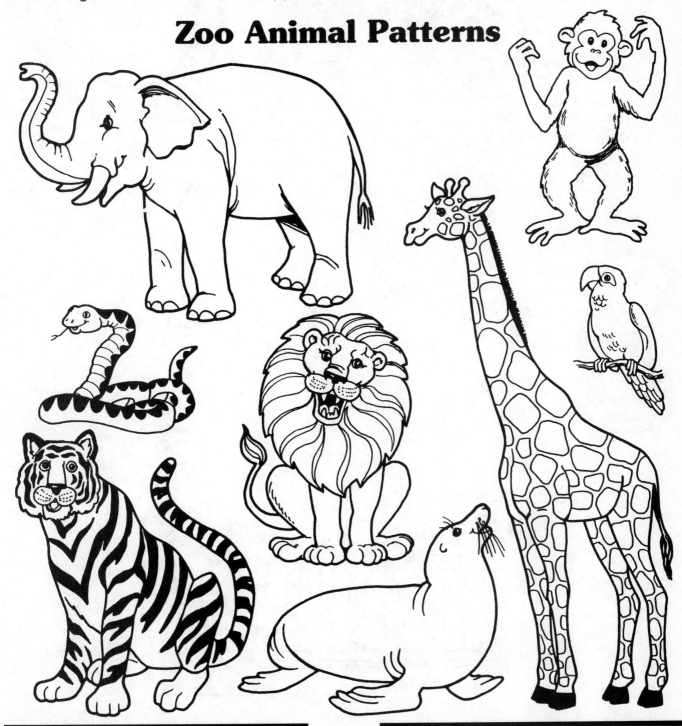

Z Pictures for Miscellaneous Activities

Letter/Picture Match Bingo

Objective: To reinforce the letter sounds

Materials: capital letter boards - one for each child (See page 273.)

lower-case letter boards - one for each child (See page 274.)

picture boards - one for each child (See page 272.)

picture cutouts   (See page 272.)

12 buttons for each child

Method: Make copies of the capital letter boards, lower-case letter boards, and picture boards. Have one for each child. Mount them on oaktag or cardboard and laminate if possible.

Make an extra copy of each board and cut to separate the letters and pictures. These will be used by the "caller" in the Bingo game.

Either you or a child is the caller. Each child gets a gameboard. You can work with all capital letters, all lower-case letters, all pictures, or you can mix and match depending on the abilities of your class.

It would be a good idea for the caller to use the letter pictures first. The children will then have a letter board. The caller says the name of the picture. If the child has the letter that the picture begins with, he/she covers that letter with a button.

When the caller uses the letters, the children will have the picture boards. When the letter is called, the child will use a button to cover the picture word that begins with that letter.

Continue the game until everyone has covered their board. You can do this by designating a first winner, a second winner, etc.

Picture Boards

IF8661 The Alphabet

Capital Letter Boards

B	V	Q	J
N	G	D	X
☺	S	L	Z

M	C	T	P
K	R	W	H
Y	☺	F	☺

Lower-Case Letter Boards

h	s	n	q
l	b	f	j
t	🙂	z	v

c	g	w	d
m	p	k	r
x	🙂	🙂	y

Alphabet Book

Activity: Each child will make his/her own alphabet book

Materials Needed per Child:
    13 sheets of 9" x 6" white construction paper
    1 sheet 9" x 6" colored construction paper
    1 sheet 9" x 6" oaktag
    scissors
    white glue
    1 shoe box
    3 worksheets - capital letters on page 277,
        lower-case letters on page 278,
        pictures on page 276

Method: Staple or bind together the 13 pages of white construction paper, the colored paper for the cover and the oaktag for the back page. Have the children design their book covers and put their names on them. Number all the pages first, using the front and back of each page. Explain to the children that they are going to make their own alphabet book. They will do one page each day in consecutive order.

Put a name on each shoe box and tell the children that they will each keep their own book and pages in their own boxes. Keep the boxes in an area that is easily accessible to the children such as a countertop, cubby or desk.

Now, you are ready to start the alphabet. Using the worksheets on pages 276, 277, and 278, each child will cut out and paste the capital A and the lower-case a on page 1. Look at the picture worksheet (page 276). Help the children find the apple, cut it out and paste it on the A page. The children can then further decorate the page. On the next day, work the B page in the same way.

The letters on the capital letter worksheet are in consecutive order. On the lower-case worksheet they are placed at random, but in such a way that the letter they are up to will always be at the edge and so can be easily cut out. It will not be necessary to cut all the letters at one time. The picture worksheet is arranged in the same manner.

Do the first two pages as a class activity to illustrate how the book will be made. Then tell the children that now they can do the books on their own. Indicate the time frame in which they may select this activity. (Center time or free activity time is a good time for this selection.) However, they may do only one page a day. When they finish each page, be sure that they show it to you to make sure that they are doing it correctly, using consecutive order and not skipping any pages.

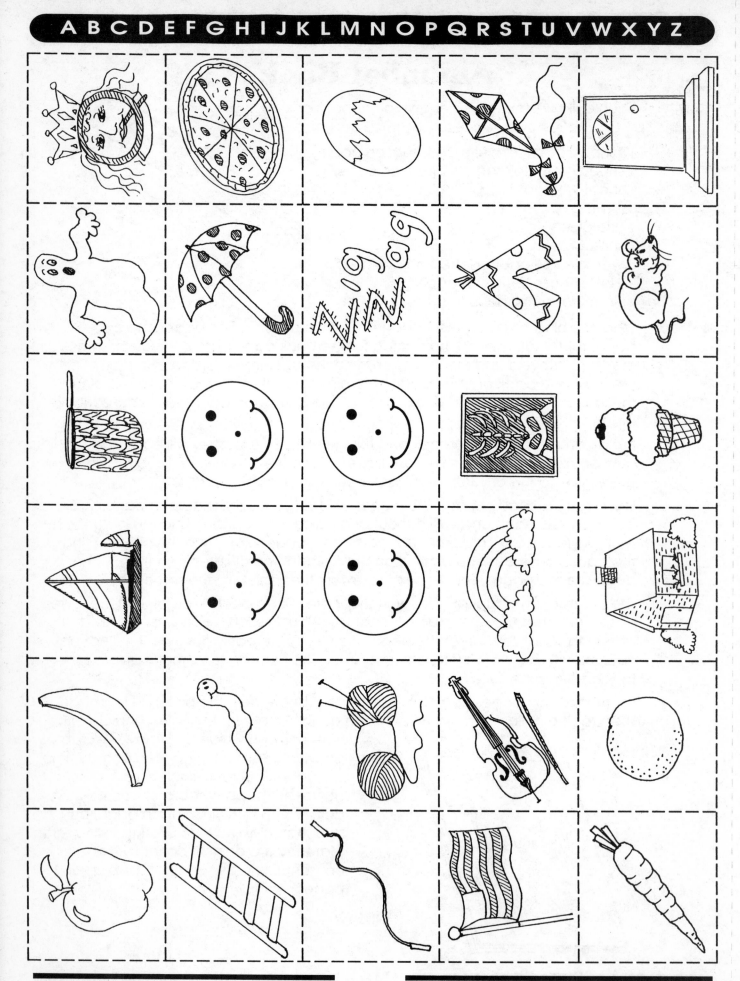

F	L	R	X	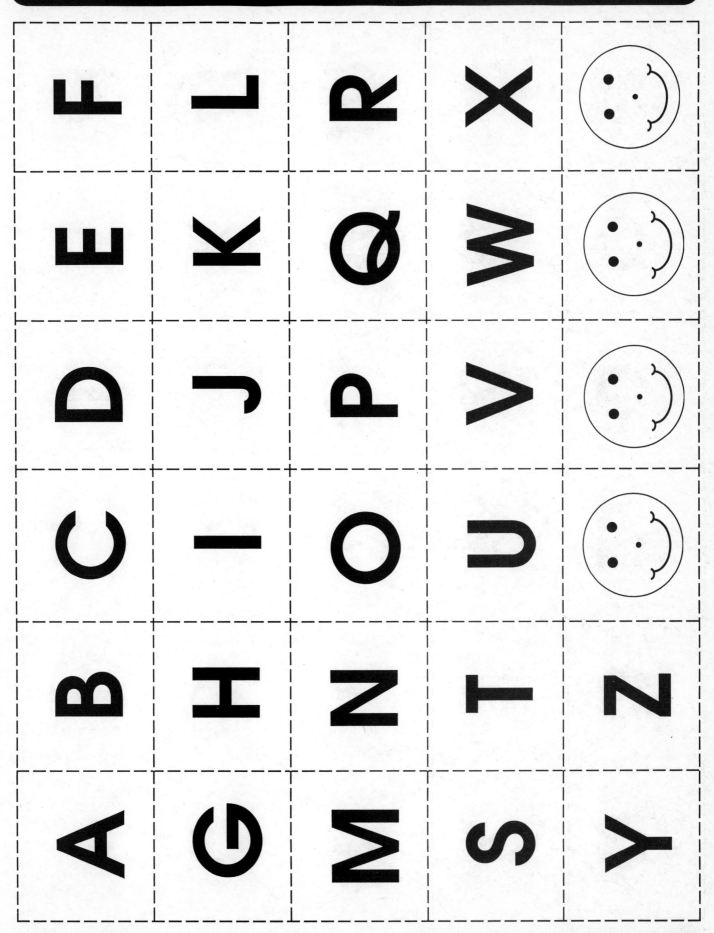
E	K	Q	W	
D	J	P	V	
C	I	O	U	
B	H	N	T	
A	G	M	S	Y	Z

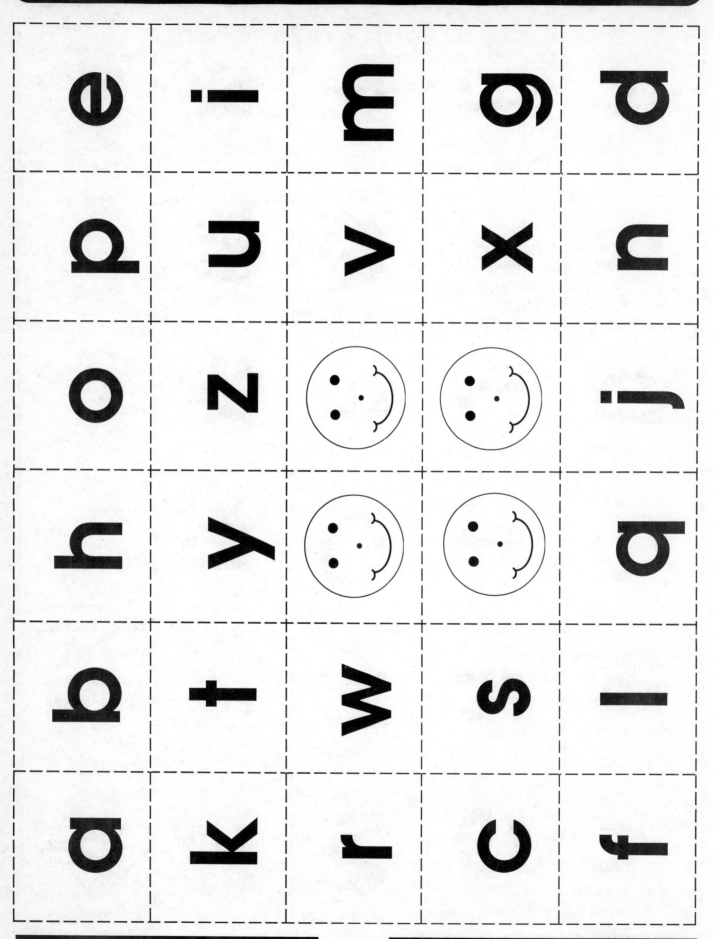

Picture Find Worksheets

Activity: To locate pictures with initial consonant sounds b-m (Worksheet 1, page 280) and n-z (Worksheet 2, page 281).

Materials: a copy of the worksheet for each student, crayons, the directions (below) to accompany the corresponding worksheet

Method: Distribute the worksheet to students and name and discuss the objects pictured. Next, explain to the students that you will ask them to look for pictures that begin with certain letter sounds. Tell them to look at their worksheets while you speak. Read the following:

Put a line under the object . . .

Worksheet 1 - Directions

1. Color the object that begins with the sound for b, blue. (boat)
2. Circle the object that begins with the sound for c. (cat)
3. Put a line under the object that begins with the sound for d. (dock)
4. Color the object that begins with the sound for f, green. (fish)
5. Circle the object that begins with the sound for g. (girl)
6. Color the object that begins with the sound for h, yellow. (hat)
7. Put a line under the object that begins with the sound for j. (jet)
8. Color the object that begins with the sound for k, red. (kite)
9. Color the object that begins with the sound for l, orange. (life preserver)
10. Color the object that begins with the sound for m, brown. (mountain)

Worksheet 2 - Directions

1. Color the object that begins with the sound for n, green. (nest)
2. Make an X on the object that begins with the sound for p. (puppy)
3. Circle the object that begins with the sound for r. (rabbit)
4. Color the object that begins with the sound for s, yellow. (sun)
5. Color the object that begins with the sound for t, red. (tree)
6. Color the object that begins with the sound for w, blue. (water)
7. Put a line under the object that begins with the sound for y. (yak)
8. Circle the objects that begin with the sound for z. (zebra, zoo sign)

Note: Be sure all the objects have been named before beginning. This activity could be used for evaluation.

A B C D E F G H I J K L M N O P Q R S T U V W X Y Z

Interactive Bulletin Boards

The following are bulletin boards for each of the letters of the alphabet. They are designed to be interactive to help reinforce the letter and the letter sound. The main theme and use of the bulletin board is indicated on each page. The choice of materials such as paper, fabric, crayons, paint, yarn, etc., is left to your discretion.

Interactive Bulletin Board

Activity: To monitor progress in the study of letters

Materials: construction paper, pictures, crayons/markers, paste

Method: At the onset of the study of the alphabet, tell the children that you are going to start to construct a class flower. Each petal will represent a letter, and as you learn about each letter, you will add that petal to the flower. However, when you start, it will be a "naked" flower - just a center, stem and leaves, but no petals.

As you study each letter, add a petal to the flower. Put the letter on the petal with a marker. Have the children draw objects or paste pictures of objects beginning with that letter sound on the petal. Your flower will soon begin to blossom!

Add An Apple!

Have students color, cut out and write their name on an apple from page 284. Each day, let one child attach his/her apple to the bulletin board.

**Apple
Pattern**

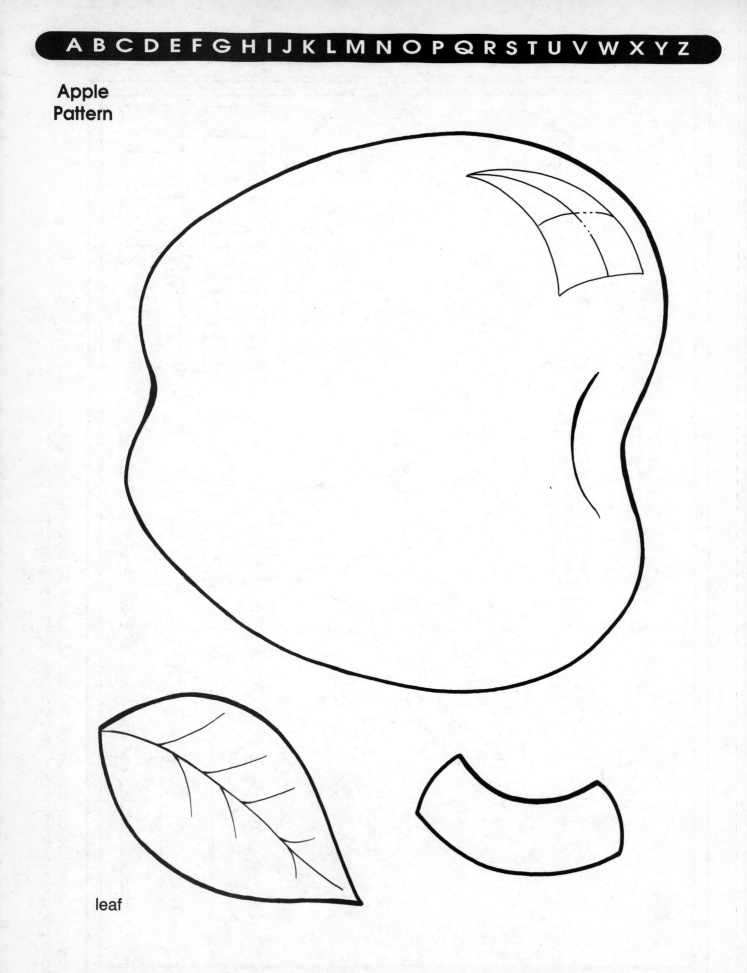

leaf

SAY ... ACORNS!

Make copies of the acorn pattern on page 286 on light brown construction paper for students. Have students make colorful faces on their acorns and write their names on the top.

**Acorn
Pattern**

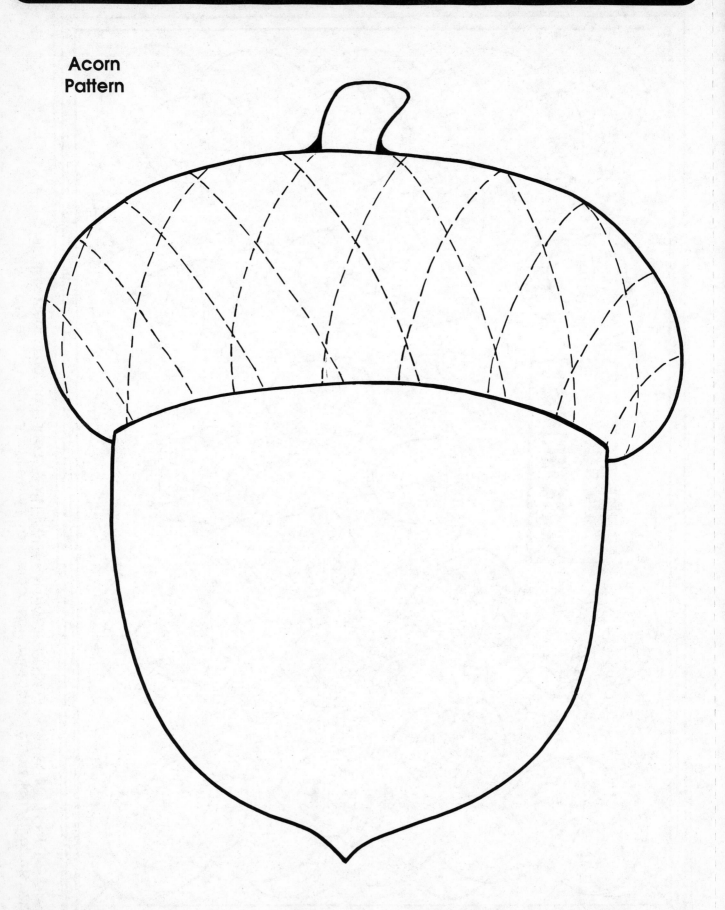

Balloons

Up, Up and AWAY!

Write each child's name on a balloon. When the child is able to identify the name of the beginning letter or sound, give the balloon to the child to take home.

IF8661 The Alphabet

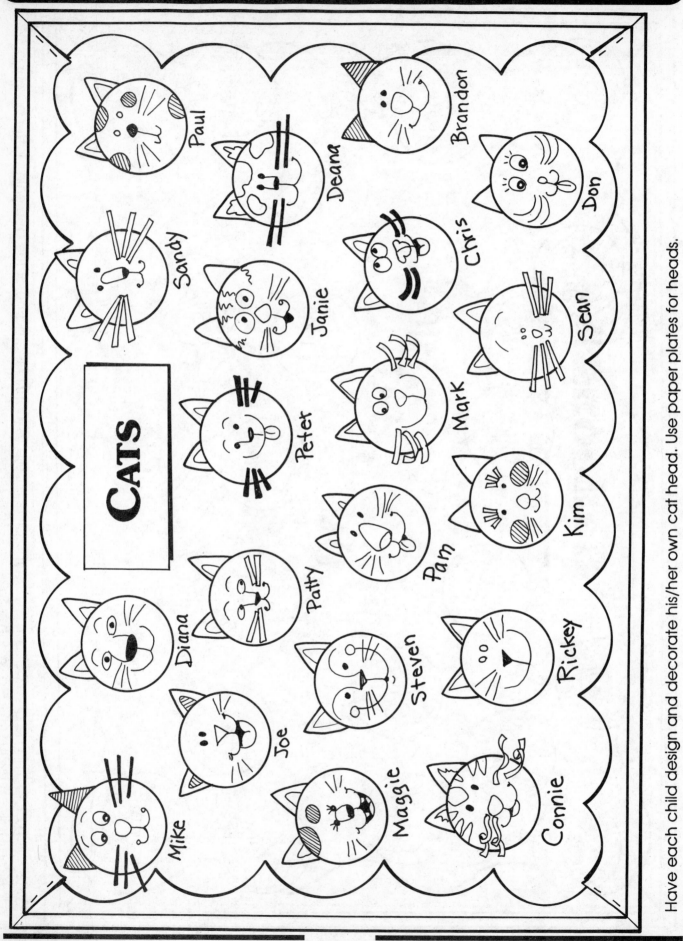

CATS

Paul
Deana
Brandon
Don
Sandy
Janie
Chris
Sean
Peter
Mark
Pam
Kim
Diana
Patty
Steven
Rickey
Mike
Joe
Maggie
Connie

Have each child design and decorate his/her own cat head. Use paper plates for heads.

Design a Dinosaur!

Brontosaurus

Becky

Joe

David

Tyrannosaurus Rex

Triceratops

Have children design and draw their own version of a dinosaur with either the child's or dinosaur's name.

"EGG"CITING EGGS!

Give students copies of the egg pattern on page 291 to design and make "egg"citing eggs. Cut out, color and assemble the paintbrush from page 291 to display also.

**Egg
Pattern**

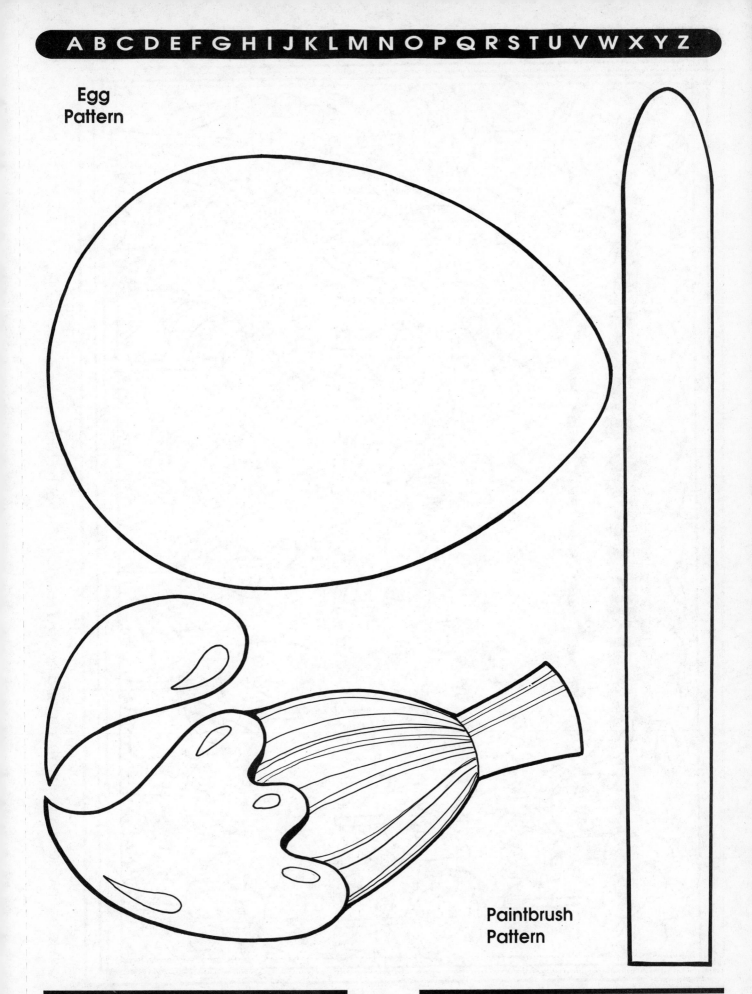

**Paintbrush
Pattern**

291

IF8661 The Alphabet

Flower Fun

Bob

Nick

Nat

Dee

Trish

Chuck

Zoe

Rhonda

Matt

Joy

Martin

Ted

Amanda

Adam

Carla

Larry

Dedre

Sam

Ken

Tony

Have each child design, draw, cut and paste a flower. Write each child's name on his/her flower.

Gorgeous Green Ghosts

Peggy
Franny
Mae
Tanya
Jerry
Marty
Toby
Jeff
Lana
Mary Jo
Sara
Tom
Wade
Phil
Ilsa
Barb
Annie

Using green construction paper, have each child draw, design and cut out his/her own gorgeous green ghost.

IF8661 The Alphabet

Happy

Faces

Everywhere!

Even the youngest child can draw a happy face! Display the happy faces with the child's name underneath. From time to time, reinforce the word "happy" and ask what makes the child happy.

IF8661 The Alphabet

Itsy-Bitsy Insects

Let students use their imaginations to create all kinds of insects—real or pretend.
Let students tell about their insect.

A B C D E F G H I J K L M N O P Q R S T U V W X Y Z

IF8661 The Alphabet

I Like Ice Cream!

Using the ice cream patterns on page 297, have students color scoops of ice cream to show their favorite flavor.

IF8661 The Alphabet

Ice Cream Patterns

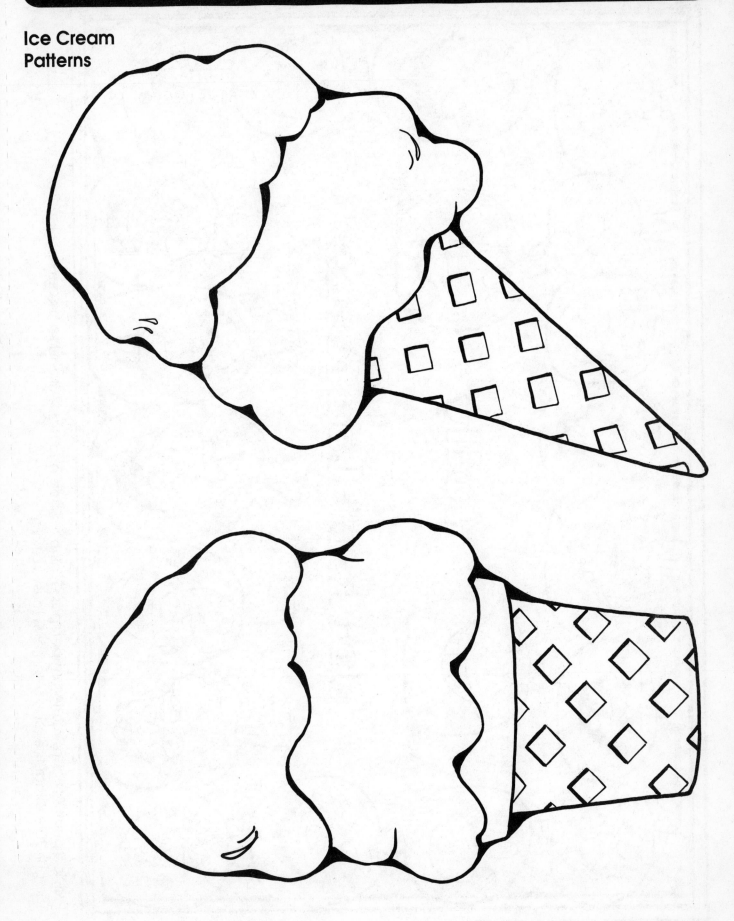

IF8661 The Alphabet

Jolly

Jack-o'-Lanterns

Provide plenty of construction paper, paste, glue, scissors and markers and let the fun begin!
The only rule is that the jack-o'-lanterns must be jolly!

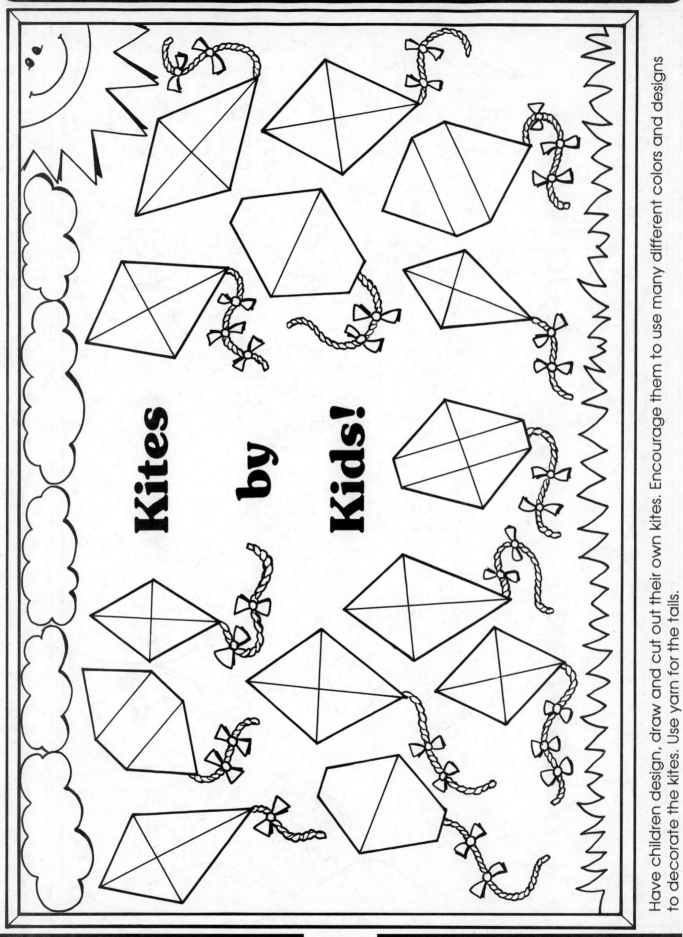

Kites by Kids!

Have children design, draw and cut out their own kites. Encourage them to use many different colors and designs to decorate the kites. Use yarn for the tails.

Leafman

Laughing

Have children collect leaves from home and the playground to bring to school. Combine their leaves to make a large leafman - or encourage the children to make their own.

IF8661 The Alphabet

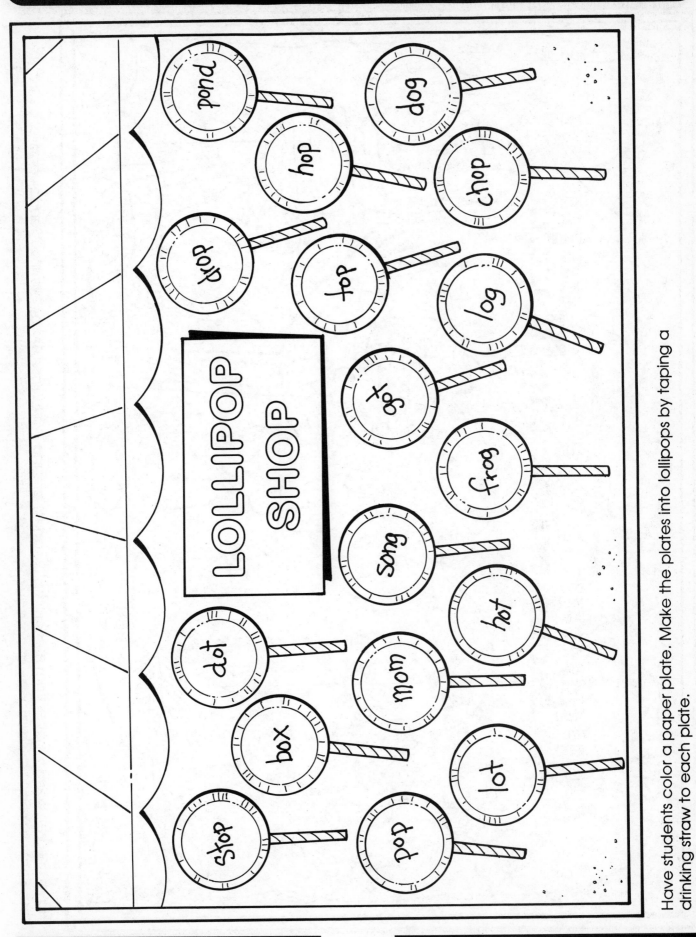

pond

gop

hop

chop

drop

top

log

got

frog

bug

LOLLIPOP SHOP

dot

mom

hot

box

tot

stop

pop

Have students color a paper plate. Make the plates into lollipops by taping a drinking straw to each plate.

Monsters on the March!

Have children design their very own monsters! Read *Where the Wild Things Are* by Maurice Sendak and let their imaginations soar. Provide plenty of collage materials.

The Number Net Game

Use Velcro or stick pins to attach number nets to a bulletin board. Play games involving numeral recognition, numerical order, numerals before and after, and addition or subtraction.

Oh, Ocean Ovals!

Give each student a piece of paper having a large oval drawn on it. Instruct the students to make the ovals into things found in the ocean.

IF8661 The Alphabet

The Pumpkin Patch Match

Attach pumpkins to bulletin board with Velcro or stick pins. Children select pairs of pumpkins to make a match. This game may also be played with letters, pictures and sounds.

A Quilt of Queens

Have each child draw a picture of a queen using crayons and markers. Assemble and display the drawings together in the form of a quilt.

A B C D E F G H I J K L M N O P Q R S T U V W X Y Z

Rockets Away!

Have children draw, design and personalize rockets with their names. The sky's the limit!

Sailboats on the Sea

Harry
Grace
Ann
John
Shelly
Ben
Kevin
Nancy
Tom
Joel
Rosie
Stephen
Sid

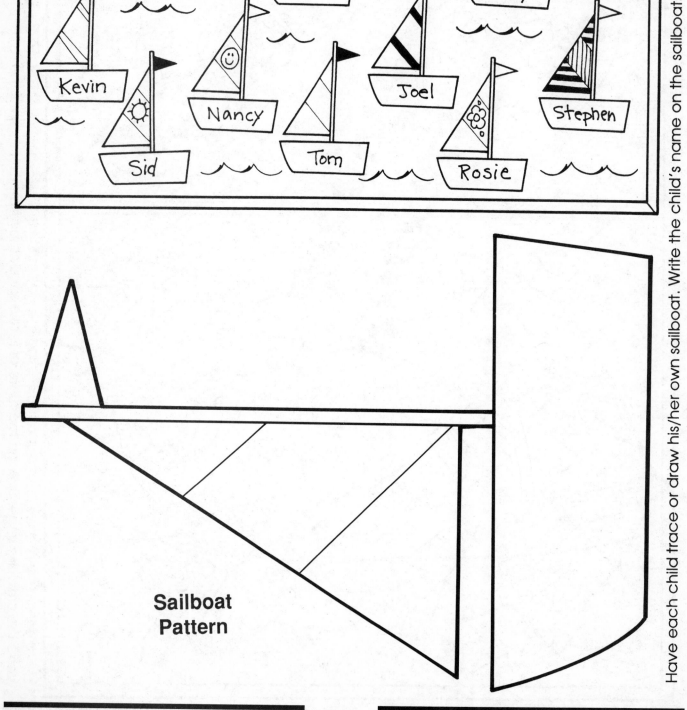

Sailboat Pattern

Have each child trace or draw his/her own sailboat. Write the child's name on the sailboat.

Turtle Talk

Pattern

UNUSUAL UMBRELLAS

Use the patterns on page 311 to make umbrellas. Have each child write his/her name on an umbrella, color, and put on the board.

**Umbrella
Pattern**

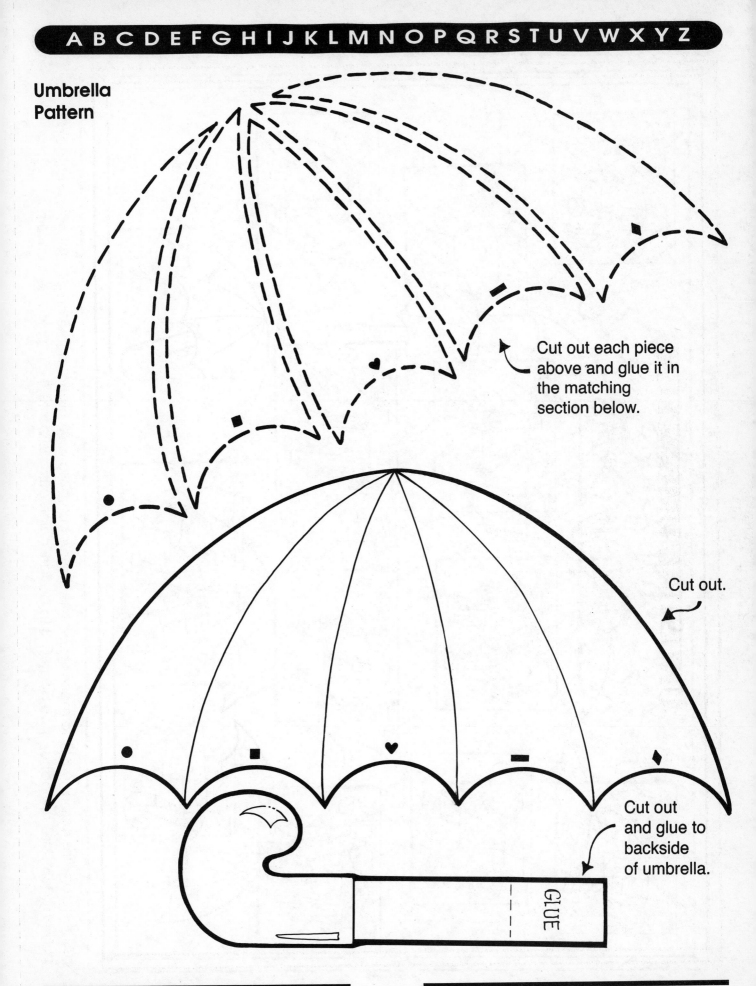

Cut out each piece
above and glue it in
the matching
section below.

Cut out.

Cut out
and glue to
backside
of umbrella.

GLUE

IF8661 The Alphabet

Unicorns in Uniforms

Have students use the patterns on page 313 to design, color, cut and paste their "unicorns in uniforms."

IF8661 The Alphabet

**Unicorn
Pattern**

Design
and color
a uniform.

Cut it out
and glue it
onto the
unicorn
below.

Name _____

Very Special Valentines

Show children how to make a valentine out of a "V." Give each child a paper with a "V" to turn into a special valentine. Have each child write his/her own name.

Winter Wonderland

Have each child draw and color a picture about winter. Provide cotton and pom-pons for snow. Make paper snowflakes and sprinkle them around the drawings.

Bulletin Board for Letter X

Preparation:

1. Cover a bulletin board with white construction paper.
2. Cut out letters for the title, **Project X**, and staple them at the top of the bulletin board.
3. Staple ½ inch graph paper (white if possible) to the bulletin board, horizontally, 4 sheets across and 4 sheets down.

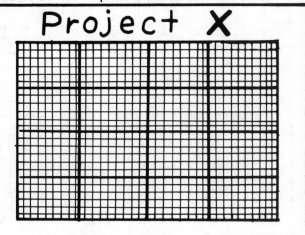

Directions:

1. Use a red marker to make a dot (•) in each of the squares that will form the word Hugs and Kisses.

2. Use a black marker to make a dot (•) in each square that will form the **X**'s and **O**'s.

3. Use a red marker to make a dot (•) in each square that will form the heart.

4. Use a brown marker to make a dot (•) in each square that will form the bear.

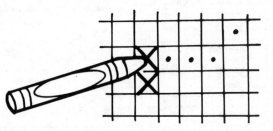

Use a black marker to draw and color in the bear's eyes, nose and mouth.

Give each student a black, red, or brown crayon or marker.

Call on one student at a time to find dots that are the same color as the crayon/marker he/she is holding. Then, the student makes an X in 5 squares that have his/her color of dot.

Continue in this way until all of the squares with dots have an **X**.

When completed, have everyone stand back from the bulletin board. Read the words and explain that **O**'s are used to represent hugs and **X**'s are used to represent kisses. Often these are used at the end of notes or letters.

Have students cut **X**'s from scrap construction paper. Staple these in the border section of the bulletin board.

Project X

Yellow can be . . .

the sun

a flag

corn

a flower

a bird

a bus

a coat

a ball

a butterfly

an egg yolk

Encourage children to think of the color yellow and all the things that can be yellow. Provide black markers for drawing and yellow crayons and markers for coloring.

IF8661 The Alphabet

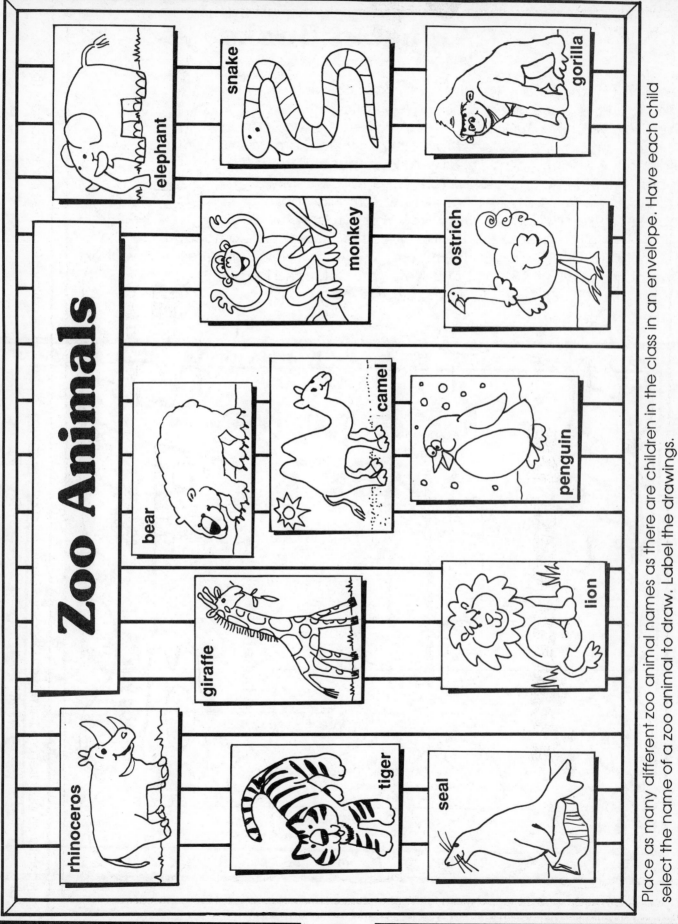

Zoo Animals

elephant

snake

gorilla

monkey

ostrich

bear

camel

penguin

giraffe

lion

rhinoceros

tiger

seal

Place as many different zoo animal names as there are children in the class in an envelope. Have each child select the name of a zoo animal to draw. Label the drawings.

IF8661 The Alphabet

Alphabet Books

Anno, M. (1975). *Anno's Alphabet.* New York: Crowell.

Kuke, K. (1983). *The Guinea Pig ABC.* New York: Dutton.

Gág, W. (1933). *The ABC Bunny.* New York: Coward McCann, Inc.

Garten, J. (1964). *The Alphabet Tale.* New York: Random House.

Grossbart, F. (1966). *A Big City.* New York: Harper and Row.

Hoban, T. (1982). *A, B, See!* New York: Greenwillow Books.

Kitchen, B. (1984). *Animal Alphabet.* New York: Dial Books.

Lobel, A. (1980). *On Market Street.* New York: Greenwillow Books.

Miles, M. (1969). *Apricot ABC.* Boston, MA: Little, Brown and Company.

Neumeier, M. and Glaser, B. (1985). *Action Alphabet.* New York: Greenwillow Books.

Oxenbury, H. (1983). *ABC of Things.* New York: Delacorte Press.

Wildsmith, B. (1962). *Brian Wildsmith's ABC.* Franklin Watts.

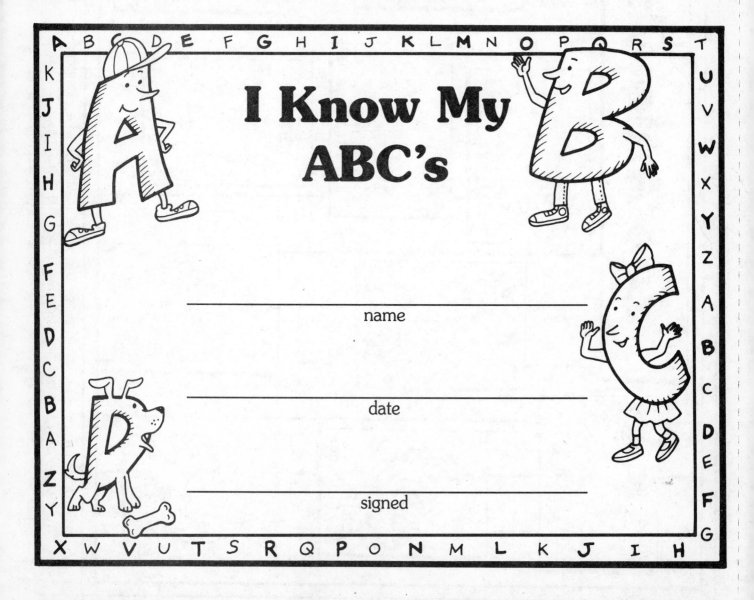

I Know My ABC's

_____
name

_____
date

_____
signed

IF8661 The Alphabet